THE MAN WHO BUILT THE BERLIN WALL

This book is dedicated to the loving memory of Chas, adventurer, companion, gourmet and dear friend.

THE MAN WHO BUILT THE BERLIN WALL

THE RISE AND FALL OF ERICH HONECKER

NATHAN MORLEY

PEN & SWORD
HISTORY

AN IMPRINT OF PEN & SWORD BOOKS LTD.
YORKSHIRE – PHILADELPHIA

First published in Great Britain in 2023 by
PEN AND SWORD HISTORY
An imprint of
Pen & Sword Books Ltd
Yorkshire – Philadelphia

ISBN 978 1 39908 882 4

A CIP catalogue record for this book is available from the British Library.

Typeset in Times New Roman 10.5/13 by SJmagic DESIGN SERVICES, India.
Printed and bound in the UK by CPI Group (UK) Ltd.

Pen & Sword Books Limited incorporates the imprints of Atlas, Archaeology,
Aviation, Discovery, Family History, Fiction, History, Maritime, Military,
Military Classics, Politics, Select, Transport, True Crime, Air World, Frontline
Publishing, Leo Cooper, Remember When, Seaforth Publishing, The Praetorian
Press, Wharncliffe Local History, Wharncliffe Transport, Wharncliffe True Crime
and White Owl.

For a complete list of Pen & Sword titles please contact
PEN & SWORD BOOKS LIMITED
George House, Units 12 & 13, Beevor Street, Off Pontefract Road,
Barnsley, South Yorkshire, S71 1HN, England
E-mail: enquiries@pen-and-sword.co.uk
Website: www.pen-and-sword.co.uk

or

PEN AND SWORD BOOKS
1950 Lawrence Rd, Havertown, PA 19083, USA
E-mail: uspen-and-sword@casematepublishers.com
Website: www.penandswordbooks.com

Contents

Introduction

This is the story of Erich Honecker, his life and his work.

It has been nearly thirty years since he died in exile and disgrace at a small villa in Chile. However, in today's Germany, Honecker and his era are enjoying increasing popularity which, in part, comes from the trend of Ostalgie or Ostalgia – newish words which describe a feeling of longing or desire for life in the former German Democratic Republic (GDR). In recent years, long-defunct East German products like 'Softee' ice cream, malted coffee, Spreewald gherkins, sparkling wine from Freyburg, and Halloren chocolate balls have appeared on the market. Honecker postcards and t-shirts sit alongside spray-painted chunks of the Berlin Wall at most gift shops in Berlin.

Across the country, newspapers often remind readers that the former chancellor Angela Merkel grew up in the GDR and even served as a cultural official for the FDJ, Honecker's youth organisation. (Curiously, Merkel was recently allocated the former office of Margot Honecker on Wilhelm Straße, from where she now conducts her activities).

It is also common knowledge – especially since the brutal war in Ukraine – that Vladimir Putin cut his teeth in Dresden serving as a KGB officer alongside Honecker's security services during the 1980s. It was in East Germany where Putin learned about the frailty of authoritarian regimes. With the collapse of the GDR, he returned home full of a bitterness that lingers to this day.

The attractions of Erich Honecker as a biographical subject are obvious enough. At the simplest level, it is a tale of ambition told amid the background of economic depression, Nazi tyranny, global conflict and Cold War. Of all the leaders in the communist world, he was the most unexpected. Even his political master Leonid Brezhnev dithered about supporting his leadership of the GDR in 1971.

A short bespectacled man with steely eyes and rigid posture, Honecker hailed from working-class stock and grew up in the totalitarian ideologies of the twentieth century – first as a victim and then a perpetrator.

Remarkably, he managed to survive a decade of imprisonment in a Nazi jail and emerged unscathed from the Second World War and the 1953 uprising against communist rule in East Germany. Over time, he became Walter Ulbricht's hatchet man, carrying out a purge of progressive functionaries.

Though well-read with rigorous political indoctrination, Honecker lacked formal education and observers considered him an unassuming functionary, unaware of his vital role in constructing the Berlin Wall.

Although frequently on the verge of being relegated to obscurity, he managed to overthrow Ulbricht in 1971 and set his stamp on German politics.

He was a stubborn man who claimed to understand the East German people. Beneath his affable exterior, there was a character of infinite guile.

Walter Ulbricht was only the first to fall before him. Honecker's agents unintentionally secured the demise of West German leader Willy Brandt, and he outwitted his political master Leonid Brezhnev with the greatest of ease.

However, some things can be set unarguably to his credit.

In foreign affairs, he secured the recognition of East Germany, signed the Helsinki Accords, and eased tensions with the West. Although his motto, 'Vorwärts immer, rückwärts nimmer' (Always look forward, never look back), made for a great rallying cry, Honecker's failures and omissions were legendary. Shortages were common, political liberties virtually non-existent, as was the freedom to travel.

During his historic visit to West Germany in 1987, as perestroika and glasnost swept across the socialist world, Honecker commented that 'socialism and capitalism can be no more united than fire and water'. But his downfall was always on the cards once the new openness devised by his political master Mikhail Gorbachev challenged his rigid loyalty to old-style socialism.

Then, as tumultuous changes swept through the Soviet bloc, everything in and around him collapsed in 1989. His health, his certainties, his ideology, his apparatus of power and his beloved SED party.

Terminally ill, he was brought to court to answer for his crimes.

In the last resort, detractors called Honecker a political opportunist long out of touch with his own people, while supporters described a man of conviction who – during his imprisonment and eventual exile – remained devoted to the communist cause.

Even as his world collapsed, Honecker retained a sense of humour and is said to have laughed out loud at a popular joke that lampooned his legacy. It told how he returned to East Berlin late one evening from an official visit abroad. Although the whole city was brightly lit, the streets were deserted. Eventually, Honecker's car passed the Berlin Wall, where he let himself be driven along only to discover a huge gaping hole and a painted sign saying: 'Erich, as you're the last one to leave, please turn off the lights.'

Although haunted by the fall of the Berlin Wall, Honecker died in 1994 still believing the GDR was the envy of the world: no unemployment, no drugs, no capitalistic exploitation and virtually no crime. But as will become clear, the reality was quite different.

The Miner's Boy

Erich Paul Honecker – General Secretary of the Socialist Unity Party of Germany, Chairman of the State Council, and Chairman of the National Defence Council – was born at number 26 Karlstrage in Neunkirchen at 6 pm on 25 August 1912. His birth certificate – issued five days later – shows both parents were Protestant and Erich, the 'Sunday Child', was also baptised as a Protestant.

Nowadays, little remains of the dusky black Saarland landscape where he first opened his eyes to the world – the coal basins and slag heaps have long gone. Back then, noise in this colliery town of 9,000 inhabitants began early in the day and continued long into the night: the creaking of coal wagons, the roar of steam turbines and the shriller outbursts of pit sirens filled the air.

As the son of a mine worker, Honecker's roots were purely working-class. He was the fourth child of 31-year-old Wilhelm and 29-year-old Karoline, along with two brothers – Willi and Karl-Robert – and three sisters, Katharina, Frieda and Gertrud.

His parents – although not given to overt displays of affection – were a devoted union and enjoyed a strong happy marriage. It was perhaps inevitable, then, that Erich looked back affectionately on his childhood, as part of a large, loving, close-knit family. He was proud of his Saarland heritage and never lost the accent or memories of his upbringing in a tiny two-up two-down in Wiebelskirchen, a northern suburb of Neunkirchen. The region was once part of the French Lorraine district, which came to France in the eighteenth century – then back to Germany following its annexation after Waterloo. Like most kids, Erich Honecker took his surroundings in his stride and found them unexceptional. At home, there was no hot water, the family shared an outside lavatory, gas-lit the bedrooms and there was no electricity. 'On the ground floor there were two rooms with a door in the middle,' Honecker recounted. 'On the second floor again, there were two rooms, one with three windows, and above that there were the two attic rooms in which the children lived.' Throughout his life, in interviews and profiles, he spoke of his father with intense pride. A short man, standing at 5ft 9in tall, Wilhelm had piercing brown eyes and wiry tan hair which turned greyish in his late twenties. He must have had a strong character, both physically and mentally, to cope with a life spent in the mines as works' steward and safety officer, which, as Erich recalled, 'meant he must go in and

1

decide whether there was clean air below. He had to conduct the wages struggle. He was a member of the miners' union – he had the trust of the workforce.' Given the high levels of sickness, Wilhelm developed his own reputation and was permanently in conflict with the pit's management. 'I honoured my father before everything because he was a straightforward person, an honest man. I honour his stand for the miners at his pit. I can say that my father was always the role model for my entire life'. Outside work, Wilhelm also attained, and then held for more than ten years, a seat on the local council.

Two years after Erich's birth, when war broke out in 1914, his father was mobilised into the German Navy. Like everyone else, he could have hardly imagined the conflict would spiral far beyond Europe and introduce the world to the horrors of chemical weapons and air-raids – as well as the toppling of a Tsar, a Kaiser and an Emperor. Never would so many men take up arms in a conflict that would leave nine million dead.

All this weighed heavily on the family, given Wilhelm's low military salary squeezed their daily lives. 'My mother,' Honecker confided, 'had to care for the five urchins herself, including clothing. It is well known that during the First World War there was hunger at home everywhere, not only in our family.' Rationing allowed eight grams of butter and two loaves of bread per fortnight, one egg and a half-pound of meat per week. When times got tough, the family was thankful for their skinny-ribbed cow, rabbits, vegetable patch and fruit trees. The bread was often indigestible; and potatoes, milk and lard were scarce. Despite this, Karoline kept the children clothed with home-tailored coats, shirts and undergarments. 'I cannot remember that anyone, other than my mother, made our clothes. She also had to earn money for the family by wafting from house to house delivering newspapers.'[1] The war, it seems, left its most powerful mark on Honecker's childhood. It ended in late 1918 when the Austro-Hungarian Empire and Germany agreed to an armistice closing the war in victory for the Allies.

Although unlikely, Erich afterward encouraged (or created) the legend that his father took part in the Kiel mutiny – the revolt by German Fleet sailors in November 1918 which triggered the revolution, sweeping aside the monarchy and giving birth to the Weimar Republic. (In fact, in the final days of the war, Wilhelm was posted to Belgium before finally returning home.)

With Germany defeated, British troops marched into the bomb-shattered Rhineland in December 1918 to begin an occupation that would last a decade.[2] In the Saarland, the Treaty of Versailles gave the green light for the French to reoccupy the area as they sought to recoup losses sustained during the war – especially after the destruction of the collieries in northern France by German troops. (Versailles had placed the area, which was formerly part of Germany, under the administration of the League of Nations for fifteen years.)

The Allied occupation – combined with an economic downturn – guaranteed Wilhelm's lot down the mines contained increasing degrees of misery. 'That's why,' said Erich, 'my father joined the communists because he saw them as the best representatives of the interests of the workers.' Evenings became a time of almost continuous political activity, given the fluid politics of the early 1920s. Reminiscing about those years, classmate Arthur Mannbar recalled, 'people usually met up at Erich's small, simple but beautifully clean house. And while the young hotheads passionately debated the work of their union, Mother Honecker was busy making sandwiches and coffee for the whole group.[3] During a period of inflation, unemployment and militant political action, Erich Honecker never forgot experiencing the '100-day strike' in 1922, when unions terminated miners' wage contracts, leading to a mass walkout. As a young Pioneer communist, he helped supply the pickets with food and newspapers, and collected donations. Peddling another legend, Honecker arranged a lively account to be published in a 1952 edition of *Junge Welt*, the communist youth paper:

> They organised a demonstration and Erich marched in the parade to Neunkirchen, with the group from the Communist Youth League, to take part in it. They sneaked past the police guards and joined in the strikers' demonstration. As it was beginning, the local police were incited to attack the workers. The children immediately moved to the front, and the police fell back. Some of them, however, were getting ready to attack the children. Then the women and the workers surged forward and pushed the police back, and the demonstration began.[4]

Honecker later mused:

> Thinking back to those days, I must say that the Pioneer organisation can be enormously effective in developing class consciousness in young people. What you absorb at that age may not have much ideological basis, but it makes such a deep impression that you never forget it. At least that's the way it was with me.

Along with his siblings Willi, Frieda and Gertrud, he became an enthusiastic member of the Young Spartacus League – a small, but vocal communist youth group made up of around fifty boys and girls, designed to awaken class consciousness, promote education for the proletariat and to continue the 'struggle against the exploiters'. Kids were encouraged to stage dramatic productions such as 'Spartacus – the slave liberator' – sometimes; afternoon rehearsals of songs and marches took place in the Honeckers' attic.

As he grew, friends remember a robust child who enjoyed football and athletics. He joined his pals on rambles and exploits into the countryside and could often be found rowing up and down the banks of the River Blies aboard a rickety homemade raft. A surviving photograph from the period shows his young face smiling brightly with other enthusiastic members of the Pioneer musical band, known as the Schallmeienkapelle. They had their own songs, and Erich could play just about every marching number on the drums and the entire repertoire of Communist tunes.

At Wiebelskirchen Protestant elementary school, a rather rambling edifice in a poor state of repair, he proved an indifferent pupil with a keen sense of humour. In fact, according to a fellow student, a curly-haired boy named Kurt Humbs, even when Honecker got a beating, he always laughed. 'Erich just couldn't cry,' Humbs marvelled, saying his young friend gained the reputation as a bit of a joker.[5]

Lively accounts suggest there certainly was a lot of physical punishment; with masters amassing a collection of paddles, birch twigs, rulers and belts. 'At school, we fought physical punishment,' Honecker recorded in the pamphlet *Vorbild des Pioniere*. 'When our singing teacher, a former army sergeant, was about to paddle one of us, the whole class would protest. The Pioneer paper, *Die Trommel*, gave a lot of help in this campaign'. He never forgot how that teacher, Herr Bock, kept his whipping cane in a violin case.

> When he forgot to take along the violin case, which happened now and then, he sent pupils to fetch it. Once, when I was ordered to do so, I opened the case on the way, broke the cane, this instrument of submissiveness, and threw it into the River Blies. Of course, the teacher who beat us procured a new cane. However, a signal had been given, and our self-confidence increased. Later we put a newspaper on his desk. On the last page there was a column entitled 'Bock, the Flogger'. Of course, we also had good teachers and wanted to learn.[6]

It is perhaps not surprising that students preferred outdoor pursuits to classes. 'There was no great striving upwards,' Erich said, remembering his German language skills were weak but arithmetic above average.[7] His uncle, Peter Weidenhof, encouraged him to try harder in German, saying that in politics, a good command of the language was essential. The story has often been told, in slightly differing versions, about how his parents made a successful request for him to be exempt from religious instruction, but as Honecker proudly asserted,

4

that did not mean he was left without knowledge in that sphere, 'whether the Bible, the Old and New Testaments or the problems of the philosophy of life'. He certainly never attended church when Katharina, his blond, blue-eyed sister, died of tuberculosis – a deadly condition stalking areas plagued by malnutrition and poverty. Looking back, he rather touchingly recounted how she had been 'especially good' at taking care of the family. 'She was the eldest, besides that, she was a lovely girl. My parents were anxious to do everything for her, so because of her illness, she was given as little as possible to do. Of course, her death meant a drastic alteration in our family.' Given the fear of contagion, Erich was briefly packed off to the safety of the countryside to avoid contact with Katharina as she slowly withered away.

To the outsider, Wiebelskirchen and the grasslands around Neunkirchen can appear bleak and a little uninviting. But this small corner of Europe left a powerful mark on Erich Honecker's childhood. By the age of 14, he had joined the KJVD, the Young Communist League of Germany and was stomping around the region handing out propaganda. With the approach of manhood he avoided clambering down mine shafts, choosing instead to work on a farmstead in Neudorf with a smallholder named Wilhelm Streich, who along with his wife, daughters and elderly father, became as good as family.

He discovered an interest in agriculture and proved good at his job of milking cows, feeding cattle and chopping firewood. 'The farmer,' he pointed out, 'had a bad hand and could only carry out the sowing, so the whole tilling of the field was done by the labourer and me, and later by me alone, on an 80-hectare farm. It was a big farm with forty-four cows, eight horses, and twenty-five to thirty pigs.' For the cereal harvest, Polish reapers strained every muscle harvesting rye, wheat, barley and oats with the scythe. 'I worked with the scythe, too,' he radiantly declared.

> It was all still manual work. I received no pay there. For me, what was important was that I performed my work with pleasure and at the same time obtained shelter and provisions. And the farmer provided clothes as well. The farmer had hoped that I might marry one of his daughters, but I was still too young and was not motivated in that direction.[8]

After two years, he was back in Wiebelskirchen hatching grandiose plans to work on the railways – alas, to no avail. 'Every lad has some kind of dream,' he proclaimed. 'That was my dream.' There was some consolation, however. Almost at once, he found himself mastering the basics of roofing with his uncle, Ludwig Weidenhof, a lanky ex-army gunner. The work was hard, but Honecker thrived on it. He acquired on-the-job experience stripping tiles and slating before starting an apprenticeship with Wiebelskirchen master roofer Franz Müller. 'I fell in love with my job because it involved a certain freedom of movement. You got around, saw the world from above. It was a job not without its dangers and always demanded attentiveness, prudence, precision, and skill.'[9]

Away from work, Honecker committed himself to the KJVD and attended the 1929 national youth rally and joined the Communist Party, which then recorded 120,000 members in industrial areas like Hamburg, Berlin, Leipzig, the upper Silesian coal-mining areas and northern shipyards. As this was happening, over in New York, Americans were reeling from a devastating stock market crash that led to the most destructive depression in modern history. 'I joined the party in 1929 at a time of heightened social tensions and political controversy,' Honecker noted. 'The worldwide economic crisis was already looming on the horizon.' In fact, it didn't take long for the contagion to reach Weimar Germany, sending the country into the abyss. A well-known saying at the time stated: 'New York sneezed, London caught cold, and Germany nearly died of influenza.' In the winter of 1928-29, unemployment had stood at 2.5 million, by the following winter the figure was pushed up to 3 million, as the economy contracted, and thousands of small firms folded. There was an almost constant state of anxiety as other predictable traumas, including tuberculosis and pneumonia, spread among the population in epidemic numbers. But there was more going on at this time. Before long, the situation handed impetus to an upstart political party from Munich – the National Socialists, or Nazis, led by Adolf Hitler, a man of monumental vitriol who used victimhood to spout a mishmash of banal ideas. Although vague on actual policies, Hitler gave the people enemies such as Jews and communists, blaming them for the financial crisis and for 'stabbing Germany in the back' during the war.

Amid this tumult and stress, the KJVD Central Committee delegated Honecker to visit Moscow to study Marxism-Leninism for a year. 'My parents agreed to my taking this course,' he remembered. 'And so, just before my 18th birthday, I went filled with expectations.' According to his own account, he packed his few belongings in August 1930 and set-off filled with boyhood optimism. There was a brief stop in Berlin for an interview with the Central Committee at the Karl Liebknecht House, near Alexanderplatz – the gritty district known for street battles and brawls between communists and increasingly confident Nazis, both fighting for influence in the city. While he didn't experience any violence, he did glimpse the dying days of Weimar Berlin, thick with risqué cabarets, prostitutes and black marketeers. Strange as it sounds, his most exciting moment was seeing a stage performance at the Volksbuhne – the people's stage – a 3,600-seat theatre opposite the KPD headquarters. A short course at the 'Reichsparteischule der KPD' – the Communist Party school in Fichtenau followed, where teachers marked him diligent and competitive.

Mother Russia

Arriving in Moscow, Honecker faced a city bigger, but significantly less elegant, than some he had passed through on the journey. But that didn't matter, the young communist had found his utopia – the epicentre of a country undergoing colossal upheaval, where workers and peasants were creating a socialist paradise as Stalin's 'Piatiletka' – or 'Five-Year Plans' thrusting the country into modernity.

As his train clattered into the Byelorussia station, he caught a glimpse of a huge sign above the platform displaying the words: 'Workers of all countries unite' – a moment of overwhelming excitement. With his political views already settled, he would spend the next year diligently confirming them at the International Lenin School, a Georgian-looking establishment located off the famous Arbat at 25 Vorovskogo Street – an upscale area, nowadays referred to as Ambassadors' Row.[1]

The school was founded in the mid-1920s by the Comintern – a Soviet-controlled organisation that governed communist parties around the globe. In practical terms, the Soviets directed enormous resources to 'educating' foreign students and, as sponsors, picked up the tab for operating such establishments. Using the cover name 'Fritz Malter' (all students and teachers used pseudonyms), Honecker was surrounded by the most promising young communists from Europe, America, Africa and Asia. He shared a room with Anton Ackermann – who would later become a close collaborator in the East German government. Fred Oelsner, who after 1945 would also shine in the GDR administration, was a lecturer at the school. Teaching methods combined lectures, study and discussions, and for the entrance examination he wrote an essay on the global economic crisis, which, he said, was well received and 'the way was opened for me to study Marxism-Leninism'. From then on, long hours were spent in the library brushing up on his Russian language skills, which he never perfected. He devoured (and memorised) the *ABC of Communism* – a tome penned by Nikolai Bukharin and Yevgeni Preobrazhensky (a paperback copy soon joined his prized possessions).

Away from the classroom, students were obliged to work once a week in a labour brigade and Honecker proved sharp enough to be allotted to a team as a welder in the Elektrozavod electro works, handling an oxy-acetylene welding

7

torch. There were carefree moments at the cinema and theatre, he developed a lasting interest in the performing arts and discovered a love of beer, a taste which stayed with him, though rarely indulged. With a stubby Zenit cigarette welded to his lips, he cut a dashing figure, standing at 1.68m, with a mop of ash blonde hair and appealing facial features. A robust 18-year-old in 1930, he felt the normal stirrings of any red-blooded teen and broke several maidens' hearts. Most memorably, he embarked on a passionate liaison with Natasha Griyenda, an auburn-haired Elektrozavod employee who he met at a dance. 'This relationship ended because I only stayed in Moscow for a year. It was hard,' he later confided. In fact, by dating Griyenda, he breached the strict rules of the Lenin school which forbade students from fraternising with strangers. Natasha's photograph travelled in his wallet long after, but they would never meet again.

As well as working at Elektrozavod, the young communist was active in Osoaviakhim, a volunteer organisation tasked with instilling militarist values into the population by providing civil defence and helping modernise the country. 'I received good military training in accordance with the teaching programme and was particularly attracted to equestrian sport,' he said. 'Sometimes it happened that I was late for classes because of the cavalry training ... but just imagine what it meant to be a cavalryman in those days!'[2]

He scrutinised his Soviet surroundings and his new Russian friends with care, spotting, for example, the huge education drive in Moscow, where citizens learnt to read, write and do arithmetic. 'Young and old were seen on the street, reading and learning at every opportunity.' Since his arrival coincided with the first preparations for the brand-new metro, the first underground railway system in the Soviet Union, it is a fair guess that he inspected the early earthworks, overseen by a young Nikita Khrushchev. Whatever his views really were, Honecker's memoirs skip over the primitive conditions other than a hesitant mention of pre-revolutionary wooden houses, scarce merchandise sold at black market prices, and orphaned youths, who he described as 'flotsam and jetsam of the civil war'.

> Despite the many homes and children's colonies, they slept in the open air and warmed themselves in winter at the public fires in streets and squares. Accelerated industrialisation helped to solve such problems too.[3]

In later life, as his importance grew, Honecker painted this period in a predictable light, a time of personal political development. 'You know, my first public appearance on an international issue was in Moscow,' he told the Soviet magazine *Ogoniok* in 1983.

I had to give a speech to the members of the railway union. I still remember crossing Red Square and to the left of the Moskva, this big meeting was taking place. Suddenly someone asked that one of us should address the audience. It was decided that Fritz Molter speaks – I had been given this code name in Moscow. I didn't know what to say, but somehow, I managed the speech. Many years have passed, but I can remember my speech to this day![4]

Another lasting experience was joining twenty-eight members of the Young Communist Labour Brigade in the far-flung Ural Mountains in Siberia to help build Magnitogorsk. It took four days by train from the capital to get to this vast new-fangled iron and steel combine, set to become the second greatest industrial district in the world. Honecker spoke often of his part in its development, describing working conditions as 'incredibly difficult', but he romantically recalled relaxed evenings when the working noise subsided, and the sound of Russian folk songs and refrains of the revolution wafted throughout the plant.

I remember it was terribly hot in Magnitogorsk, up to 40°C … There were neither trees nor greenery. We worked day and night, lived in tents and in the earth. We were housed in wooden barracks. The building was impressive, although there was no technology at the time – our muscles, that was all the technology.

He not once mentioned the 50,000 dispensable prisoners in a neighbouring camp used as forced labour on starvation rations. Even forty years later, Honecker only reminisced about the 'heroic struggle with the pioneers of socialism':

Where Magnitogorsk stands today there was nothing but bare, barren steppe forty years ago. Building on the foundation of Soviet power and led by their Leninist party, the Soviet workers and Komsomols built the new factories and the new residential section at the cost of tremendous effort and sacrifice. I have vivid memories of their heroism in those days, of how they overcame extreme difficulties and of the unequalled achievement of our Soviet class-brothers.

While in Moscow, Honecker had two 'in the flesh' encounters with his hero Stalin – albeit from a distance: 'It was the greatest thing I have ever experienced,' he gushed.[5] His first glimpse of 'the great man' occurred in January 1931 during the Congress of the Leninist Young Communist League at the Bolshoi

Theatre, where he sat four rows behind the Russian dictator. Sometime later, he saw him again at a meeting of the Supreme Soviet in the Great Hall of the Kremlin. 'The Moscow, which I left in the summer of 1931,' Honecker later stated, 'was already clearly another Moscow than when I arrived a year earlier. It had become familiar to me.'

On returning to Germany, Erich Honecker delivered accounts of his experiences at youth discussion evenings arranged by the KJVD. He rhapsodised about Magnitogorsk, Moscow, and Stalin's ambitious five-year plans. His enthusiasm was quickly rewarded with the post of local secretary for agitation and political director of the Saar Young Communist League, for which he was paid a monthly salary of 250 francs. From here on, he was able to apply what he had learned in Moscow in a leading party function. 'Honecker was a brilliant orator,' according to Erich Voltmer, the late editor of the *Saarbrücker Zeitung*. 'He avoided the rough and tumble of street clashes' with political opponents, choosing instead to leave 'that to his comrades, who regarded him as their unchallenged leader and spokesman – although most of them were a lot older than he was'.[6] Honecker, Voltmer said, was a toughened and dedicated activist and wouldn't recognise any opinion but his own. 'And he got results, because in the November 1932, election nine Communists, five Social Democrats, five Democrats, three representatives of the Centre Party, and only two Nazis, were elected to the Wiebelskirchen town council.'

Although the National Socialists fared poorly, their leader, Adolf Hitler, campaigned by crisscrossing Germany by air, and managed to swell Party membership from 129,500 in September 1930, to 450,000 in mid-1932. Remarkably, during this threatening climate, communist propaganda largely ignored the Nazi menace, choosing instead to denounce the SPD as '1,000 times worse than an open fascist dictatorship', and reminding voters that without the support of the SPD, Germany would have been unable to make war in 1914. Ernst Thälmann, the thickset, balding KPD leader, failed to trigger adequate alarm by declaring 'some Nazi trees must not be allowed to overshadow a forest of Social Democrats'.[7] Even graver accusations, first made in 1924, were reheated. The KPD charged the SPD with making Germany a paradise for capitalists and speculators.

> Social democracy appears under the mask of a workers' party. It has promised a thousand times to represent the interests of the exploited, and a thousand times it has betrayed the masses of the working people to German and foreign big business. The Social Democrats have always stabbed the fighting proletarian in the back ... Social Democracy must be defeated so that it no longer dares to call itself a workers' party...

In the KPD calculus, the Nazis were less sophisticated and thus less dangerous than the SPD. It was a major strategic miscalculation, and Hitler benefited greatly from the inability of the KPD and SPD to cooperate. After a noisy propaganda campaign for the 1932 presidential elections, the incumbent, Paul von Hindenburg, kept his position, and Ernst Thälmann managed to snatch 13.2 per cent of the vote, compared to Hitler's 30.1 per cent. Throughout, the KPD was swamped in the preparations for a propaganda blitz, and cadres, including Honecker, were key to transporting their message. In addition to speeches, the communists were helped by technical innovations like cheaper printing, which helped flood the market with illustrated pamphlets and posters. In the federal elections – in which Honecker was involved in intense campaigning – the KPD won 16 per cent of the vote, coming third. Honecker remembered it was the last time 'I saw our unforgettable Ernst Thälmann, the first and last time that I was able to talk to him personally.'[8]

Although the Nazis saw a reduction of votes in 1932, as is known, Hitler was assisted to power by a group of conservative politicians led by Franz von Papen, who – convinced he could tame and manipulate Hitler – persuaded President Paul von Hindenburg to nominate the Nazi as Chancellor on 30 January 1933.

From here on, one man's magnetism proved to be Germany's fatal attraction. Once in the saddle, the National Socialists squashed opposition, as they raced to transform Germany into a police state. The communist headquarters at Liebknecht House in Berlin was raided on 4 February and all demonstrations organised by the KPD were forbidden in Prussia, Thuringia, Brunswick and Mecklenburg. By 2 March, the Swastika was hoisted over Liebknecht House, communist propaganda was confiscated as were socialist, and other democratic newspapers. Nazi action against political opposition was not only swift but thorough, right down to the village level. As KPD deputies and officials were traumatised or detained, Thälmann ordered measures to protect the party and to continue its fight underground. Soon after, though, Thälmann was seized and dispatched to prison. According to Honecker's memoirs, of the 360,000 members which the KPD counted in December 1932, at least 18,000 were arrested and detained during the first six weeks of the Hitler regime.

To make matters worse, one more twist of fate in favour of the Nazis occurred on 27 February when an arson attack by a Dutch communist destroyed the Reichstag. From that moment, the whole machinery of Nazi disinformation blamed the fire on communist agitators. The KPD was formally banned on 14 July, when the Nazis were declared the only legally permitted party in Germany.

From this point on, Erich Honecker – the young propagandist – lived a precarious existence. When away from the autonomous Saarland – separated from Hitler's grip by the Treaty of Versailles, he worked underground, existing in a world of impoverished resisters, code names and secret gatherings. During the spring and early summer of 1933, he crossed over several times into the Third Reich to attend illegal meetings at Mannheim, Mainz and Frankfurt-am-Main. 'We compared notes on the anti-fascist struggle and discussed measures to support the illegal work of the KJVD in Hitler's Germany,' he recounted.[9] In Essen, he tossed anti-Nazi leaflets from the roof of the Althof department store near the city centre and formed an alliance with Catholic and Protestant youth groups, including the young members of the SPD-affiliated 'Friends of Nature' (the KPD's aversion to the SPD was abandoned after Hitler came to power).

Across Germany, tens of thousands of communists were sent to concentration camps such as Dachau near Munich where 5,200 anti-fascists were squeezed into prison huts. According to the Red Aid organisation, 5,000 communists were murdered before mid-1935, while 21,000 were sent for trial, and 19,000 were taken to execution sheds or slapped with lengthy prison terms. During this period, Honecker attended the Central Committee conference of the Communist Youth League in Amsterdam and the Antifascist Workers' Congress of Europe in Paris, organised by trade unions in Germany, Italy and Poland. Delegates called for Ernst Thälmann – still shackled in a Nazi prison – to be freed. 'Hitler's murder gang mean business against Comrade Thälmann, but the workers of the world can save him from these murderers,' British socialist Harry Pollitt declared. 'Let us just ask ourselves what it must mean to sit in a prison cell for over a year, never knowing which day might be the last.' From Paris, Honecker travelled to Basel, then made his way to Zurich, where he spent three weeks at a hotel near Lake Lucerne.

With the Saar preparing to hold a plebiscite on union with the Third Reich in January 1935, he joined the KPD's canvassing effort which urged residents to vote for the region to remain a League of Nations mandate territory. 'During those weeks we were on the move every day and on many evenings spoke in more than one location,' he remembered. 'We fought right up to the last minute.'

Yet, fighting the Nazi claim that the Saar was tied by blood to the German fatherland –turned out to be an uphill battle, made worse by Hitler's sabre-rattling propaganda minister, Joseph Goebbels, a club-footed loudmouth who whipped up a propaganda campaign. He dubbed communists 'the sworn enemy' of God, and found many believers, especially among the large Catholic community. Although the mood was increasingly hostile (many communist speakers were booed and hissed), Honecker fared well in Wiebelskirchen. He bragged how, years later, a local resident told West German television he had admired the mettle of the young KPD campaigner: 'Honecker told me that this was his conviction, and it did not require special courage.'[10] In the end, the morale of communist activists was dealt a bitter blow when voters opted for unification with Hitler's Germany on 13 January 1935 – making the KPD in Saarland an illegal entity. 'The referendum result turned out even worse than I had expected,' Honecker lamented.[11] 'Of the 540,000 voters, supposedly 470,000 voted for the return to Germany and only 4,000 for the status quo.'[12]

As Nazi muscles arrived in the Saarland, Honecker was deployed north to the Ruhr with the approval of the Saar KVJD. After receiving 180 Francs and being installed in a safe house in Essen, he set about making a personal investigation of attitudes towards the Reichsarbeitsdienst (the official state labour service) and compiled a report on mining conditions and unemployment in the district. Unaware he had been under police surveillance, he was forced to abandon his work after being arrested in Gelsenkirchen, north of Essen, on 15 February, after being detained outside a cinema under the pretext of suspected theft. 'As Honecker presumed that his arrest had to do with his political activity, he left the same day for Saarbrucken,' a police report noted.[13]

Unnerved by what was happening, he briefly visited Forbach in the Moselle on 27 February, before steaming unmolested into the Gare Montparnasse in Paris where he brooded for several weeks until the KPD in exile instructed him to lead Communist Youth League activities in Berlin, a role which required a new identity. His mission was to replace Bruno Baum, who was preparing to flee into exile because of his Jewish faith. 'I had to change by gradual stages into the sailor Martin Tjaden, born 21 September 1911 in Amsterdam, living in Amsterdam,' Honecker explained. A passport photograph was taken in Paris, and he received a Dutch passport in Switzerland. Via Basel, he journeyed to Zurich. 'Then I moved on, from Switzerland via Austria and Czechoslovakia.' By the time he reached Berlin during the blistering August of 1935, anti-communist purges had swept through the entire city which was in the midst of a beautification campaign for the 1936 Olympics. Baum briefed his replacement on the status of underground KJVD work and gave pointers on how to percolate with members of the former Socialist Working-Class Youth, the Socialist Youth League, the free-trade union groups and the Hitler Youth. Ostensibly, Honecker's mission was to receive underground literature (often printed on frail onionskin sheets) from neighbouring states to distribute throughout Berlin. With Baum's help, he found modest lodgings on Brusseler Straße and, still relatively lean and fit, was able to make covert handovers of clandestine material and even smuggle a small printing press into the heart of the Nazi capital. His situation was not enviable. Money was a real problem, and as Berlin swarmed with Gestapo, police kept watch on interminable working-class districts such as Wedding, while all suspicious post was seized.

Although careless risks were frequent, overconfidence led to his luck running out on 3 December after a rendezvous on Solinger Straße near the Tiergarten with Sarah Fodorová, a pretty young Czech girl. Fodorová had been duped by a friend into delivering a suitcase, unaware that it was stuffed with communist literature, such as the *Rote Fahne* and the Moscow paper *Deutscher*

Zentral Zeitung, hidden under a false bottom. She did, however, manage to deposit the case at the Anhalter railway station luggage office and slipped the ticket to Erich. Later that night, he set about retrieving the suitcase. 'While I waited, I saw that the station officer was disturbed about something when he went with the luggage ticket towards the suitcase and compared the numbers,' he said, describing the experience. 'He vanished quickly. I saw two men come near me and immediately thought, caught!' In a desperate attempt to save his skin, he grabbed the case, dashed to the taxi rank, and told a waiting driver to stomp on the gas. After a few minutes – with his wits still intact – Honecker was back on foot running alongside Zoologischer Garten station before vanishing into the neighbouring Tiergarten. But his luck ran out. After receiving a tip-off, gun-toting Gestapo officers burst into Honecker's apartment the next morning, he was not treated gently. All too carelessly, he had left a stash of propaganda leaflets and literature hidden throughout his flat. Erich Honecker was about to gain his sobering introduction to Nazi justice.

The Prison Years

Honecker's experiences in captivity would change the trajectory of his life and in turn the lives of millions of others. The clandestine manner of his propaganda work provided sufficient evidence for a crime by the low standards of Nazi justice. However, nothing in his imagination, before entering Gestapo headquarters, had prepared him for the merciless, degrading misery of prison. The building on Prinz-Albrecht-Straße, which housed the office of Heinrich Himmler, sat above a sprawling complex of airless subterranean cells and interrogation rooms.

From this moment, there was a year and a half of struggle with the state advocate who, as Honecker explained, was sniffing for blood. 'He wanted to impute us to deeds that would warrant a death sentence. These are not my words, but those of my official defence, an SS leader.'[1] Lack of information about proceedings and scant contact with friends and family contributed to his mental anguish. And although pre-trial detention provided time to dwell on what was to come, Honecker maintained that resistance to Hitler proved there 'was another Germany' and claimed to have helped 'convert' members of the Hitler Youth, Labour Front and the SA members to the anti-fascist cause.

Honecker's survival in the Nazi prison system is nothing short of incredible. During 1935–37 he endured a tough, miserable existence at three infamous Berlin prisons: Columbia-Haus, Moabit and Plotzensee – all desolate, impregnable and oppressive places. The latter, in the northwest of the city, was being used as a remand detention centre for political cases at the 'Special Courts' and the notorious 'People's Court'.

The sequence of events that followed could not have been more predictable. On the third of July 1937, the boyish-looking Honecker was escorted a few hundred meters past the famous Sports Palace (where Hitler made his big speeches) to the second floor of the old Kammergericht building in Kleistpark – later the scene of show trials under the fiery Nazi fanatic Roland Freisler. The fruit of the prosecutor's labours was a twelve-page appreciation with three annexes, outlining why Erich – along with Bruno Baum, who had also been apprehended – was a danger to the state. Throughout the session, Honecker sat silently, his eyes wide open, his head sometimes cupped in his hands. That morning, the court handed him a sentence of ten years penal servitude for the 'preparation of high treason alongside the severe falsification of documents'. Trembling like a leaf, Baum was passed a twelve-year stretch, while the luckless Sarah Fodorová, the Czech girl with the suitcase, was released.

After judgment, Honecker – marked prisoner 523/37 – was moved to Brandenburg-Görden prison, a hulking behemoth hidden in thick fir forests to the west of Berlin. Known as the 'German Sing Sing', this multi-story structure grouped around courtyards, could hold 1,800 inmates, making it the largest penal institution in Germany. 'A few of the supervisors treated the political prisoners with the utmost brutality,' Honecker said. 'Conditions regarding food, sanitary facilities and health were often appalling.'[2] Discipline was administered by warders made up of old Nazi fighters absorbed into the state after Hitler's appointment.

In the seven years that followed, Honecker's relations with fellow inmates were generally good; however, his commitment to the KPD cause remains a matter of conjecture and speculation. Despite strict isolation and surveillance, inmates formed an illegal KPD group to organise resistance and unite imprisoned anti-fascists. The saying, 'Where there is a comrade, there is the party' became well known. The KPD grapevine kept inmates posted on developments from the outside world, such as Hitler's march into the demilitarised Rhineland in 1936, the annexation of Austria, the Sudeten crisis, and the vicious pogroms against the Jews.

Once released from isolation, Honecker moved into a three-man cell in 'Building 2', and after the outbreak of war in 1939, good behaviour earned him the position of a Trusty, a role he committed himself to wholeheartedly by serving the prison doctor, Johannes Muller. According to former colleague Heinz Lippmann, many prisoners described Honecker as being reserved, 'snotty', and showing few signs of solidarity. (For his part, Honecker looked back on these years as a time of unity, fellowship and brotherhood and later mythologised it in his own mind). It is, however, almost certain that he did not belong to the inner circle of resistance, though he did provide 'political and moral solidarity' by helping comrades keep up the fighting spirit. Because of his job as a doctor's orderly, he slipped extra provisions to sick inmates and facilitated illegal meetings.

> We arranged things like telling some prisoners they should report
> ill. Then we locked them in the waiting cell and conducted them
> to the doctor. In that way, we created a possibility for some
> comrades to discuss things with each other.[3]

Fellow inmate, Max Frenzel, vouched for Honecker's underground work, saying he was 'always the comrade who did his duty in these difficult years in this hostile environment, despite Nazi terror and daily threats'.[4] Likewise, Wilhelm Thiele, sentenced to life imprisonment, found himself temporarily in a cell with Honecker. 'When comrades spend the difficult times of their lives confined together in a tiny cell for years, they not only get to know each other inside and out, but a close feeling of togetherness also develops. Erich was animated by an unshakable optimism, he radiated friendliness.'[5] Good news from the outside world was scant. Honecker was saddened to learn his brother, Robert, was dispatched with the newly formed Afrika Korps to shore up the Italian effort in the Middle East in March 1941. Robert endured a difficult time in North Africa and Greece, where he eventually became ill and was taken prisoner.

However, a morale booster came a few months later when Germany invaded the Soviet Union on Sunday, 22 June, ending the much-hated Molotov–Ribbentrop pact, which had allied the Nazis with Stalin.

Honecker suffered from intense homesickness and often treated cellmates to imaginary tours of Wiebelskirchen. He found distraction by devouring the works of Goethe, Schiller and Shakespeare: 'There was hardly a field I was not interested in, from natural sciences to classical literature.'[6] His good behaviour was enough to allow his parents, Karoline and Wilhelm, and sister Gertrud and her husband, Hans Hoppstädter, to visit twice annually. On one occasion, after a long, exhausting train journey from Wiebelskirchen, Wilhelm pleaded for his son's draft into the army like his other brother, Willi, who was wearing the Wehrmacht uniform, courageously fighting in the Soviet Union (but was later killed during the retreat from Romania).[7]

Despite penning two petitions for clemency, Wilhelm was informed his son was denied parole because, as the SS declared, he remained a 'convinced communist functionary' and an 'incorrigible supporter of communism'.[8] Furthermore, it was reckoned that, if released, he would immediately return to the underground KPD.

Shortly thereafter, with the Allied bombing of Germany having taken a more dramatic turn, Honecker was drafted to conduct roofing work at the Arado airplane factory, though the unit was more often employed in bomb disposal in central Berlin: 'When necessary, we carried the bombs some distance away, un-defused, on our shoulders,' he explained. Before too much time passed, with trembling fingers, he was digging out the dead and wounded from caved-in air raid shelters and removing rubble from the streets. 'When we got caught by a new bomb attack in the process, which happened more and more often, we were detailed to throw incendiary bombs down from roofs.' (He was even commended by Attorney General, Erich Kolb, for his bravery in rescuing women trapped in a detention centre).

Throughout those days, as raids flattened homes and factories, the roofing detail mustered one hour before dawn for rations – bread, cheese and ersatz coffee. With the onset of winter, as travelling to Berlin became trickier, the team moved to Barnimstraße women's prison, a squalid red-brick facility in Friedrichshain, near Alexanderplatz. It was there in November 1943 that Honecker witnessed 'an image of hell' when – in sub-zero temperatures – the RAF unloaded 2,500 tons of explosives in two attacks, which killed 4,000, injured 10,000, and left 45,000 homeless. 'Alexanderplatz and Lichtenberg were turned to rubble,' he observed. 'That afternoon the sun was obscured, the day turned into night, lit only by the many fires. All hell broke loose. Time and again incendiary bombs fell on the roofs of the women's prison, and we tossed them off.'

In this remarkable atmosphere – horrific though it was – Honecker's roving eye spotted Charlotte Schanuel, a former civil servant in the Prussian civil service who had been conscripted as a prison warder. Although nine years his senior, the attraction was mutual, and sex was fast and rewarding, presumably snatched in dark cells and washrooms. Charlotte, though, was no passing fancy. Their illicit encounters would out-see the end of the conflict and beyond.

As the war's problems became more intractable, senior military leaders carried out a failed assassination attempt on Hitler in July 1944. Revenge was swift. Within days, thousands were arrested and imprisoned in the most appalling conditions – Brandenburg-Görden was suddenly crammed with 4,000 inmates and, in an orgy of bloodshed, at least 2,000 resistance fighters were murdered either by guillotine or hanging. 'I could have gone, like anyone else into a concentration camp or a probation battalion,' Honecker reflected.[9] 'That could have been my lot. Not one of the political prisoners at Brandenburg knew what tomorrow would bring him. But we didn't give this a great deal of thought. We fulfilled the tasks of the day.'[10]

Amid the carnage, Erich received the shattering news that Hitler had also taken the opportunity to order the execution of KPD leader Ernst Thälmann, who had been languishing at Buchenwald concentration camp under the most harrowing and humiliating conditions. Predictably, the Nazis blamed his death on an air-raid, as the Völkischer Beobachter reported:

Killed by Terror Bombs!
During a terrorist attack on the area around Weimar on 28 August 1944, the concentration camp was also hit by numerous high-explosive bombs. Among the prisoners who died are the former Reichstag deputies Breitscheid and Thälmann.[11]

In the course of time, Thälmann's death would provide German communists with a martyr – a man cast as a pivotal historical figure: a myth and legend in propaganda. But that was all in the future.

As autumn of 1944 progressed into winter, the Allies pushed as far as the Rhine. Despite his best efforts, Hitler's Ardennes offensive failed, leaving German military reserves exhausted. In January 1945, the vastly superior Soviet army pushed over the Vistula bridgeheads, overrunning Germany's eastern provinces. By the end of the month, Stalin's men were digging into positions in Küstrin and Frankfurt an der Oder, near the German-Polish border. As this was happening, Anglo-American pilots continued to unload bombs on Berlin, Dresden and many other German cities. However, as the country rapidly disintegrated, there was no sign whatever of revolt, as the power and omniscience of the police kept the regime firmly at the rudder. The Führer himself – joined by senior aides – assumed residence in a bunker underneath his once-majestic Chancellery, which resembled a jumble of collapsed walls and crushed interiors. Fearful of losing grip on power, authorities cracked down on defeatism and potential threats. Believing his life in danger, Honecker took advantage of lax security when working at the juvenile women's prison on Magdalene Straße. Just after 11 am on 6 March 1945, along with former KPD activist and fellow inmate Erich Hanke, wearing filthy prison garb and carrying bricklayer's buckets, Honecker clambered over a lightning rod to a neighbouring house, navigated a maze of landings and walked out to freedom on Alfred Straße. For all their eagerness, however, the men stepped into the full horror of wartime Berlin, as Honecker reflected in his memoirs.

> When we turned into Frankfurter Allee there were hundreds of policemen and soldiers busy clearing away rubble from the latest heavy bombing raid. It was too late to turn back. But apparently, nobody got suspicious. We reached Siegfriedstraße near Berlin-Lichtenberg railway station. From there we wanted to go to an uncle of Erich Hanke in the Wotanstraße, but he was not at home. Nearby there was a bombed-out house where we got rid of the eye-catching stripes on our prison clothes. Now we looked like foreign workers.

Soaked by rain, they roamed the streets of Lichtenberg and Neukölln in constant danger of being caught as they sought shelter with friends who were either not there or whose apartments had been bombed out. Without identity papers and money, the fugitives could use neither the underground, tram nor bus. 'Besides,' Honecker said, 'public transport was frequently put out of operation by bombing raids.'[12] Their first night was spent huddled in the basement of a gutted tenement in Hallesches Tor, where they snatched what rest they could. When they awoke the next morning, the pair went their separate ways. Exhausted and desperately cold, Honecker made a short journey across the rubble-strewn streets to Landsberger Straße and the apartment of his lover, Charlotte Schanuel. However, conscious of the possibility of being discovered and handed to the Gestapo, Charlotte spirited him back to the women's prison a week later. With some luck, he was never punished, despite his absence having been reported by Hauptsturmführer Seraphim, an over-zealous SS man. 'The acting Attorney General at the Berlin Court of Appeal stood up for me against Seraphim,' Honecker later explained. 'So, I was lucky in my misfortune.' (In fact, the wheels had been set in motion for an arrest warrant, but the document was destroyed during an air raid). Predictably, though, his escape caused a rumpus in the KPD group at Görden and he was called to provide an account before a cadre commission, which, after much debate, exonerated him as no 'retaliatory measures' were inflicted on his comrades.[13] In later life, Honecker pooh-poohed suggestions of wrongdoing and held an almost invariably spoken belief that his escape was a heroic enterprise. Likewise, Erich Hanke – who afterward enjoyed a long career in the SED administration – blarneyed the episode in his 1970 autobiography:

> Under the difficult living conditions, in which human weaknesses and human strength quickly become apparent, I was impressed by the personality of comrade Honecker. He is a man of excellent qualities. Modesty, a sense of justice, the ability to make any personal sacrifice for the good of the people, courage, willpower and energy are coupled with great intelligence, extensive knowledge, great experience, a clear view of the essentials, and perseverance. The demands of imprisonment and the many hours of discussions revealed a good person and an outstanding communist.

In later years, the story of Honecker the prisoner became an essential part of the communist construction of his persona, perhaps the most critical part.

As Hitler governed from beneath the ruins, the Nazi chain of command was breaking down. By April, when a tidal wave of near-starving refugees snaked into Berlin from East Prussia, chronic supply problems worsened. And as Germany's situation grew ever more perilous, the Red Army began assaulting Berlin from its bridgeheads on the Oder River on 16 April. Four days later – Hitler's birthday – Honecker witnessed the first Soviet salvos into the heart of the capital.

> I shall never forget the midday hours of this last Führer's birthday. The first Soviet artillery shell landed right opposite the Barnimstraße women's prison, the second one immediately

beside the prison where we were held. The next hits were already in the city centre. Obviously, the Soviet artillery was ranging on the Reich Chancellery, the last refuge of the big Nazis.[14]

The following morning, 21 April, Soviet tanks sped towards the Berlin motorway ring road to cut off the Reich capital and sever supply routes. Amid this chaos, Honecker's construction crew began a hastily forced march to the prison at Plötzensee and loaded onto trucks destined for Görden, where the warders were 'noticeably more nervous' and uncertain.[15]

As the battle for Berlin raged on in all its bloody fury, the northern and eastern suburbs of Tegel and Reinickendorf were captured. Fighting erupted in Charlottenburg, Moabit and Schoeneberg and, by 25 April, Russian forces were swarming through the ruined capital as civilian defenders threw down their guns. 'Wilma D', a sixth-grade pupil from the 41st school in Prenzlauer Berg, felt the full horror of the onslaught when a so-called Stalin Organ struck her backyard: 'my mum was standing there with seven other women when the grenade hit. Her legs were ripped off.'[16] At the Zoologischer Garten in central Berlin, the scene was apocalyptic after artillery shelling destroyed roofs and killed most of the animals.

Two days later, on 27 April, the area near Görden was awash with Soviet troops who later conducted a floor-by-floor release of prisoners. Honecker never forgot the enthusiasm with which he embraced the Russian soldiers. 'They came as liberators, as class brothers and friends, as pioneers of a new, better future for mankind!'[17]

In their last hours before liberty, some prisoners had planned to launch an attack on their captors, but many guards vanished, while others surrendered rather than fight. Amid emotional scenes, KPD inmates mustered for a planned foot march to the capital. Honecker, though, would have none of it. Late on the afternoon of 27 April, after snatching a little sleep, he undertook a three-day trek back to Berlin, desperate to find Charlotte. Feeling a powerful mixture of excitement and apprehension, he reminisced how 'heavy fighting was still going on in the city centre, it was not easy and certainly not without danger'.[18] He had a long and tiring march before him. 'To reach the destination by a direct route was impossible. There were still some isolated units of the Wehrmacht and the Waffen SS between Brandenburg and Berlin who were trying to get through to the Elbe.'[19] By the time he arrived in Berlin on 1 May, news of Hitler's death – portrayed as a heroic stand at the head of his troops – was spreading like wildfire.

Climbing The Ladder

When the fighting was all over in Berlin and the shells quit exploding, Honecker resurfaced. Over the years, a multitude of conflicting stories have been published concerning the period between his gaining freedom and rejoining his communist cadres.[1] However, it is almost certain he lingered at Charlotte's apartment at 37 Landsberger Straße for a week, before emerging onto the streets of Berlin. After a chance encounter with former comrade Hans Mahle, he was introduced to Walter Ulbricht, the leader of German communists in exile who had been preparing in the Soviet Union for the establishment of a (communist) post-war Germany.

After the Nazi surrender, Germany was split into four occupation sectors and Berlin into four zones. The USA, USSR, United Kingdom and France held supreme authority, while the Commanders-in-Chiefs of the occupying powers held almost absolute authority across the land. Western Allies moved into Berlin in June 1945, a month after the Russians had occupied the city.

During the first month of sole Russian occupation, Berlin resembled a 'picture of hell', according to Ulbricht's youngest associate, Wolfgang Leonhard. There were 'flaking ruins and starving people shambling around in tattered clothing ... all of them looking terribly tired, hungry, tense and demoralised.'[2] Ulbricht's daily sessions at the 'Rose' restaurant became a Mecca for functionaries released from Nazi prisons looking for jobs. Ulbricht later explained:[3]

> Our advantage lay in being well prepared. When the Soviet troops crossed the Vistula, a commission had already been set up within our party leadership to plan the first essential measures in the struggle against Hitlerite fascism. We worked out every detail, including the organisation of cultural life. We also had a list of anti-Hitler people we assumed to be in Berlin, with names of communist and social democratic members of the Reichstag and other opponents of Hitler from bourgeois groups. So, we arrived in Germany on 30 April 1945 well prepared. We reached Berlin on 1 May, and then our work began.[4]

What endeared the Russians to Ulbricht was his neurotic allegiance to Stalin. He was adept at creating controversy. Any failures or misjudgements by the Soviets were rarely discussed as, time after time, he stubbornly supported Russia on a multitude of issues. For example, when there were complaints that German factories were being dismantled and shipped to the Soviet Union – increasing the suffering of the local population – he backed Moscow. From the moment the Red Army rolled into Berlin, military units had set about dismantling AEG, Borsig, Osram, Siemens and hundreds of other industrial concerns.

Another thorny issue concerned his point-blank refusal to entertain discussion on the rape of German women by Russian soldiers, an outrage which also compromised the Soviet claim to be a liberator. Devoid of emotional intelligence, Ulbricht remained unmoved by calls from victims to have abortions, dismaying many in his own ranks. Moreover, his faithfulness to his Soviet mentors knew no bounds, even before the war, he wrote in defence of Stalin's despised 1939 non-aggression pact with the Nazis.

For his part, Honecker remembered Ulbricht as an earthy, thick-set fellow with thinning hair, wire-rimmed glasses, goatee beard and a high-pitched voice. He could be brusque and was not a man people relaxed around. 'Walter Ulbricht, whom I did not know until then, went from table to table,' he recounted of their first meeting. 'He also came to the table where I sat with some comrades and asked about our past, insofar as he did not know about it, and what plans we had.' Honecker's prison misdemeanours were not mentioned, but after a long chat, Ulbricht felt he had the right sort of experience to offer him the daunting assignment of working out a framework for a youth organisation. As several associates gave approving nods, the old man talked for another hour, ending – as he put it – with 'a call for action'. After the meeting, with the help of Ulbricht's contacts, Honecker was able to make a surprise visit to Wiebelskirchen for a family reunion, which 'after more than ten years away was indescribably great'. His weight had fallen sharply. His sister remembered being shocked by his gaunt appearance, leading to his mother cooking him three hearty meals a day. The rest and relaxation at home proved a pleasure, a splendid diversion from the filth and desolation of Berlin. 'We had a lot to tell each other, but unfortunately, we didn't have enough time. Just a few days later I had to start my return journey.'[5]

At first, the Soviet occupiers seemed to be advocating a form of democracy by allowing old parties to resurface, including a reformed Christian Democrat Union (CDU), Social Democrats (SPD) and the Liberals (LDP). This, however, was a premeditated plan to legitimise the organisation and promotion of the KPD. But to Ulbricht's distress, because of its close links with Moscow, the KPD failed to gain public support as indignation continued at the extent of Russian raping and pillaging that accompanied the occupation. Concerns about the electability of the KPD worsened after elections in Hungary and Austria saw the communists record dire results.

In an effort to solve the problem, the Soviets identified a natural sympathy between the KPD and the more-popular SPD (which emerged as a significant rival in the eastern zone) and pushed for a merger. However, the proposal suffered a humiliating setback in a West Berlin referendum (the Russians prevented it in theirs) where SPD members crushingly rejected merging by more than six to one. However, after months of coercion and intimidation, SPD representatives finally accepted a merger to create the Sozialistische Einheitspartei Deutschlands (SED). The union was cemented on 21 April 1946 at the Admiralspalast, opposite the Friedrichstraße railway station. 'We all rose from our seats enthusiastically and sang the *Internationale*,' Honecker remembered. The newly fused party, with the help of SMAD, the Soviet military government, swept to victory in the 1946 elections for local and regional assemblies held in the Soviet zone.

Predictably, for the SPD, the forced union was disastrous. After enjoying largely equal rights with the KPD, they played hardly any role from 1949 onwards when level representation was abolished, and the communists seized the most influential posts. By the time of East Germany's formal founding in 1949, the SED was a full-fledged communist party – a 'rebranded' KPD.

Prior to this sequence of events, Honecker had settled into the role of chairman of the central youth committee, working from an office at 39-40 Kronenstraße, near Goebbels' old propaganda ministry. 'I could draw on my experience in youth work as a member of the KJVD's Central Committee, as political chief of the KJVD for the Saarland, Ruhr and Berlin Brandenburg Districts,' he recounted. 'The sheer scope and complexity of the task which I had now been entrusted in a completely different situation was only to dawn on me in the following weeks and months.'[6] Soon after, he was appointed chairman of the Central Antifascist Youth Committee and six months later, in February 1946, he organised a petition to SMAD requesting permission to form the 'Free German Youth' (FDJ), a 'supra-partisan, united, democratic youth organisation.' The application was approved within two weeks and the Politburo,* then known as the Central Secretariat, appointed thirty-four-year-old Erich Honecker as FDJ chairman.[7] He took credit for uniting former members of the KJVD, Socialist Workers' Youth, members of the Protestant and Catholic youth federations 'in other words, young people from all classes and sections of society united in the Free German Youth'.

---

* The principal policy-making and executive committee of the SED.

With Ulbricht looking over his shoulder, the 'Free German Youth' was unveiled at the State Theatre on 10 March 1946. The more astute observers wrinkled their noses, recognising that although 'unity and non-partisanship' were invoked from the start, the FDJ – like the SED – would develop as an arm of the communists. 'Everybody understood that,' said Ed Stuhler, biographer of Margot Feist, a young FDJ functionary. 'That was Ulbricht's ultimate intention. It was a charade that just played out,'[8] (for example, while the key areas of FDJ finance and public relations fell into communist hands, the CDU, on the other hand, received the less important culture department).

Throughout this period, Honecker cast his net far and wide to enlist recruits to the FDJ by adopting the posture of a young go-getter, full of gung-ho spirit and vitality. SED photo archives show him dribbling a football during a sporting afternoon, whistling up a group of teenagers for a cycle ride and helping clear rubble in Prenzlauer Berg. Using the four-point slogan 'unity, work, construction and peace,' he found male teenagers generally enthusiastic, but recruiting girls, he complained, became a reoccurring headache as they were mostly interested in dancing, chocolate, cosmetics and cigarettes, like young women in the West. 'We have to meet their desire for a happy life,' he grumped. His talent stretched to designing a colourful uniform stitched from mustard yellow and sea blue fabrics with the FDJ logo of the rising sun sewn on the left shirt sleeve. The ceremonial parade uniform, which included a bright red neckerchief and side-cap, was, according to Honecker, intended to 'develop young people's sense of togetherness and promote their fighting spirit'.[9] The logo represented that 'after the pitch-dark night of fascism, a new day was dawning for the German youth'.[10] All youngsters between the ages of 14 and 25, apart from former full-time Hitler Youth members, were eligible to join the FDJ at the counters of local offices springing up across the Soviet zone. But unlike the Hitler Youth, the FDJ avoided torch-lit parades and semi-military training, instead emphasising character building, indoctrination and physical training. It was mixed-sex and provided educational activities for those from disadvantaged backgrounds.

In later years, when SED 'court historians' wrote Honecker's biography, a chapter devoted to 1945–46, painted a portrait of a heroic man inspired by the 'indomitable will to do everything possible to seize the opportunity offered to the German people by liberation from fascism'.[11]

As an activist from the very beginning, he used all his strength to eradicate fascism and militarism, to establish a new anti-fascist democratic state and to steer social development along the path of socialism.[12] 'Honecker's tremendous effort,' the biography explained, was focused not just on gathering working-class youth, but ripping an 'entire generation misled and abused by fascism out of hopelessness, to give their lives new meaning and new goals, and to involve them in the struggle to overcome fascism, militarism and imperialism'.[13]

In a quiet interval during his strenuous work-life, Honecker tied the knot with Charlotte at the Berlin-Mitte registry office before a small group of friends. The marriage certificate states his employment as 'Secretary Honecker', and Charlotte – full name: Gertrud Margarete Charlotte Schanuel – as a 'Wachtmeisterin' (constable/patrol woman). There was no wedding album nor honeymoon, and Honecker's comrades turned a blind eye to Charlotte's Nazi past. However, despite a seemingly happy start, the groom soon tired of his new wife – there were violent tantrums, made worse by her refusal to join the SED. He was deeply hurt when she refused to stop working – saying she enjoyed her career and wanted to continue with it. From here on, relations cooled rapidly and Honecker devoted more time to work.

He grew in stature as a rising figure in the Party and frequently mixed with Wilhelm Pieck, widely regarded to be the most charismatic figure in the German communist movement, a man Honecker thought the embodiment of decency, duty and tradition: 'I was filled with joyful excitement that suddenly I was faced with a man who epitomised the best traditions of the German Workers Movement.' Remembering this period, Honecker's right-hand man at the FDJ, Heinz Lippmann, recounted when it came to personal relationships, his boss was not a man to act impulsively nor rush into anything. 'He had a very unassuming manner and seemed very receptive to other people's ideas and suggestions and always ready to learn.' Fraternising with bourgeois and clerical types was something he never enjoyed. 'In a closed group of comrades, he made no secret of it,' Lippmann divulged. 'It was hard for him to feign friendliness and tolerance with middle-class people.' Ivan Bedin, a youth officer with the SMAD, thought Honecker displayed an unassuming demeanour, 'he was a lean man,' he recounted, 'more than humble, but charged with colossal energy, who was able to inspire others'.[14]

During this period, he became a much more confident writer, penning articles on sport, agriculture, class unity and threats to the socialist way of life. He set the presses rolling on the first issue of the youth journal 'Neues Leben' by appealing for readers to work shoulder to shoulder in clearing away the 'visible and invisible debris of the past from the streets and from people's minds'. We would, he recorded, 'have to put in our best efforts to bring about the reconstruction of town and countryside'.[15] Since the cessation of hostilities in Berlin, every kind of public service had been either seriously impaired or left unworkable and accommodation for those who survived was often primitive in the extreme. After entering Berlin, it took the Russians six weeks to get electricity and water supplies functioning to a reasonable degree, while sanitary engineers endeavoured to purify the water supply. But, amid the filth and misery, signs of recovery emerged. Pubs and makeshift canteens served construction workers, along with barter markets springing up everywhere.

On the outskirts, lakeside beaches attracted bathers on warmer days and at one of Berlin's biggest libraries – where huge shell holes were blown into the walls – a lending service operated from the basement.

As well as helping in the clean-up effort, FDJ members deployed in June 1946 to deliver propaganda in a campaign calling for a referendum in Saxony 'to expropriate war criminals and Nazis'. With 77 per cent of voters in favour of nationalisation, the ballot retrospectively legitimised the confiscation of thousands of companies by the Soviet occupying power the previous year. Without any further referenda, nationalisations were expanded to the entire occupation zone. The action came ahead of the first so-called 'parliament' of the FDJ from 8 to 10 June 1946, when the political character of the organisation became abundantly clear. Honecker chose the term 'parliament' deliberately to show off the 'democratic nature' of the FDJ.

Watching the parliament, William Forrest, a British journalist, was struck by 'the storm of applause which greeted the appearance on the platform of Wilhelm Pieck and Otto Grotewohl, joint leaders of the communist-inspired Socialist Unity Party'. Reporting that 'this showed where the political sympathies of the delegates lay'. The keynote speaker, Colonel Tolpanov from the Soviet Military Government – a loud, brash, man with a penchant for large cigars – rhapsodized that the young must imbibe the culture of the whole world and 'above all the most progressive culture in the world, the culture of the Soviet Union'.[16] At the closing ceremony, Honecker mounted a floodlit marble stage to present dozens of youngsters with gilt-edged certificates of attendance, signed by himself.

Soon after, the FDJ manifesto was tweaked to state that a good understanding between the 'German youth and the most progressive youth movements in the world, especially the Russian youth, is one of the main objectives to be sought in order to regain equal rights for the German people.' Writing in *Einheit*, the SED's theoretical newspaper, Honecker had already described the Party's task to 'educate the young to become socialists and never to forget that they were the sons and daughters of the working people and the bearers of mankind's greatest idea'.[17]

In private, Honecker could not stomach statements from church groups on Christianity, and Herman Axman, also a SED member of the FDJ, poured out scorn on political rivals. Lighting a slow-burning fuse, Honecker set about limiting the influence of Christians at the FDJ's central training school and restricting them to delivering just two lectures (out of sixty on the programme).

Over the coming years, Christians and churches were singled out for persecution, culminating in the 'Jugendweihe' in 1955, an action undermining the church youth work and endangering the future of Christianity in East Germany. As the FDJ peeled off its democratic camouflage, leading CDU members and representatives of other political colours began quitting the movement.

No one was prepared for the brutal winter of 1946–47 when Germany slowly froze, succumbing to electricity cuts, burst pipes and coal shortages. As the situation worsened, Honecker deployed the FDJ to Saxony and Brandenburg to chop firewood and help shore up the fuel supply – placing the movement at the forefront of the public's consciousness. For a brief period, he hogged the limelight when helping hundreds of teenagers working at a coal mine. He also joined a group of boys dispatched to clean up farmland for the spring sowing. 'Many leaders and groups of the FDJ helped to ease the extremely arduous situation of the people during the long and hard winter,' he proudly recounted. As the snow mounds melted, he sent truckloads of FDJ boys to spearhead relief efforts during floods in Oderbruch near the Polish border. This kind of activity dispelled any doubts about Honecker's physical stamina and showed the FDJ not to be just a theoretical organisation but a practical one. By March 1947, it boasted 425,000 members, with 1,500 young people elected to municipal and district parliaments and thirteen members to state parliaments. In works council elections, over 8,000 young people became members, 80 to 85 per cent of whom were supporters of the FDJ.[18]

While in terms of visible achievements, Honecker's work life was remarkably successful, his home life remained turbulent. He endured an anxious period after Charlotte spent the winter in virtual seclusion under treatment for neurological problems, aggravated by heavy depression. A physician brought to the house was glum. There was nothing to be done except for his ailing wife to remain in bed. For the next few months, Honecker nursed Charlotte, administered medication, and read to her late into the night. But when her condition took a turn for the worse, she was moved to the St Joseph's hospital where she died on 6 June 1947, physicians said her passing was due to 'degeneration of the brain tissue'.

For years after, her medical records, death certificate, autopsy and burial details were closely guarded. As Ed Stuhler observed, 'it was as if this woman had never existed on paper'. In an attempt to wipe the slate clean, this awkward union was airbrushed from Honecker's life – with no mention made of Charlotte in biographies or his memoirs. Remarkably, though, a wedding certificate was unearthed by Stuhler at a registry office in Berlin in 1991. 'It is genuine. Honecker has done everything possible to cover up this marriage,' Stuhler told the author. 'It certainly is curious how it managed to survive the incinerator.'

After Charlotte's death, Erich Honecker engaged on several official foreign trips showing himself to be a gracious guest and enthusiastic tourist. Over the coming years, he displayed a genuine appetite for travel and wherever he happened to be, a few hours of his day were spent exploring. In Bucharest, he padded across the 'Little Paris of the Balkans,' where enough of the past lingered to give it the charm of tradition. He delighted in the sunlit boulevards and wooden houses hiding in the shadows of concrete buildings, and small white churches nestled beside modern apartment blocks. But, he observed, the poverty he saw everywhere, 'resulted from the undeveloped economy'.

From 19 July to 5 August 1947, he led an FDJ delegation to the Soviet Union to visit factories, schools and sanatoriums, treating Soviet soldiers wounded in the fight against Hitler. The journey, dubbed by the media as a 'Flight for Peace to the East', saw Honecker standing before rows of sick beds, and speaking of his gratitude 'for all that the Soviet people have done, for the trust placed in us.'[19]

The group – which included his FDJ deputy Edith Baumann – journeyed by air to Stalingrad and by train to Leningrad. In an interview with *Neues Deutschland* at the 'Astoria', the hotel earmarked for Hitler's headquarters before his failed assault on the city, he spoke of meeting German prisoners of war: 'they are not used in heavy labour,' he assured, 'and have the same food rations of the Soviet Army'.[20] He went to pains to explain that Russians did not dislike Germans, 'but hated German fascism, which destroyed their homeland so terribly. They know that the Soviet youth are sympathetic to the progressive German youth and will help them to eliminate the last remnants of fascism in Germany.'

In Moscow, away from official duties, he found time to join a procession of people filing silently past Lenin's dimly lit tomb in Red Square. In deference to this magnetic figure who had loomed over him since childhood, Honecker took off his hat and walked slowly in silence. He didn't kiss or touch the glass encasing Lenin's corpse, nor lay flowers ... but just stared.

During this trip, he nursed any grief he may have felt for Charlotte by embarking on a relationship with his deputy Edith Baumann, who was three years older but no dazzling bauble. Surviving photographs show a short, stocky, frumpy, plain-looking woman. According to friend Gerhard Schürer, what he felt for her was probably not physical attraction: 'I was always a bit surprised,' he stated, 'because politically they were an experienced couple. He was a handsome man with a good physique, whereas she was an elderly comrade,' a lady with a clear sense of morality. 'I was in need of support at the time,' Honecker said of Edith in 1990. 'We often sat together, including at her home in Mühlenbeck.' It is possible, that perhaps, Honecker sought security – and motherly love – which Baumann was able to provide. The daughter of a bricklayer, she was born in the working-class district of Prenzlauer Berg in 1909. While working as a typist, she joined the SPD in 1927 and belonged to the Socialist Workers' Youth. During the Nazi era, she served three years in prison and after 1945 was attracted to the KPD but joined the SPD to promote the idea of a unified party. After the KPD-SPD merger, she joined the SED executive, helping to set up youth committees alongside Honecker, as his deputy.

After months of courting, marriage followed. Honecker lost no time in demonstrating his credentials as a family man when Edith presented him with a daughter, Erica, in 1948. They moved into a handsome apartment at 12 Puderstraße, an elegant lane in Treptow, opposite the Russian memorial dedicated to Soviet soldiers lost in the battle for Berlin. 'Baumann's influence on him was positive in every respect,' Heinz Lippmann recounted. Increasingly self-assured, he 'looked better groomed and had more poise than before'. Her influence also stretched to the workplace, where decisions concerning his staff – especially those involving the disciplining of other officials 'were often made less harsh or obviated altogether by Baumann. At that time, Honecker made the impression of a very unassuming man who lived quite unostentatiously.' Life at Puderstraße was a time of happiness. He loved playing skat, a trick-taking card game with bidding, and, like Edith, adored films, theatre and dining out. In restaurants, he derived 'childish pleasure' by wolfing two full dishes of pig's trotters while his friends struggled with the first course. He had the constitution of a cockroach but as many comrades were afloat on a sea of alcohol, Honecker stuck to the occasional beer and avoided spirits. He rarely became snappish but detested the countless vodka toasts at official receptions. 'He was usually ill after these affairs,' Lippmann noted.[21] Wolfgang Ghantus, a government translator, recollected Honecker's weakness for American filter cigarettes:

> When I first met him in 1950, he offered me a Camel ciggy. Back then he was still puffing away like a chimney. He had no knowledge of foreign languages, which surprised me because he was in the Soviet Union for some time. But linguistically nothing could be done with him.[22]

Edith failed to convince Erich to visit Wiebelskirchen when his brother, Robert, returned from years in British captivity in the Egyptian desert. Having contracted Schistosomiasis, an infection caused by a parasitic worm in the blood, Robert was left drained. After spending several months bedridden, he died on 30 October 1947. Too full of grief for his brother, Erich could not bring himself to attend the funeral.

At this time, he was focused on establishing the Young Pioneers Association in the FDJ, which launched to a barrage of criticism from parents demanding children should be shielded from politics. 'We were of a different opinion,' Honecker explained. 'As early as at the age of 10, I saw that children were confronted with politics. They were either with the workers or with those who were against the workers.' He preached that imparting state ideology to schoolchildren was essential in order to 'convey the feeling of social responsibility to them'.[23]

With this in mind, Honecker was also busily improving *Junge Welt*, the central organ of the FDJ, which was morphing into a considerable success.[24] Behind the scenes, Edith used her contacts to procure interviews, and help compose Honecker's opinion pieces – which evolved a style like that of Russian periodicals. There was no luxuriance of rhetoric, his articles were stuffed with atrocious technical terms outside of the ordinary lexicon, such as: classless society, peasantry, bourgeois, capitalist and Narodnik. From here on, this became the distinctive Honecker tone – blunt, factual and without creativity or emotion. Although hardly a marvel of journalism, Honecker insisted *Junge Welt* was committed to 'progressive democracy' and exposing 'all those who, under the guise of democracy, are hostile to young people'.[25] Over the coming decades its circulation thrived and even exceeded one million, making it the most widely read newssheet, even outselling *Neues Deutschland*, its only real national competitor.

The paper was especially active during the Berlin Blockade, the first major international crises of the Cold War, sparked when the USSR cut off the Western Allies' rail, road and canal access to the sectors of Berlin under Western control. Everything, not just foodstuffs, but coal, gasoline, clothing and a staggering range of supplies for 2 million people had to be flown in. Day in, day out, week after week for fifteen months, British and American transport planes, army and civil, flew to West Berlin. A flight every ninety seconds was the average, with turnaround – landing, unloading and taking-off – averaging six to seven minutes.[26]

With mounting irritability, *Junge Welt* also fumed during the creation of NATO, as battle lines were drawn between East and West. At the same time, as Soviet and Western zones became politically, economically and socially more like their respective occupying powers, mistrust and suspicion grew.

Before long, two divergent Germanys had developed without direct reference to the German people themselves, as their destiny played out against the background of American–Soviet rivalry. When the Berlin airlift began, the United States and Britain had already agreed to establish a West German state as a federal parliamentary republic – which was formally born in Bonn during May 1949, with Konrad Adenauer as chancellor. As integration with the West developed as the foundation of Adenauer policy, West Germany became a major recipient of reconstruction aid under the Marshall Plan.

Amid this mass of seething tension, the SED screamed about Bonn's new 'separatist government' and set about establishing the 'German Democratic Republic' (GDR) across the territory administered by Soviet forces. Predictably,

Junge Welt sat at the forefront of a full-scale propaganda campaign, reporting that works' councils, political party leaders and workers' organisations demanded that the communist-led 'People's Council' should proceed immediately with the formation of a German Democratic Republic. Honecker commissioned leading articles by communist leaders to denounce in savage and blistering phrases the FRG parliament at Bonn. 'The time had come,' it was said, for the 'Bonn colonial state and the British-American capitalistic splitters and warmongers to be answered by a government of the people.'[27]

In a brief address, Wilhelm Pieck proclaimed the German Democratic Republic on 7 October 1949, with an appeal to all Germans to fight against 'NATO warmongers,' and 'German traitors in the service of American imperialism.' The founding manifesto demanded West Germany be abolished, occupation troops withdraw, the creation of a unified German currency, the prohibition of foreign investment (unless approved by Germans) and increased trade with the Soviet Union. Watching events unfold from over the border, the British, French and US High Commissioners for Germany, denounced the SED as having no title to represent Eastern Germany with the 'artificial creation of a popular assembly' which possessed no mandate for this purpose. Leaders in the 'so-called' German Democratic Republic, they charged, 'were not freely' chosen but instruments of Soviet foreign policy.

On paper, the first GDR constitution looked remarkably progressive, guaranteeing basic political rights and demands of the labour movement. In the first section, state authority was defined with 'Article 19' stating that economic order must 'correspond to the principles of social justice'. Although private initiative was desired (Articles 21 to 23), private ownership could be nationalised without compensation (Article 24). Furthermore, natural resources were declared 'public property' (Article 25). More ominously, provisions prohibiting strikes and walk-outs opened the possibility of repression under criminal law (Article 6). A few days later, when Pieck was elected president, Honecker sent 30,000 FDJ teens to march in procession along Unter den Linden. Honecker remembered:

> Torches were alight as far as one could see. After the World Youth Song had been sung, Berlin's Mayor Friedrich Ebert opened the demonstration. As FDJ chairman, I was given the floor to present to Wilhelm Pieck the oath of the German youth. It ended with the vow: 'We, the German youth, swear loyalty to the GDR, because it wants to and will bring peace and a better life to the young people. ... We want to be builders of our new house of peaceful work and militant humanity!'[28]

That night, FDJ lads carried life-size cardboard portraits of Pieck and his SED co-chairman Otto Grotewohl, the new Prime Minister, who declared that friendship with the Soviet Union was the greatest guarantee of peace: 'It will be the basis of our foreign policy. The government is willing to have friendly relations with all countries which desire them on a basis of equality'.[29]

By this point, Pieck was well into his seventies and content with fulfilling a patriarchal role with little power. Western journalist Michael Gray acidly observed that the old man pottered around on his farm, occasionally attended press interviews, and his speeches were read by an assistant, 'while he himself dozes off gently'.[30] Grotewohl, like Pieck, did not enjoy good health and within a year, his power was reduced as the SED restructured along more orthodox Soviet lines by electing a Central Committee, a Secretariat and a Politburo, a structure identical to the former KPD.[31] Ultimately, Walter Ulbricht, as First Secretary of the Politburo, would hold the keys to power.

A girl called Margot

On 14 December 1949, two days after arriving in Moscow with a delegation to celebrate Stalin's 70th birthday, Erich Honecker embarked on his first serious love affair with Margot Feist, one of the brightest young stars in the FDJ. Margot was short, she had a bun of brunette hair, fair skin and high cheekbones – and uncorked a stream of passion that he found impossible to resist. 'Margot first fascinated me because she was a pretty young girl,' Honecker recalled. 'Second, I was fascinated by the fact that she was also very active in the party.' Feist's biographer, Ed Stuhler, said she was 'lively, fun and had an infectious loud laugh'. He described a wild, impromptu affair, very spur-of-the-moment, which quickly took a different course. 'It has often been said that Margot got involved with Erich primarily to advance her career in this way,' Stuhler explained. 'But that's nonsense because at that time it was a great risk to enter such a relationship. The affair was extremely risky for Honecker because it violated the party's moral standards. But to be with Margot, he was willing to pay almost any price.' Born on 17 April 1927 in Halle, Margot was a fellow-spirit, having endured a childhood marked by poverty and struggle. Her father (a cobbler) and mother (a factory worker) were both members of the KPD and held onto their convictions after 1933, bringing her father to various prisons and concentration camps.

During their time in Moscow, the young lovers enjoyed Stalin's birthday junket – they attended the Bolshoi, where Erich watched – open-mouthed – as a crowd converged on stage. 'In the middle was Stalin! Then came Mao Tse Tung. I can still remember that the representative of the People's Republic of Poland first gave his good wishes in Russian,' he marvelled. 'The 70th birthday of Stalin was a historic moment, just as the foundation of the German Democratic Republic and the foundation of the People's Republic of China had been.'[1]

There was an aura of guilt about Honecker when he returned home to Edith and Erica in Berlin. At first, he tried to hide the romance but couldn't resist endless encounters at Margot's bedsit. Realising her husband had strayed, Edith penned a desperate letter to Ulbricht complaining that Erich never came home before one o'clock in the morning. 'Something burns like a fire in him,' she lamented. 'He can't get away from the girl … I found out that she asked him three times to divorce me.' The solution, she suggested in a postscript, was

34

to 'kick Margot Feist out of the FDJ and send her back to Sachsen-Anhalt'.[2] Although Ulbricht – a strict moralist in such matters – was appalled by the affair, the lovers found a powerful supporter in Wilhelm Pieck, who tried to defuse the issue. Honecker quietly moved out of Puderstraße, but Baumann resisted being convinced, or coerced, into divorce. She quit the FDJ and took a position in the secretariat of the SED Politburo.[3] Outwardly, she remained stoic and defiant, but her bitterness was immense and before long, she upped sticks to Pankow where she lived with Erica and her elderly father. In the months that followed, Erich's love affair with Margot reached its climax. As her star rose, she undertook several training trips to Moscow, and with her lover's help, climbed the ranks of the FDJ, ending up in Baumann's old job.

Paradoxically, Honecker had every reason – and more so as it turned out – for optimism as 1950 dawned. His messy private life failed to disrupt his career or efforts to transform the FDJ into a vehicle for Soviet indoctrination.

With the calming presence of Edith gone, he adopted an authoritarian working style to control the FDJ bureaucratic apparatus across departments dealing with working-class youth, rural youth, West German work, culture and education, students, sport and young pioneers. According to Heinz Lippmann, a dominant style of leadership evolved which saw Honecker speak more often and more loudly. Whenever there was criticism, there was a ready defence – he brooked no dissent, and 'abandoned efforts at collective leadership and returned to the old style of decreeing. There were hardly any fundamental discussions or criticism.'[4]

In terms of productivity, Honecker helped draft the first youth laws, including measures to promote sport, hiking and recreation. Furthermore, he devised a 'sports badge' for athletic accomplishments and pushed for the increased production of sporting goods and the construction of new stadiums.

From this time – the early 50s – the threat from the West was to be Honecker's theme to the exclusion of almost everything else. As world events shook the foundations of ordered society, US President, Harry S. Truman, prepared the development of the hydrogen bomb in response to the detonation of the Soviet Union's first atomic explosive device. In Europe, a joint declaration by America, Britain and France amounted to a virtual guarantee of German security, when it was announced that any attack on West Germany would be considered by them as an attack on the so-called 'Big Three'.

Furthermore, Paris, London and Washington ended the state of war with Germany and permitted the formation of a West German Ministry of Foreign Affairs, which could establish embassies abroad. From here on, the outward look of the FDJ adopted a much more militaristic tone – marching in columns, carrying flags, and discipline on parade became the norm. Honecker sent his young warriors to help fan anti-Western flames in Heligoland, a small archipelago in the North Sea, where squatters forced the British Royal

Air Force to abandon target practice. The situation was reddened by Prince Hubertus Loewenstein, a nationalist campaigner, who claimed the RAF was a menace to Germans and cited a series of incidents, one being the crash of an RAF Hornet fighter into a house in Dusseldorf. Honecker fuelled anti-British sentiment by encouraging author Peter Martin Lampel to write a play about the struggle. When first performed, *Kampf um Heligoland* was a far greater success than any of its participants anticipated. Over time, the theatre became a fruitful place for the FDJ to spread its message. Honecker persuaded Gustav von Wangenheim to write a Whitsun play which, he recalled, 'proved that an artist can be inspired by such a commission if it agrees with his own basic aims. In fact, when staged, the play *Du bist der Richtige* (You are the Right One) enjoyed considerable success.'[5]

Buoyed by such triumphs, he personally prepared a highly choreographed all-German youth gathering in Berlin, where 700,000 'young peace fighters' joined together in one of the mightiest demonstrations the capital had ever seen.[6] Among the privileged guests, Walter Ulbricht could be seen beaming at his young protégé. He was deeply impressed. Summing up his achievement, Erich recounted:

> I declared that the youth of our country would never bear arms for imperialist interests and that it would never fight against its liberator, the socialist Soviet Union. In a telegram to J.V. Stalin the delegates of millions of young people confirmed their determination to exert all their might to bring about the banning of the atom bomb, to shirk no effort or exertion in order to thwart the criminal designs of aggressive circles in the West, and never again to permit the German people and its youth to be driven into a war against the Soviet Union, against other socialist countries, or against progress.[7]

Bowled over by the spectacle, Ulbricht nominated Honecker as a candidate member of the Politburo, the actual government of the GDR. 'At the age of 38,' Erich wrote sheepishly, 'I was the youngest in a collective body of workers.' From here on, his star was firmly hitched to Ulbricht, who also engineered his protégé's membership to the Central Committee.

Meanwhile, over at the FDJ, Honecker was busily preparing for the Third World Festival Games of Youth and Students, which drew 2 million youths from 104 nations to East Berlin between 5 and 19 August 1951. Before the event, he described the festival as a chance for German youth to thank Soviet mentors who had both sheltered them from 'capitalist exploitation and guided them toward socialist solidarity'.[8] Wilhelm Pieck set the tone, telling the opening ceremony that 'British and American warmongers, despite their overwhelming defeat in Korea, have not given up their war plans.' Observing events, a West Berlin spokesmen called it a 'most dangerous manifestation of Soviet mass influence on German soil'.[9]

Despite the good start, behind the scenes, the event was swamped by leadership chaos. Instead of attending discussion seminars and rallies, many visitors slipped over to West Berlin, strolled along the Kurfürstendamm, took rides on double-decker buses, and enjoyed the famous Zoologischer Garten. Over the next few days, hundreds of young East Germans decided to defy orders and took similar jaunts. Through it all, West Berlin's mayor, Ernst Reuter, exploited the chaos by arranging his own 'capitalist' events and offering free drinks and snacks to the young tourists. Furious, Honecker mustered FDJ members to march into the Western sectors, flags flying, singing communist songs. The effort, however, turned into a fiasco when West Berlin police officers – untrained in patience or tolerance – pushed a column of 3,000 FDJers back from the sector boundary at Schlesische Brücke, arresting sixty-two. There were scattered incidents of violence at Neukölln, where two cordons of FRG policemen assembled at either end of the high street, trapping 4,000 FDJ marchers between them, and after ten minutes of scuffles, cleared the streets by force. Movements were also underway in Wedding, where police blasted water cannons to end a protest.

All of this was captured on film by SFB, the West German TV, and broadcast repeatedly on both Berlin and European television. Later that afternoon, Honecker arrived at the Schlesische Brücke to condemn the 'brutal actions' of the West Berlin police, which, he barked had 'unmasked itself and openly expressed what it understood freedom to be'.[10]

Ignoring taunts from West Germans, he made fantastic claims that 'numerous agents' had been arrested in East Berlin: 'We have clamped down on quite a number of agents including several who tried to poison the food of festival participants with certain tablets.'[11] As this was happening, Margo Feist – who was equally quick on her feet – was at Arkonaplatz in the Mitte district, perched on a garden wall protesting the 'hypocrisy of the West Berlin administration,' which, she screamed, 'attempted to lure the youngsters and then beat them down with truncheons'.[12]

Honecker's sanitised account, completely lacking in any real sense of proportion, stated that 'when 100,000 young peace fighters demonstrated in West Berlin, they got a bitter taste of the political system of capitalism. In brutal police attacks, ninety-six young people were injured. This too was part of the scene in those days.'[13]

In reality, he was embarrassed by the incident and reportedly paid a personal call on Ulbricht to apologise. The Politburo lamented Honecker's impulsiveness, calling it reckless and irresponsible. In FDJ circles too, it went down badly.

The Model Stalinist

By the early 50s, Soviet relations with many Western nations, including the United States, were at their worst levels since the Berlin Blockade, prompting extensive militarisation across the eastern bloc. Moscow was horrified when Washington detonated the first atomic bomb in the Marshall Islands and prepared nuclear war exercises in the Nevada desert. And, as if that wasn't bad enough, the United Nations declared China an aggressor in the Korean War and, at the same time, Stalin accused Britain, the US and France of organising a regular West German army. In response, he sent fresh troops and equipment into East Germany.

Stalin also pushed Ulbricht to form an army, but 'without making much noise, without propaganda. Once the army is already organised, then you can shout about it.'[1] Thus, over time, the GDR People's Police became a military force, training in armaments: 'You should have combat police,' Stalin told Ulbricht. 'You should change their instructions, improve their equipment and training.'

From then on, Honecker, too, was urged to reinforce the home front by gearing FDJ members to handle weapons, parachute and learn map reading in order 'to defend the peace'. Starting with the Pioneers, youngsters across the GDR sat through classes featuring anti-Western movies and newsreels. They were given a steady dose of lectures on topics like the 'American enemy', and the 'oppressed and their oppressors'. In addition to a regular solemn flag-raising ceremony, they were introduced to lessons celebrating the German 'rebirth' under the banner of socialism.

Over time, Honecker made a pronounced effort to organise special 'shooting games' (target practice) and rifle lessons, while the *Children's Hour* on GDR national radio, introduced toddlers to the song: *We must defend our homeland*.[2] Propaganda in *Junge Welt* took on a particularly virulent form by accentuating the peril of foreign threats. 'German youth is ready to defend its Republic,' the paper reported, in summing-up a number of 'letters' from young readers on the question of homeland defence. A 17-year-old apprentice toolmaker, Roland Schumacher, wrote: 'We might just as well save ourselves the trouble of rebuilding and working if we were not prepared to protect and defend our gains in the German Democratic Republic.[3] A student at an East

German university added: 'Should the warmongers dare to fall upon our homeland, I will follow the great example of Korean students and fight against the plague. In the ranks of the national armed forces, I will defend our gains and my opportunity to study.'[4]

As part of the militarisation scheme, Honecker was also commissioned by the Politburo to set up a paramilitary labour structure, based on the model of the Nazi Reich Labour Service (Reichsarbeitsdienst). While the new 'Dienst für Deutschland' was mainly developed by the Interior Ministry, Honecker was responsible for a large part of the planning to provide basic military training to teenagers, however, his commitment could not be described as passionate. During the spring and summer of 1952, over 100,000 youths headed to the countryside with little or no preparation for the hardships that awaited them.

Almost immediately, the Dienst für Deutschland developed into an organisational fiasco. Training camps erected on bog land flooded; there were shortages of food and sanitary facilities, and medical care was poor. After just a few weeks, some camps reported a sickness rate of 40 per cent, and furthermore, in addition to stomach and intestinal infections, it was learned sexually transmitted diseases had spread, as the camps were not separated into areas for young men and women, leading to accusations of moral degeneracy. As the complaints increased, a delegation from the Politburo – headed by Ulbricht's devoted crony Hermann Matern – was sent to inspect the camps but absolved Honecker of responsibility for the fiasco.[5] Though the details were damning enough, Ulbricht too – who bore a certain amount of accountability – set about reorganising the Dienst für Deutschland, before finally throwing in the towel in early 1953.

The episode proved a considerable blot on Honecker's copybook. His embarrassment wasn't helped that summer when the Politburo finally dealt with the problem of his exotic love life, given Edith Baumann was still resisting divorce. Despite her emotional distress, she reluctantly backed down when Margot Feist fell pregnant, and later gave birth to a 6½ lb baby daughter, Sonja. Some weeks later, with Honecker's parents Wilhelm and Karolina in attendance, Sonja was christened at a name-giving ceremony in Pankow.

Soon after, Margot and Erich married. However, Margot was then packed-off on a one-year course to the Soviet Union, leaving Sonja in the care of her parents. Speaking in 1990, Margot lamented this 'almost inhuman' decision and blamed Ulbricht for what she saw as some kind of perverted punishment for past indiscretions.

Characteristically, while Margot was away, Erich – as one associate delicately put it – did not lack female attention. Markus Wolf, a member of the state security services, recounted how Honecker remained discreet, but on one occasion was spotted 'surreptitiously slipping' through the backstreets of East

Berlin. Left in no doubt that he was visiting a secret girlfriend, Wolf informed his superior, who reacted with no surprise but insisted on filing details of the indiscretion.

On the work front, Honecker began to restore his reputation as a fearsome supporter of the SED's tightening political course. A year earlier, he had backed the first five-year plan which pushed a more assertive agenda to increase production, especially in the industrial sector.[6] He cheered loudly at the Second Party Conference in July 1952 when Ulbricht promised to codify his socialist ambitions by expanding heavy industry at the expense of consumer goods. Over the summer, the plan was put into practice as the SED set to work forming agricultural cooperatives based on state-controlled Soviet collectives.

However, amid the 'propaganda' success of the scheme, the reality was a disaster, as the forced collectivisation of agriculture proved one of the greatest traumas Germany had experienced since 1945. The pattern was familiar to Soviet historians, who watched in horror as chaos erupted on farms, sparking food riots and industrial unrest. By November, the GDR government was scraping the bottom of the food barrel to tide itself over.

In a tactic to deflect blame, Otto Grotewohl attributed the crisis to 'Western speculators, imperialist hate propaganda, the weather, saboteurs, failings in the supply ministry and too little imports'.[7] During this time, the situation looked so bleak that butter rationing became more stringent, salt and dried fish was substituted for meat and lard, and quark (skimmed milk cheese) took the place of butter. For many, memories of Hitler's wartime rationing came flooding back. 'It means wartime austerity again,' the West German press observed, predicting a clean-out in the GDR trade and supply ministries. (On cue, Dr Karl Hamann, Supply Minister, and his chief assistant, Rudolf Albrecht, were suspended from office).

The paradox of this drama was the Politburo's ill-judged decision to increase work quotas by 10 per cent across all state-owned factories, meaning workers had to produce more for the same wage. As if that wasn't bad enough, hikes in the price of sugar, milk, bread, healthcare and public transport caused outrage. At the notoriously threadbare HO government grocery stores, real coffee had not been sold for more than a year, while tea was a luxury few could afford, and eggs were scarce. Most cafes had nothing to sell – no soup, beer, or even sandwiches.

When added up, Ulbricht's Stalinisation amounted to a 33 per cent cut in the monthly wage, prompting a mass exodus of people to flee West. The sense of deflation in the SED worsened when a coal crisis emerged, prompting Ulbricht to appoint brigades of inquisitors to ferret out sabotage and failures in pit management. Ironically, at the same time, Grotewohl was still deceiving himself about responsibility by promising ruthless punishment of the 'men responsible' for the food shortages. Under an absurd new scheme, he set up fifteen commissions to make village-to-village tours, urging farmers to deliver more meat, wheat and other produce. Another directive called on farmers, officials and the public to 'leave desks and homes' and gather in the last of the crops. Labourers and tractor drivers on collective farms were called to 'mobilise all women and youths' and 'feel [themselves] responsible for every single sugar beet or potato'.[8] The theme of every citizen doing their bit became a constant feature of SED propaganda during 1952.

Meanwhile, with the crisis deepening, the military sealed off the 600-mile East-West German border, leaving only crossings in Berlin accessible because it was administered by all four occupying powers. Thus, from this point, Berlin became the main route by which East Germans fled West via eighty-one sector crossing points. More than 15,500 disenchanted souls of all creeds and political views (including 2,000 farmers) fled to West Berlin during October, marking the highest number of any post-war month.

This drain on manpower worsened during the first week of December when 600 farmers laden with personal baggage took flight, leaving large areas of land lying idle for want of labour.[9] Few knew where they were going, or for how long. The vast majority would never return. Officials in the Western sector said refugees were fleeing 'iron discipline, grey routine, blind purges and the fear of something worse happening'. Some left to avoid army call-up, others because their property was confiscated, or they were persecuted as Christians. In the latter area, Honecker was particularly active. Already by 1951, he had managed to contain church youth work by having 3,000 boys and girls expelled from school for being members of the 'Junge Gemeinde', the Protestant Church parish youth group. Under his aegis, an ongoing campaign of demonising Christians would continue throughout 1952. And as if that wasn't bad enough, the SED recommended the abolition of workers' Christmas bonuses, describing the traditional system as 'a disgraceful hangover from the capitalistic era'. For many East Germans, Ulbricht's socialist paradise was worse than living in Nazi Germany.

A Fragile Foundation

Basic attitudes toward the SED did not change with Stalin's death on 5 March 1953. What did change, though, was Moscow's attitude towards Ulbricht's disastrous reforms which were roundly criticised by a new power group revolving around Soviet Prime Minister Georgy Malenkov and KGB chief, Lavrentiy Beria.

During April and May, Stalin's heirs repeatedly warned Ulbricht to soften his reforms, but without success. As a result, on 5 June, Beria went for the jugular and gave Ulbricht a final warning to implement a 'New Course' and ditch reforms instigated the previous year. Aware that Beria considered Ulbricht to be a woolly-headed 'idiot' – several old hands in the SED Politburo felt secure enough to support Moscow. Among them, Beria's confidante Rudolf Herrnstadt, editor-in-chief of *Neues Deutschland*, the party daily, Wilhelm Zaisser, the GDR Minister of State Security, Anton Ackermann and Fred Oelssner. These men, and others, had long mouthed anti-Ulbricht sentiments and duly lined up to launch a carefully orchestrated broadside.

After being verbally mauled by the group, Ulbricht approved a reversal of policy by promising relief to hard-pressed farmers and an easing of anti-church measures but oddly, the unpopular 10 per cent rise in production quotas was kept in place, leaving workers furious.

It was in this ugly atmosphere that the first main crisis of the SED began to unfold. On 13 June, builders in East Berlin began slow-downs, followed two days later, on 15 June, by the dispatch of a small deposition to protest to aides of Otto Grotewohl – but there was no response. 'Anger,' one worker observed, 'was the emotion that dominates all others.' Feeling ignored and dejected, the next morning – 16 June 1953 – builders at Stalin Allee – East Berlin's most prestigious building project – along with workers at a new hospital in Friedrichshain, downed tools and took to the streets to demonstrate. As the number of protesters grew, they kept up an almost solid front as they carried a single banner reading: 'We, the building workers, demand production quotas be lowered.'

By 10 am, they were marching shoulder-to-shoulder singing *Bruder, zur Sonne, zur Freiheit!** across Alexanderplatz to Friedrichstraße, before tramping

---

* The principal policy-making and executive

42

down Leipziger Straße, the wide street leading to the House of Ministries, where they demanded the termination of work quotas, an improvement in earnings and better working conditions. Some complained about exploitation and meaningless striving, and the constant round of obedience to authority, whether it be showing ID papers or meeting quotas. As protestors chanted, the furore was ratcheted up a notch when neither Walter Ulbricht nor Otto Grotewohl – who were both hidden away within the House of Ministries – refused to meet the marchers. (Throughout his career, Ulbricht never took the chance to confront those who despised him.) Watching events unfold, Czechoslovak diplomats saw demonstrators' yelling slogans like, 'Down with German-Soviet friendship,' 'Down with the government ... Long live Western freedom.'; 'We want a new government.'; 'Long live the general strike ... We want butter, not armed police.' and 'We want free elections in Berlin.'[1] The Czechs also witnessed:

> FDJ members in blue shirts threatened, and shouts were heard that they should take their shirts off and that they had outlived their time. The SED has sent all its functionaries among the demonstrators to try and win them over.[2]

As the crowds swelled, the absence of clear orders from the administration baffled Russian officials. Only Fritz Selbmann, minister for heavy industry, attempted to quell the storm by addressing the crowd, but his speech was drowned-out by catcalls and curses. As the day wore on, there were also calls for a general strike. Then – in what must have been horrifying for Honecker – a young girl dressed in a FDJ shirt pushed to the front of the crowd and gave a speech. *Pravda* Correspondent P. Naumov recalled:

> We could not understand what she was speaking about, but after some hours, the American radio in West Berlin, RIAS, reported that she cautioned the workers to be careful. She said: 'We in the FDJ were sent here to spy on you.' The throng of people supported her. They applauded with roaring approval.

Naumov was flabbergasted at the SED's 'complete ignorance of the mood of the masses, lack of connection with the classes, an inability to speak to the people'.[3] Having witnessed the chaos in the House of Ministries, Honecker dashed over to the FDJ headquarters, a broad-beamed building near the Brandenburg Gate. After bounding up the stairs, he told subordinates, 'It's getting serious, we'll defend the building in an emergency, weapons are ready. The most important thing is that we, as the Party's cadre reserve, stand firmly and united around

Comrade Ulbricht, on whom the class enemy is now aiming fire.' Never before had the SED so obviously lost control of its own patch. Back in the House of Ministries, chaos mounted, as fevered discussions moved from room to room and across corridors. By mid-afternoon, Ulbricht was forced to withdraw the higher productivity quotas but as word of his decision spread, events were already careening out of control as calls for a general strike mounted. The die was cast, and by eventide RIAS was broadcasting news of the planned strike with details of times and locations: 'Tomorrow morning, 6.30 am at Strausberger Platz,' a square in the Friedrichshain-Kreuzberg district. In contrast, GDR radio aired emergency programmes, with all scheduled broadcasts, including news bulletins, dropped.

Before too much time passed, Soviet representatives convoked a meeting to discuss evacuating the families of Politburo members. In no doubt about the gravity of the situation, a visibly upset Honecker attempted, albeit unsuccessfully, to convince Margot to seek haven with the Russians. 'That night,' wrote Heinz Lippmann, 'I witnessed the first quarrel between Margot Feist and Erich Honecker, when he tried to justify this resolution as necessary.'[4] Sometime between eight and nine, Erich Honecker was back on the streets rallying 600 blue-shirted FDJers to stage a pro-Government counter-demonstration. Armed with a loudhailer, he arranged a quick rehearsal before the group hoisted banners declaring: 'I have confidence in our government,' and marched off down Stalin Allee singing patriotic songs, following the route taken earlier by the strikers. By nightfall, the disturbances had calmed as demonstrators prepared for a general strike.

In the small hours of 17 June, Walter Ulbricht took his entourage – including Erich and Margot – to shelter at the Soviet military headquarters in Karlshorst, the same place where Germany's unconditional surrender was signed in 1945. Couped up in the canteen, they sat restlessly preparing to follow events with a phone and transistor radio. Karl Schirdewan, second only to Ulbricht in the national hierarchy – had clear memories of Ulbricht and Grotewohl lingering over small talk and tea, 'nobody made any decisions. I thought the Party was leaderless.'

Then as the sun poked through storm clouds, workers began marching from outlying districts toward the House of Ministries. Across the GDR, similar marches got underway in Halle, Leipzig, Dresden, Gera, Merseburg and Görlitz. Along with SED and FDJ lackeys, police officials tried – and mostly failed – to encourage the marchers to return to their homes and workplaces. However, by 09.10, over 25,000 people had congregated in front of the House of Ministries, and tens of thousands more were en route to Leipziger Straße or in Potsdamer Platz.

As the crowds grew in Berlin, events took an ugly turn when around 100 demonstrators overpowered police at the House of Ministries. As all hell broke out, protestors attacked the entrance, breaking windows, throwing in burning pieces of wood, and battering the doors. Bruce Rothwell, a journalist from the *Daily News*, reported that: 'books by Marx, Engels, Stalin and Lenin were burned in street bonfires. Fire brigades turned hoses on the packed crowds – but in vain, they were already soaked from the rain.'[5] Over the coming hours, kiosks were overturned, and the red flag was torn down from the Brandenburg Gate and set alight.

The unrelenting violence unfolded with such extraordinary speed that the Russians declared martial law and sent in T-34 tanks, the same machines that had ploughed through Berlin in 1945. 'The Russians were ready,' Rothwell continued. 'Their machine guns opened up. The men were hit – and the Berlin workers retaliated with a shower of stones on the Red troops.'[6] The crisis was so grave that Russian tanks began crawling down Leipziger Straße to Potsdamer Platz, approaching the border with West Berlin. 'When the first shots came, I sought cover,' remembered teenager Peter Bruhn, who found himself in the thick of the action. 'Shortly afterwards, I got to Potsdamer Platz. There, I saw people running in wild panic to get over to the Western sector. Constantly, they had to throw themselves to the ground to seek cover. Some did not get up again.' From his place in the surging crowd, British reporter, Reginald Peck, 'watched the steel-helmeted Red Army men train the machineguns of their tanks onto the workers. Then volleys cracked into the air.' Despite the indomitable spirit of the demonstrators, as daylight faded, so did the Berlin 'uprising'. That evening, full of bravado, the Russian military commander, Andrei Grechko, sent a radiogram to Moscow: 'The following number of active provocateurs were caught and executed: one in Berlin, two in Magdeburg, two in Gorlitz, one in Jena. The population was told of the execution of the sentences.'

After anxiously awaiting the outcome of the demonstrations, Ulbricht, along with the Honecker's and other Politburo members, were chauffeured from Karlshorst back to their homes in Pankow.

That evening, as authorities cleaned up the plaza outside the House of Ministries, West German Commentator, Karl Willy Behr, took to the airwaves of Radio Hamburg (from a studio in the British sector of Berlin) to denounce the state of emergency imposed by the Soviets, which he called 'a state of war against the population of East Berlin'. It was significant, he said, that the SED government could be protected in no other way but by Soviet bayonets.[7]

On 24 June, in the presence of about 500,000 Berliners, Chancellor Adenauer pledged the entire nation's 'sincere will and desire' to continue its efforts to bring about German reunification in peace and freedom. Speaking at the West Berlin funeral ceremony commemorating the death of victims on 17 June, Adenauer pointed out that their uprising had demonstrated before the whole world that force cannot break the will for freedom. Soon after, Ernst Reuter,

West Berlin's charismatic mayor, renamed the Charlottenbuger Chausee – a long thoroughfare cutting through the Tiergarten to the Brandenburg Gate – 'Strasse des 17 Juni', as a memorial to those who died.

Oddly enough, the great irony of the unrest was that it secured Ulbricht's grip on power. Though its causes remain clouded, Ulbricht dubbed it a 'fascist coup attempt' and blamed 'saboteurs of peace'. He claimed the disorder was systematically provoked and organised by provocateurs from West Berlin and members of a clandestine American network. In support, socialist media ran a flood of stories transmitting the same line. 'It is known that in West Berlin, controlled by the Americans,' Radio Prague noted, 'there are a number of espionage agencies and fascist organisations which organise sabotage and terrorism in the German Democratic Republic in return for American dollars. Adenauer turned to these professional criminals.'[8]

Shrill propaganda was backed up by supportive articles from the likes of Kurt Bartel, secretary of the Writers' Union and Ulbricht apparatchik. Feigning indignation, he claimed to have been 'embarrassed by the immaturity of the workers', and penned a booklet entitled: *How Ashamed I Am*, addressed to builders, painters and carpenters. 'Repairing destroyed houses is easy,' he emotively explained. 'Restoring destroyed trust is very, very difficult.' He went on to thank the Red Army for wiping the city clean and blamed the uprising on:

> scum from the other side [West] who stole on silver bicycles through the city, like swallows before the rain. But you could go to sleep in your beds by nine that night, like good children. For you and for the peace of the world, the Soviet army and the comrades of the People's Police kept watch. Are you not ashamed, as I am? For you will have to build much and well and wisely in future before this shame of yours will be forgotten.

At first, the GDR's most eminent writer, Berthold Brecht, placed himself behind the regime. However, after reading Bartel's booklet, he penned an extraordinarily provocative poem, 'The Solution,' which, remarkably, managed to pass the censors of *Neues Deutschland*.

> After the uprising of the 17th of June
> The Secretary of the Writers Union
> Had leaflets distributed in the Stalinallee
> Stating that the people
> Had forfeited the confidence of the government
> And could win it back only
> By redoubled efforts. Would it not be easier

In that case for the government
To dissolve the people
And elect another?

It was Ulbricht who 'cracked the whip' and restored discipline by detaining construction workers, wayward functionaries and the intelligentsia. Over the next six months, 1,500 people were sentenced to prison terms on trumped-up charges, two were executed.

In a moment of high drama, Karl Schirdewan – a dour figure with tinted glasses and a baldpate – sent out a memo to all SED district offices on 21 June to deploy members to discover the true attitude of workers: 'This evening they must go to the bars, and, so to speak, listen in on the conversations.'[9] When completed, Schirdewan's probe noted countless thousands of FDJ members had taken part in the protests. This was enough to make Honecker's restless mind wander off as he sensed plots and resentments everywhere.

The Russians also fed his insecurities after complaining that the FDJ education programme 'only existed on paper'. Albert Norden, a member of the Central Committee, later rounded on him. He carped that his administrative talents were uneven, and he shouldn't confront young people as a politician. 'He should be their friend and fool about with them for a bit. His speeches shouldn't consist of great political theorems.'[10] For all these reasons, Otto Grotewohl feared that the party was losing its grip on young minds, and complained he had 'not observed the slightest tendency towards development' in Honecker's work in recent years.[11] Fred Stamp, a personal assistant to Grotewohl, even recommended Honecker be replaced by a 'more capable, more experienced comrade'.[12]

As ever, Honecker tried to bear tribulation stoically by flitting around the Berlin region in the wake of 17 June. With the fiery zeal of a preacher, he sold a new gospel of openness to the workforce, assuring the SED would solve existing problems and improve living conditions. 'During the two preceding days,' he explained, 'I had talked to workers in all departments of the VEB Engine Works factory in Babelsberg. Thus, I got to know their thoughts, ideas and desires and could explore the causes of their discontent.'[13] Displaying more personality and less authority, he admitted 17 June showed some FDJ members had not recognised the nature of the 'fascist provocation' and were, therefore, not in a position to counter 'enemy propaganda' with effective arguments. He added: 'This is to be attributed to a lack of political knowledge and the lack of well-organised youth-orientated political training within the organisation.'

To weed out dissent, Honecker requested the State Secretariat for University Activities oust 183 students from academies and universities, accusing them of expressing opposition to the policy of the Government by both words and actions.

At a thrilling Politburo meeting on 8 July, Ulbricht's unpopularity became evident when every member – except Hermann Matern, chairman of the Party Control Commission and Honecker – demanded he step down. However, there was no question of the Soviets risking further instability by helping unseat Ulbricht – the Kremlin stuck with the tried and true.

Amid this upheaval, Beria had been eliminated in the first post-Stalin purge in Moscow, leaving his supporters in the SED Politburo, Wilhelm Zaisser and Rudolf Herrnstadt, at the mercy of Ulbricht who declared them 'enemies of the German people' and replaced them with uncritical supporters. Honecker later recounted that Beria wanted to liquidate the GDR as a socialist state and give up the goal of a comprehensive construction of socialism. 'Just at this time, in 1953, Herrnstadt tried with Zaisser to topple Walter Ulbricht, at a point in time when the Party required firm leadership. After the arrest of Beria, this plan collapsed.'[14] (In fact, Beria wanted to ditch East German communism entirely, and seek the reunification of a neutral Germany in return for generous Western compensation).

As the atmosphere calmed, Ulbricht was feted in Moscow during August when the Soviets promised more economic aid, an end to reparations payments, and elevated the diplomatic missions between the two governments to embassies. Damage-limitation to heal the wounds of 17 June saw some citizens granted travel concessions and, for a brief moment, the tense relationship between church and state became friendlier when seventy church officials were released from detention and Grotewohl promised more tolerance to the Christian community. Even Honecker, who had been staging a campaign against Evangelical youth groups, graciously received a delegation of leading church representatives and heard them out sympathetically. He expressed no objections to involving young people in church community work and promised that all young people who had lost their apprenticeships for belonging to Christian youth groups would be reinstated. On top of that, the Protestant youth magazine *Die Staffette* was allowed to reappear after being banned. Predictably though, six months after Honecker's assurances, bands of FDJ youths were targeting young Christians again. On one occasion, twelve FDJ activists roughed up a young nun at Berlin Ostbahnhof, ripping a small silver cross from her coat. Decrying this state-sponsored persecution, the provost of St Marien church recounted a chain of similar incidents and suggested a new meeting with the FDJ. He recalled that:

> Honecker did not respond. New incidents against young Christians were reported in Karl-Marx-Stadt, Leipzig, Dresden, Magdeburg and Schwerin. A state youth convention scheduled for 13 June 1954 in Güstrow was not allowed to take place and all efforts to get in touch with Honecker failed. Twelve months after July 1953, we were faced with closed doors.

Reactions in the international press to the treatment of Christians were almost universally condemnatory.

Unsurprisingly, the events of 17 June laid the groundwork for Ulbricht's increased interest in the Ministry of State Security (MfS) – the so-called 'Sword and Shield of the Party'. Its failure to sniff-out dissent in June sealed the fate of Minister Wilhelm Zaisser, who was expelled from the Politburo and the Central Committee and deposed as minister. Commonly known as the 'Stasi', the MfS was set up under the direct guidance of the Soviet Cheka to serve as a secret police, investigative agency and foreign intelligence service. Zaisser was replaced by Ernst Wollweber, a man of unstable temperament and defective judgement, known internationally as a specialist in shipping sabotage. Under Ulbricht's guidance, he worked overtime conducting a wave of arrests against opponents of the regime, as well as putting emphasis into monitoring the population within the GDR, as opposed to operations in West Germany and elsewhere.

In order to track down and eliminate 'hostile-negative elements', MfS functionaries penetrated all areas of life, building-up dossiers on the entire population (More than 100 miles of files were amassed in Berlin alone). Unofficial collaborators were recruited to spy on neighbours, workmates and friends. Known as 'IMs', collaborators reported what was happening in companies, at universities, in the arts, medicine and sport, or even in their own family circles. In a number of cases, 'IMs' infiltrated opposition circles and provided information about colleagues or fellow students.[15] Over time, Stasi agents were even able to listen in to telephone conversations at NATO headquarters with no difficulty, and – using state-of-the-art snooping techniques – they could eavesdrop on any telephone call in Europe. As the MfS pulled in suspects, the judiciary assumed a dominating role. The Minister of Justice, Hilde Benjamin, known as 'Red Bide', oversaw numerous show trials against agents and saboteurs, working under the slogan 'no impartiality towards the enemies of the State'.

Return to Moscow

The shockwaves of the June uprising finally caught up with Erich Honecker in May 1955 when he was 'retired with honour' as chairman of the FDJ and packed off to Moscow to begin a one-year study course at the Party college. Despite a faint whiff of disgrace – given Grotewohl's, Norden's and Schirdewan's earlier criticisms – Ulbricht pinned a 'National Gold Medal for Merit' on Honecker's blazer and, for good measure, named a trawler from the Baltic fishing fleet in his honour.[1]

Ulbricht deemed it essential that his protégé expand his academic knowledge, given that during his decade at the FDJ he had hardly found time for thorough political training, despite the SED demanding leadership cadres be properly schooled.

'So, for the second time I was taking a protracted study trip to the land of Lenin,' Honecker mused in his memoirs. He recognised that there were large gaps in his education and later wrote he was glad 'that my party was now giving me yet another opportunity to broaden my knowledge systematically'. The school pushed a stiff regimen on students, requiring tedious lessons on the history of the Soviet Union and the CPSU, basics of Marxism, dialectic and historical materialism, the history of the international labour movement, economics, and political and economic geography. 'For us, study meant still more thorough comprehension of the laws of social development and the generalised experiences of socialist construction.' Honecker also attended lectures at other Soviet academies and was particularly interested in talks on military history and political issues. Like in 1930, he was obliged to take an intensive course in Russian, but was a hopeless linguist and still failed to grasp the language.

His education continued smoothly until a bolt from the blue stunned the communist world on 25 February 1956. That evening, Soviet leader Nikita Khrushchev astounded a closed session of the Twentieth Congress by denouncing Stalin as a vicious, half-mad, power-crazed despot: 'The cult of the individual acquired such monstrous size chiefly because Stalin himself, using all conceivable methods, supported the glorification of his own person.' In the speech, Khrushchev repeated Lenin's warning that Stalin was likely to abuse his power, and cited countless instances of excesses, including purges, a cult of personality, foreign policy errors, secret plots to kill critics, and military blunders which cost countless lives.

When informed about the speech, Honecker could scarcely believe his ears. In a 1990 interview, he admitted to tearing down a picture of the late dictator from his bedroom wall. 'This was so to speak, my first emotional reaction. It was all very shameful for us, those of us who had honoured Stalin so much.'[2]

As details of the speech passed from lip to lip, Ulbricht was asked what he should say to East Germans studying at the party school in Moscow: 'You can tell them Stalin is no longer considered a classic,' he snorted.

But joking aside, Ulbricht was soon under pressure to join in the anti-Stalin onslaught. Loathe to push his hero into the shadows, he made half-hearted criticism of the former dictator, accusing him of 'self-adulation and disfigurement of the history of the party' in his post-war writings. Beyond that, he resisted all efforts toward supporting Khrushchev's de-Stalinisation which – over time – heralded in economic reforms and on the cultural front, opened new contacts with the outside world.[3]

As Stalin was consigned to a no-man's land of history, a new wind blew across the Soviet Union, as thousands of former dissidents were released from jails, and once banned foreign books, movies and music became available. Soviet agriculture, which Stalin had virtually destroyed, was resuscitated, and a new surge in housing construction allowed hundreds of thousands to move out of jammed collective apartments.

But those expecting the winds of change to whistle through the streets of Berlin were left sorely disappointed. The Soviet ambassador, Georgi Pushkin, along with Karl Schirdewan – now considered one of the brightest lights in the SED, and viewed by Khrushchev as a potential successor to Ulbricht – expressed displeasure at the lack of reforms.[4]

The atmosphere soured further at the third SED conference in March 1956, when those hoping Ulbricht would tackle the issue of the Khrushchev speech, and interpret what it meant for them, were left bitterly disappointed. Instead, he was ambivalent and evasive and launched into lectures on everything ranging from transport to corn cultivation, prompting several participants to walk out.

In an awkward effort to find a point of agreement, Ulbricht approved the establishment of a 'Commission for the Review of Matters of Former Party Members' to examine the 'unjustified persecution' of SED comrades in the late 40s and early 1950s. At the time, around 13,000 people were serving sentences in East German jails for 'crimes against the state'. Soon after, as a gesture of conciliation, seventy-three SED members were rescued from official obscurity, including Anton Ackermann, Elli Schmidt and Hans Jendretzky. Ulbricht's biggest concession was granting pardons and early releases to 11,896 others. By the end of 1956, nearly 21,000 people had been released.

Highflyer

At the age of 44, Erich Honecker could view his political career with a sense of achievement. 'Enriched with new impressions and new insights,' he returned to Germany in July 1956. 'The study results were not bad,' he recounted. 'I finished with distinction. The time I studied in Moscow was altogether the finest in my life. My study there laid the decisive basis for my abilities later on – theoretical, political, economic and cultural.'[1] As he moved closer to the inner circle of government, his *annus mirabilis* started with a change of demeanour, tidier social life and smarter image. Family life with Margot and daughter Sonja resumed at their spacious home on Majakowskiring in Pankow, a leafy cul-de-sac with century-old trees, pristine park and gilded-age mansions. Prime Minister Otto Grotewohl lived next door, and around the corner, Walter and Lotte Ulbricht occupied a spacious villa. There was thick barbed wire fences around the grounds, a private park and tennis courts, from where Ulbricht could be heard grunting and shrieking during his daily practice.

While waiting for a full-time appointment, Honecker proved his usefulness by undertaking various jobs in the youth and sports movements. For starters, he led a team repairing storm damage at a mine, appeared at a gymnastics and sports festival, and took part in a 'frank and open discussion' about problems facing athletes and the future of the Olympic team.

Finally, he was appointed as the Central Committee secretary for security issues, giving him responsibility for the police and the state security service and the 'National People's Army', which had been officially formed from the barracked People's Police. One of his most important tasks was to muster recruits for so-called combat groups, a military-trained militia recruited from among the factory workers reporting directly to the SED leadership. As Heinz Lippman observed, Walter Ulbricht showed unlimited trust in Honecker by putting the state's power apparatus in his hands: 'The old Ulbricht-Honecker alliance was re-established after a one-year break at a higher level.' The kind of values Ulbricht instilled on his protégé is entirely clear. He took lessons in learning intrigue, manipulation, patience and the deployment of innuendo and half-truths – tools essential for survival in the corridors of communist power.

With his position in the Politburo confirmed, Honecker tore off around the GDR giving rousing speeches on his usual themes about subversion, greater military strength, and launching an ideological counter-offensive against fascism and capitalism. He mixed with the rank and file, was articulate and knowledgeable, and engaged in small talk rather than shop.

Meanwhile, in the wider world, the unintended consequences of Khrushchev's speech and subsequent thaw had led to substantial disenchantment towards the Soviet Union in Poland; while in November 1956, the first flames of revolution in Central Europe saw a violent uprising of workers and students in Hungary, which brought the government such distress that only the intervention of the Soviet army could stabilise the situation. Aided by Moscow, Honecker used the Hungarian 'counter-revolution' as an excuse to further tighten security. 'He was aware that the working class would never forgive the SED and the GDR government if they had neglected to strengthen the armed forces in this situation ... he devoted himself to this task with great energy,' a state-penned biography published in 1977 asserted.[2] Through his own dedication, the hagiography added, Honecker 'did much to strengthen the cause of socialism and to raise the overall level of political and ideological work in the army'.

Around this time, the entire SED apparatus – including Honecker – moved to a new Central Committee building on Werderscher Markt in the former Reichsbank, for which Adolf Hitler had laid the foundation stone in 1934. From then on, this concrete behemoth became the supreme centre of power in the German Democratic Republic. Honecker held court in chambers on the third floor from where he kicked-off a frenzied pursuit of critical intellectuals, who, encouraged by Khrushchev's reforms, demanded liberalisation of society, or a so-called 'third way', and 'human socialism'. Dissenting voices were loudest at the University of Berlin, where the resignation of Stalinists was openly demanded. Having helped to purge resentment in the capital, Honecker spread his tentacles far and wide and choreographed a hate campaign against philosopher Ernst Bloch in Leipzig, who was ostracised and isolated from his staff and students. By then, the outlook for opposing voices was grim. Writer and professor Alfred Kantorowicz fled into exile in Berlin, as did the Rector of Jena University, Professor Josef Hämel, and the literary scholar, Hans Mayer. Many other academics followed them. In all, *Neues Deutschland* reported on 1 November, seventy-three 'agents' had been arrested on charges relating to the security and political and economic future of the GDR. Years later, Honecker recalled when the 'class enemy tried to get students from the Humboldt University onto the streets in Berlin at the end of October 1956; it was the working-class KDA combat groups that thwarted this intention simply by appearing.' The KDA, a paramilitary organisation serving as the de facto militia of the SED, was composed of party members and politically reliable working people. In a speech to members, Honecker once said:

> The class enemy hates the working-class combat groups in the GDR. That doesn't bother us. He fears it. That's a good thing and he's right to fear it. The high level of political maturity and morale, firm discipline and boundless devotion to the cause of socialism is the guarantee that the combat groups will continue to carry out all the tasks assigned to them with honour.[3]

But it wasn't just academics that fell victim to the purges. With the help of Mielke, Honecker plunged energetically into the task of gathering enough evidence of dissent to have his old rival Karl Schirdewan and Stasi chief Ernst Wollweber dismissed – both held critical views of Ulbricht and sought to 'democratise' the SED. As his investigation intensified, Mielke installed a listening device in Wollweber's apartment, where Schirdewan's friends often met for a confidential exchange of views.

Honecker explored two parallel lines of movement: a so-called faction aimed at deposing Ulbricht and incompetence. When he had amassed enough 'evidence', Honecker charged that Wollweber's 'false appraisal' of 17 June prevented state security agencies from performing their duties properly:

> *The struggle against subversive elements was criminally neglected by Comrade Wollweber. Investigations showed that he had failed in his duties. Instead, he tried to recruit other comrades for the divisive work of the Schirdewan group. This divisive activity was conducted with a lot of talk. Oppositional agencies were able to acquire information about internal party matters and use it against the party.[4]*

As for Schirdewan, Honecker barked that his deviation from the Party line became clear during the Hungarian revolt. Furthermore, he allegedly 'underestimated the dangers of NATO policy and ignored attempts by West German militarists to undermine the GDR'.[5] During this dressing down, Schirdewan glimpsed the glint of cold steel behind Honecker's affable façade: 'It was like an inquisition from the Middle Ages.' Fred Oelssner, chief party theoretician, was also expelled from the Politburo. Heinz Brandt, an SED functionary in Berlin, described the loss of Schirdewan as a bitter blow to reformers. 'When Khrushchev got into increasing difficulties after the Hungary debacle – after all, he was accused of having triggered the signs of disintegration in the hitherto 'monolithic' Eastern bloc with his secret speech and his thaw policy – he saw himself forced to concede on the Schirdewan-Wollweber issue'.

Firmly back in the saddle,[6] Walter Ulbricht issued a communique decrying the 'activities of an opportunist group which attempted to change the party line'. For his sterling efforts, Erich Mielke – Wollweber's aggressive deputy, was rewarded with the post of Minister of State Security. Wolfgang Herger, a member of the Central Committee of the SED, remembered Mielke as a tiny man with a pudgy babyish face and a constant smile that gave him the look of a mischievous, overweight kid. Whether in a car or boat, train or plane, office, or conference, or even the bathroom, Mielke's flow of instructions and commentary never ceased. Herger amplified this image, observing:

> When we Germans do something, we do it thoroughly! [...] If there is someone at the head of the Ministry for State Security for whom ideological diversion is the decisive factor, then gigantic apparatuses are set up and expanded to combat them, and with all conceivable thoroughness. [...] And Erich Mielke was, as far as that is concerned, a very typical German who really organised everything from top to bottom and who always wanted to know everything – about everyone.[7]

Under Mielke's tutelage, Honecker mastered the workings of Stasi and security machinery and shared his passion for secrecy and intrigue, using his position of undeclared heir apparent with energy and skill. He approved of Mielke's astonishing network of surveillance which employed a vast web of informants and operatives tracking opponents and detractors to the ends of the earth. Honecker's responsibility for military and security issues involved close contact with General Willi Stoph and Karl Maron, the head of the People's Police. 'They were, so to speak, placed under my control,' he explained. 'The greatest achievement of that time was that, despite all the attacks on the work of the central committee of the SED and its politburo, the GDR was successfully defended, and a secure basis was laid to withstand all the storms of that time.' In Mielke, Honecker and Ulbricht had found a dogged defender.

Endless Flight

Erich Honecker celebrated May Day 1958 in Copenhagen, where he was applauded after announcing 'those responsible for crimes against Denmark in the Second World War had been brought to account in the GDR'. An item transmitted by ADN, added that he also charged 'West German militarists' with continuing to work against normalisation of relations between the GDR and Denmark.[1]

This tirade against Bonn was delivered under the shadow of the FRG's 'economic miracle' or 'Wirtschaftswunder', which continued to impress the world and surprise even Germans themselves. This extraordinary prosperity – where possibility had no bounds – saw car production increase by 100,000 compared to 1956, while the national income shot up by 10 per cent. Furthermore, exports recorded a 16 per cent increase and shipping tonnage rose by 12 per cent. The sensational recovery was attributed, in part, to Conrad Adenauer, who was voted into office again in 1957.

While Western media celebrated Wirtschaftswunder, it followed the contrasting situation in the GDR where, in a clear attempt to tame spiralling inflation, the government called in all existing GDR bank note currency and replaced it (without devaluation) with a new issue on a strictly rationed basis. This made it almost impossible for banknotes held by people living abroad to be exchanged.[2] To make matters worse, the loss of GDR manpower to the West continued despite new laws authorising prison sentences for those attempting to leave without permission.

During this period, Honecker's security services ensured the noose around the GDR was strengthened. A permit was needed to enter a four-mile zone close to the national border, where frontier police surveyed the zone from dugouts and watchtowers. Three parallel barbed-wire fences ran along parts of the frontier, a foretaste of Berlin's future.

The size of the exodus or 'Republikflucht' from Berlin – which had already taken 3 million Germans out of the East since 1949 – rose to an alarming figure of 1,000 persons a day during July and August 1958. This endless paralysis was caused by political crackdowns and the unbeatably higher standard of living in the Western world and the opportunities for more liberal ways of life. During the first half of the year, figures revealed no fewer than 621 doctors

56

and dentists, 1,392 schoolteachers, 85 scientific assistants and 200 professors, lecturers and other academicians had fled West, leaving faculties in the world-famous universities of Halle, Leipzig, Dresden and Jena, denuded of their best men.

As the staggering exodus continued, Ulbricht tooted his own horn. On 12 July 1958, he took to the floor of the Fifth SED Congress to boast that East German living standards would quickly surpass those of the FRG. Moreover, Moscow, he said, had agreed to triple deliveries of iron, steel, copper and other raw materials.[3]

From here on, Ulbricht's great Socialist revolution would see the GDR make the transition from five to seven-year planning. In agriculture – despite the shortages of 1953 – forced collectivisation was ramped up; while private companies were more firmly integrated into the planned economy. Standing witness to the Fifth SED Congress, Khrushchev flew into East Berlin to add his endorsement.

'We want to live in peace and to attack no one,' he told a rally of 200,000 people. At a reception, a rare flash of unity between Ulbricht and Khrushchev was caught on film, it was a brief and friendly moment but probably uncomfortable for both. The two had known each other in Stalingrad in 1943, where Khrushchev witnessed Ulbricht using a megaphone to appeal to German troops to lay down their arms. 'He would crawl around at night for a long time, and when he came in, we would have dinner with him, and would report how many Germans had surrendered.'

On the same platform at the Fifth Congress, Honecker's position was also strengthened. After his status as a full member of the Politburo and secretary of the National Defence Council was affirmed, he spoke about the military in stark terms, saying training, morale and leadership all needed to be addressed.[4] He pushed for greater SED involvement in the national army and accused officer comrades of underestimating the opinion of the party: 'Some officers believed that to strengthen the party's leading role would weaken the individual performance and discipline in the armed forces.' He found more sour words for the relationship between officers and rank-and-file servicemen:

> There are still officer-comrades who fail to see their enlisted men
> as class comrades and co-fighters for the cause of socialism and
> peace on an equal footing with themselves, who pay no attention to
> their personal needs and troubles and treat them condescendingly
> even off duty. With the help of our party organisations, we
> must all quickly rectify this unhealthy state of affairs, which is
> incompatible with the character of our armed services. At the
> delegates' conferences, a number of comrades made the valid

criticism that top officers do not always respond to suggestions from the youth groups for improving military training and political work and suppress unfavourable comments on the way they perform their duties. Some officer-comrades were criticised for assuming that while the men can learn from them, they cannot learn anything from the men. During the discussions, several comrades openly posed the question of these officer-comrades' relation to the party.

Honecker stressed relations between the members of the armed forces and production workers 'must become closer, even though they have already developed well in the past'. Announcing that many enterprises had delegated members of their staff to the military to maintain close contact with them, he said: 'This will help to link the members of the armed forces still more closely with socialist construction and help them to handle the weapons which the working people have put into their hands in such a way as to protect the victory of socialism.'[5]

As a scan through the East German newspaper archives reveals, Honecker had become a minor celebrity by this point. Few military parades, tattoos, full-dress inspections or conferences were complete without his valued contribution. Once, on a visit to troops, he interrupted a display of physical exercises, stripped to the waist, and performed a difficult shoulder balance on the parallel bars.

After the Fifth SED Congress, Honecker eased the pressure on professors and intellectuals, cooling his drive to suppress liberal tendencies and freer thinking in universities. The reason for this reversal was the flight of intellectuals to the West. As the human exodus continued, a solution was taking shape in Ulbricht's head. At his instigation, Khrushchev tried to drive the Western powers out of Berlin by serving notice on France, Britain and the United States on 10 November 1958, to get out of the 'capital of the German Democratic Republic' within six months. If they refused, he promised to sign a peace treaty with the GDR, which (he contended) would terminate the legal justification for the Allied deployment in the city.[6]

However, the threat wasn't enough for the Americans, British or French to rise, and their unity and resolve remained unbroken. For the Allies, there was no doubt that the departure of the 10,000-strong Western defence force from Berlin would lead to the absorption of the 2.2 million West Berliners into the GDR. Thus, in a meeting of the North Atlantic Council, the Allies stated they were determined to maintain their position and rights in Berlin, including the right of free access. 'We are solemnly committed to hold West Berlin, if need be, by military force,' US Secretary of State Dulles crowed.[7]

Meanwhile, to the surprise of no one, Ulbricht's tone kept getting colder. In a New Year's message, he described West Berlin as a 'cancerous growth' that must be operated on during 1959. Even the decrepit president, Wilhelm Pieck, added to the drama when wheeled out to say NATO attempts to save West Berlin would fail. Unable to resist the chance to simultaneously boost his profile and yank the FRG's chain, Honecker assisted Defence Minister Willi Stoph and Interior Minister Karl Maron in issuing 'Orders of The Day' asking Soviet armed forces to be ready to go into action against 'any imperialist aggression'.

Despite the agitation, Khrushchev's ultimatum deadline for the Allies to quit Berlin on 27 May 1959 was dialled back, but nobody was deluded into thinking the matter was dead. Khrushchev's posture of restraint came after the Soviet Union achieved several key distinctions that year, such as becoming the first nation in space, the first to place a satellite in solar orbit, and the first to crash a missile on the moon, achievements which left American self-confidence badly shaken.

While these momentous events were transpiring in the Soviet Union, Honecker keenly followed a series of anti-Semitic events in the FRG, including the defacement of a synagogue in Cologne by two members of the right-wing 'Reich party', a political clique regarded as a revival of the Nazi Party. While demands were made in Bonn to ban the movement, Adenauer left the party alone. His blunder proved a Godsend for Honecker and the SED propaganda machine and a huge embarrassment for West Germany. 'Such forces,' noted *Neue Zeit*, 'could unfold again which, with old slogans, would awaken the "consciousness against the East" and stir up racial hatred.'[8] At the same time, in his capacity of defence chief, Honecker muddied the water by accusing the FRG of imperialistic intentions after clumsy attempts by F.J. Strauss, the ham-handed West German defence minister, to obtain bases for the Bundeswehr in Spain. Even Western media described him as 'the man in Bonn who scatters the heaviest Teutonic bricks'.[9] As if that wasn't bad enough, Strauss also gave the Kremlin a splendid opportunity to harvest propaganda when he encouraged the Bundeswehr to publish a blimpish pamphlet calling for the arming of the Federal Republic's forces with long-range nuclear weapons.

The Sixties

For Erich and Margot Honecker, 1960 began with a drastic change of lifestyle when Politburo members were moved to a densely wooded settlement in Wandlitz, near the B109, north of Berlin. In this high-walled stronghold, camouflaged as a 'wildlife research area', the SED hierarchy lived a gilded existence, safe from their fellow countrymen.[1] The couple was installed into a suburban-looking house on Habichtweg, next door to Ulbricht and his wife Lotte, only separated by a thin line of bushes. Erich Mielke lived at House 14, located at the extreme north-west corner of the settlement; his only direct neighbour was Honecker's ex-wife Edith Baumann, who moved in with daughter Erica.[2]

The Honecker house had just seven rooms – 180 square meters of living space – and a small private garden and patio (strangely enough, there were garden gates, but no fences). The inner ring, where the functionaries lived, was surrounded by a high concrete wall secured by a state security guard regiment. Honecker paid a monthly rent of 370 marks for the house, furniture, and fittings.[3] Although his main residence for nearly three decades, he later claimed to loathe Wandlitz; its only advantage, he asserted, was being able to sleep well, awake rested and be in Berlin within half an hour. This daily commute, according to his bodyguard, Bernd Bruckner, involved racing to the capital at 130 km/h, while in contrast, Margot explicitly told her driver to obey traffic regulations and not drive faster than 100 km/h, even on the highway.[4]

Although detached from the buzz of Berlin, there were compensations at Wandlitz; notably an onsite spa, heated swimming pool, sauna, supermarket (selling Western goods), medical centre, hairdressing salon, tailor's shop, locksmith, laundry, canteen, bowling green, cinema and garden centre. Residents were spared nothing, there was even a garage with its own petrol station also available for tenants.

SED functionary Günter Schabowski remembered the shop sold everything from Colgate toothpaste, Milkana cheese, and designer suits to Western Hi-Fi and video equipment. 'We granted ourselves what we could not give to the common man,' he revealed with merciless candour.[5] In the nursery alone – dotted with large greenhouses – up to thirty people worked to cultivate fresh herbs, fruit, vegetables and flowers.

In the beginning, there were communal evenings and Ulbricht occasionally arranged dinners and film screenings, but that 'soon petered out', Honecker was to recall. As Erich's bodyguard Lothar Herzog attested, his boss was 'quite sociable' in the early sixties and 'would come with some of his colleagues to the clubhouse' – the male-dominated Wandlitz 'F-Club' – and play skat and 'have a brandy or a beer every now and then'. Herzog, a captain in the Ministry of State Security, was responsible for Honecker's personal protection and his physical well-being. Many waiters at Wandlitz remembered the table manners of the well-lubricated Politburo were 'in need of improvement' – people told dirty jokes, slurped, farted, burped and spoke with full mouths. Honecker continued to hurriedly shovel food with a fork, like in his youth. 'He was definitely not a connoisseur,' Herzog admitted. Pyotr Abrasimov, the Soviet Ambassador, occasionally dropped in and struck up a friendship with Honecker. Unlike his predecessor, Abrasimov took a high-profile approach to his duties, visiting factories, exhibitions and appearing on television as well as fully enjoying the privileges of a Politburo member. Although, Honecker showed him respect, given Abrasimov had fought against the fascist Okku-Panten as an officer with the Belorussian partisans, their relationship would soon falter. In private, Honecker's security detail accused Abrasimov of being so vain that he used to dye his mane of silver hair, which, after rinsing, transmitted a blueish tint.[6]

As will be seen, with the collapse of the GDR thirty years later, Wandlitz cast a cloud over Honecker's reputation. 'Whenever that place is mentioned, I still feel a mixture of shame, anger and resignation,' Schabowski confessed. 'Did we, I wonder, have to further morally compromise our cause and ourselves?'[7] Honecker, though, lashed out at allegations of living a charmed existence. Put on the defensive, his former valet (another bizarre contradiction) embellished tales of his sedentary lifestyle insisting his boss ate 'simple dishes, macaroni and ham', for example, and was 'interested in animal documentaries'.

Herzog added: 'Every morning he drank the juice of a whole lemon to protect himself from the flu. He insisted on Langnese honey for breakfast, liked soluble Nescafé and preferred to drink DAB beer from the can at the end of the day.' Honecker gave a similar account: 'Every morning I ate two rolls with butter and honey. At midday, we were at the Central Committee where I ate either grilled sausage with mashed potato, macaroni with bacon or goulash, and in the evening, I ate at home, watched some television and went to bed.' Another titbit, as provided by Herzog was his boss's hatred of fish and game as well as asparagus and mushrooms. He also refused to eat fruit or desserts.[8]

While he may have genuinely disliked Wandlitz, there is no doubt, however, he loved the fresh air and peace. Then there were the early morning visits from Erica Steinhorst, a physiotherapist who provided a massage and shared breakfast with him. Every fourth Tuesday, a platinum blonde beautician arrived to administer a manicure and pedicure, making sure Honecker's hands were soft and supple.

He was not a big lover of physical activity and avoided the gym, preferring instead to stretch out on a deckchair or take gentle walks in the forest with Sonja, who was turning into a spunky, opinionated child. The Honeckers were loving parents – there can be no doubt that the couple adored their daughter and she loved them back, ardently. On weekend visits (she lived at a school dormitory during the week), Sonja would regale her father with tales from school. He never forgot her being teased by classmates because Walter Ulbricht travelled in such a big car. 'She answered,' Honecker recounted, 'by asking ironically, "Should he travel on a tricycle then?"' Unlike some of the distracted SED-leadership fathers, Honecker was attentive and cheerful with his daughter's friends when they sometimes visited, playing board games, and asking them about their lives. Another significant part of family life was vacations in resort areas of northern Germany, Poland and the Harz Mountains. The Honeckers spent time on the north coast every year from 1957 to 1960 and from 1962 to 1984, where Erich enjoyed motorboats, curative baths, entertaining guests and, inevitably, working (a courier delivered mail from Berlin daily). Like many East Germans of his generation, he could not imagine a holiday without getting a suntan and bathing in the Baltic. Moreover, the breaks gave Margot the chance to energetically 'play house' and fuss over Sonja. Margot was also passionate about skiing and often took holidays at the snow-covered Erzgebirge Forest between Fichtelberg and Tellerhäuser on the Czech border, where she was occasionally accompanied by Eberhard Riedel, the GDR's most famous alpine skier, known for his appearance at the 1960 Winter Olympics.

By this point, Margot (with eight years of elementary school on her CV) had risen to the post of Deputy Minister of Education and was involved in the socialist development of the school system. A snide joke overheard at the time asked: 'Why are the foundations of the new Ministry of Education building being dug so deep?' –The punchline: 'They are looking for the diplomas of the Comrade Deputy Minister!'

Under her watch, the curriculum was centralised, ideologically charged and obligatory. She backed a law for the introduction of polytechnic schooling, designed to further develop technical and intellectual leadership skills, increased vocational training opportunities and helped expand public childcare facilities, increasing crèche places. In March 1960, she announced a seven-year scheme to build 700 new schools, saying 'the fulfilment of the building plan was the most important task of the moment. It must be our goal to make this a matter for the whole population'. Her appointments calendar for the next decade shows ministerial duties took her to Rome, Paris, Havana, Moscow, Helsinki and countless other destinations. In July 1960, she led the first sizeable educational delegation from the GDR to China for a month-long visit to inspect colleges, universities, vocational schools, as well as secondary and elementary schools. 'Our delegation has set itself the task of rendering the cooperation between our two countries closer within the framework of the agreement on culture,' she told ADN's correspondent in Beijing. 'We have found much we have in common, since in China, too, on the basis of Marxism-Leninism, school is linked with life and tuition with production.'[9]

The death of Wilhelm Pieck on 12 September 1960 marked the end of an era for the communist old guard. In tribute, Honecker paid homage in *Neuer Weg*, praising 'his attitude to the party and his lifelong humility which bear witness to the noble character of our comrade Wilhelm Pieck, to his utter devotion to the cause of the working class.' Only five days after Pieck's death, the People's Chamber abolished the presidency altogether and replaced it with a collective Council of State. Ulbricht became chairman, with six deputies, a secretary and sixteen members reporting to him, thus formally becoming GDR head of state. It had been a busy year for Ulbricht, during the spring he implemented the last stage in the collectivisation of private farms – an effort SED propagandists dubbed 'The Socialist Spring in the Countryside'. In the event, between March and May, almost 500,000 farmers who had previously worked privately were forced to join production cooperatives. Officially, they remained the owners of their land, but could no longer freely dispose of it. As early as 25 April, Ulbricht declared the 'liberation of the farmers' was complete. However, the 'brutal method' of collectivisation prompted a rare rebuke from the US State Department which condemned 'this programme of compulsion which highlights once again the denial of Germans living in the Soviet zone the basic right to self-determination and the completely unrepresentative character of the East German regime'. Furthermore, Washington accused Ulbricht of using methods ranging from 'massive pressure campaigns to naked force'. The tragic consequence of this change, as in 1952, was many farms literally went to seed. There was a massive increase in fires, which were probably due to arson, and a sizable number of cattle and pigs perished. More seriously, when crop failures due to the weather were reported, the Soviet Union intervened with food aid, including truckloads of butter (which was put back on the ration).

Once more, fed up and exasperated, a high proportion of people from the farming community sought refuge in West Germany, many bitter at quitting a livelihood to which they had given the sweat of their lives. By the end of spring, the exodus rose to over 1,000 a day, the highest number since 1953.

Young people, especially graduates, led the charge along with doctors, dentists, chemists, clerks, lawyers, nurses, draftsmen, midwives, cabinetmakers, mechanics and others. Collectively, they were sharply aware of the discrepancy between the grand myth of a socialist paradise promised by the SED, and the facts of their present situation. Nevertheless, Ulbricht continued to keep up his courage by issuing confident statements about the progress of his economic plans and even led a delegation of unprecedented size to Moscow in November for the forty-third anniversary of the founding of the USSR.

1961: A Momentous Year

At a Warsaw Pact meeting on 28-29 March 1961, Ulbricht gave a blood-and-thunder speech, describing West Berlin as a sewer of ideological infection and political subversion. As the exodus of refugees from the GDR took a decisive turn for the worse, he presented a terrifying spur to action by claiming the Americans could use the city as a base for nuclear weapons and suggested West Berlin be blocked 'with troops, barriers and perhaps with barbed wire fences'. Berlin, he said with a weary voice, was a 'huge hole in the middle of our republic that costs us more than a billion marks a year'.

The situation, as some Warsaw Pact leaders recognised, was getting desperate. After some debate, Khrushchev gave the green light for Ulbricht to thrash out a 'tentative programme of action' for the division of Berlin, a task which landed on Honecker's desk. (Officially, he was appointed 'chief of staff' for the campaign).

In the febrile atmosphere of the day, FRG media ramped-up commentary of the refugee problem. 'If a million people, in peacetime, flee their native country like thieves in the night, leaving behind everything they own, the situation must be unbearable,' FRG Federal Minister for All-German Affairs, Ernst Lemmer, told RIAS on 17 May. 'There is a continuous and flagrant violation of human rights going on here.'[1] Newspapers such as *Bild* detailed how 19,198 people fled the GDR in June alone; a good half of them under the age of 25. Responding, Honecker accused Western media of unleashing 'nasty agitation' against the GDR. He claimed 'border violations and border provocations increased. Centres for poaching workers from the GDR had been set up in West Berlin'.[2] Throwing aside all restraint, East German media intensified reports of 'hostile acts' against the GDR economy, all of which were blamed on Western agents or people 'controlled' from West Berlin. Ulbricht described the migration from the GDR to West Germany as 'the trafficking in human beings, of the psychological warfare and sabotage directed against the GDR'.

> This is no political emigration but filthy trafficking in human lives conducted by despicable means in which the West Germans and US agents, most of which are working from West Berlin, invest large sums of money. Since large pensions have been given to all

Nazis in West Germany, many politically incriminated persons also go to the West.[3]

Meanwhile, to help sketch out a physical border, Honecker handpicked an eight-man task force. By summer, they were installed at an operations centre on the second floor of the Police Presidium on Keibelstraße near Alexanderplatz. Working from a suite of four offices with an adjoining conference room, plastered with maps and diagrammed routes, the team set about planning the dissection of Berlin. Honecker was meticulous in examining every detail personally and often ventured out to get the lay of the land. It was a massive organisational effort involving the command staff of four ministries: Defence, State Security, Interior and Transport. Those privy to the secret plans included Paul Verner, chief of the SED in Berlin, Erich Mielke, Willi Stoph and Karl Maron. Werner Hubner, a fanatically loyal army lieutenant colonel, advised on military issues, while Gerhard Exner, a police colonel, played a key role in logistical problems. Anyone holding a topographical map of Berlin could see the Wall would cross rivers, shallow lakes, streams, a canal, housing estates, bridges, woodland, railway stations and several cemeteries. They planned to quickly seal off the border with razor-sharp concertina wire which was to be gradually replaced by a brick wall. Concrete for stabilising the larger barriers would be carried in barrows, while wooden supports for the countless small barbwire fences was to be pounded into the ground by sledgehammers. Moreover, Honecker's plans were all the more impressive given they included the separation of the U-Bahn and S-Bahn lines to West Berlin. In some places along the Spree River, underwater barriers to prevent swimmers fleeing were planned. Given the difficulties, the pace of progress was remarkable. Writing ten years after the fact, General Hoffmann marvelled at the amount of preliminary work, coordination and military expertise required to carry out such an operation. Regular handwritten reports on the project's progress were handed to both Ulbricht and the Russian Ambassador, Mikhail Pervuchin.

Although Khrushchev had still not committed to building a wall, Ulbricht's impatience on the issue was highlighted by Pervuchin in a letter to Foreign Minister Gromyko on 19 May, in which he detailed plans by the SED leadership to 'immediately close the border' between East and West Berlin, against Soviet policy.

Our friends [the SED] would now like to impose a control on the sector border between democratic Berlin and West Berlin, enabling them 'to shut the door to the West', as they call it, to reduce the exodus of people from the Republic and to weaken the influence of the economic conspiracy initiated against the GDR by West Berlin.[4]

As Ulbricht was told to sit tight, the international situation remained difficult and dangerous. At a summit in Vienna on 4 June 1961, between US President John F. Kennedy and Khrushchev, the two discussed numerous issues but there was no breakthrough regarding Berlin. Then, in late July, Kennedy's disarmament adviser John McCloy met with Khrushchev in Sochi on the Black Sea, where the Soviet leader expressed doubt about whether the Western powers were willing to fight to defend their rights in Berlin. Russian diplomat Valentin Falin, employed in the Germany department of the Moscow Foreign Ministry, recounted that Khrushchev had informed McCloy 'broadly about what action [in Berlin] was to come.'[5] The tension finally came to a head on 25 July, when, in a live broadcast to the nation, Kennedy announced he had formulated 'three essentials' concerning West Berlin: using all possible means, the US was willing to maintain the presence of the Western powers in Berlin, free access to the Western part of the city and to guarantee the freedom and viability of West Berlin. A few days later, Kennedy confided to Walt Rostow, Deputy Special Assistant to the President for National Security Affairs, that 'Khrushchev is losing East Germany'. He continued: 'He cannot let that happen. If East Germany goes, so will Poland and all of Eastern Europe. He will have to do something to stop the flow of refugees.'

From here on, any reservations that Khrushchev may have held about sealing off Berlin evaporated. During a two-hour conversation with Ulbricht on 1 August, he was informed about Honecker's plan to carve up Berlin.

> In houses with exits into West Berlin, they will be walled up. In other places, barbed wire barriers will be erected. The barbed wire has already been delivered. It can all happen very quickly. It will be harder with transportation routes. We will then reconstruct the train platforms of the city trains [S-bahn] and underground trains [U-bahn] that go to West Berlin.[6]

That same day, 1 August, Marshal Ivan Konev, as supreme commander of the Soviet Armed Forces in Germany (GSSD), approved Honecker's detailed plans. Then, on 5 August, the heads of state and party leaders of the Warsaw Pact met in Moscow and gave the go-ahead for the building of the Wall in Berlin. Khrushchev sermonised:

> Let's look at it this way: if we don't take the needs of the GDR into account and don't make any sacrifices, then the German comrades won't be able to hold out [...] By strengthening their position, we strengthen our position. Therefore, comrades, this help, I would say, is not only for comrade Walter and the Germans in the GDR but for others as well.[7]

Upon reflection, Khrushchev later commented that the drain of workers was creating a 'simply disastrous situation' in the GDR, which was already suffering from a shortage of manual and specialised labour. 'If things had continued like this much longer, I don't know what would have happened.' Looking tired and drawn, Ulbricht informed the Politburo on 7 August that Moscow had given permission to control the border, as Honecker recounted: 'On 11 August 1961, the Volkskammer declared that a grave danger to the peace in Europe existed. It charged the GDR's Council of Ministers with preparing and implementing all measures which were necessary to safeguard peace.'

One of the grim ironies of the story was that many Volkskammer MPs had no inkling of what was to come. The following day, the Council of Ministers passed a resolution, as Honecker recounted, that the 'border between socialist and capitalist Europe be placed under proper control'. At this crucial moment, Erich Mielke was busily informing senior Stasi officials that measures would be taken against flight from the GDR, with the ring around Berlin of particular focus. While his language was vague, its implications were not. 'All preparatory work is to be carried out under the strictest secrecy,' he said, adding: 'The entire operation has the code name "Rose".'[8] Later that afternoon, Honecker found himself at the police operations centre on Keibelstraße. To those who saw him at close quarters, he appeared in high spirits. 'From there,' Honecker noted, 'I was in constant contact with the commanding officers and staff of the armed forces, the district committees of the SED in Berlin, Frankfurt/Oder and Potsdam, the central government departments, the Berlin Municipal Council and the regional councils of Frankfurt/Oder and Potsdam.'[9]

From here on, the operation proceeded with absolute precision. Over most of Berlin and Brandenburg, the weather was beautiful in August 1961 – relentless sunshine poured over the city and forests. Everyday life was punctuated with trips to lidos, lakes and swimming baths. In this ocean of calm, Adam Kellet-Long, a duty reporter for Reuters in West Berlin, recalls a 'vague feeling' in the city that some action was pending to stop the refugee flow. In an interview for this book, he said it 'would have been hard to avoid this feeling just from reading the East Berlin press and of course listening to West Berlin radio stations, something that the majority of the city's population did'. However, Kellet-Long was certain that the populations of neither part of Berlin had any idea that the border would be closed, and a wall built:

And, as far as East Berlin was concerned, I can vouch from personal observation that the general population was not expecting anything drastic to happen that weekend. It was very hot, and a lengthy tour of East Berlin that Saturday afternoon showed the streets almost deserted as the population crowded public swimming pools and the lakes to cool off.[10]

As the light faded into the evening on 12 August, Ulbricht ordered members of the Politburo, the Presidium of the Council of Ministers, and the Council of State, to his summer residence on Döllnsee. Only Honecker, the Stasi, Defence and Transport Ministers were not present, for obvious reasons. After dinner, Ulbricht stunned his guests by reading out the resolution on the construction of the 'anti-fascist protective wall'. There was no shock or delusory remarks, just grim nods of approval.

A few hours later, as the clock approached midnight, 'Operation Rose' commenced. 'You know the assignment,' Honecker told Army headquarters in a phone call, 'Now March!' As the army snapped into a state of high alert, streetlights along the border were extinguished, followed by the termination of underground and S-Bahn services.

As this was happening, troops blocked the windows of apartments on the border with corrugated iron, as 20,000 armed men fanned the length of more than 160 kilometres to halt all traffic from East to West. Erich Mielke was the first to inspect roadblocks and barriers, followed by Defence Minister Heinz Hoffmann, who remembered Honecker arriving to shake hands and pat a few backs. 'He spoke not only to me and other high-ranking officers but, as is his habit, also to the other ranks on the spot and explained to them why we had to take these measures.'[11] 'For Honecker, this was probably his masterpiece in dealing with the armed forces,' said Helmut Müller, then an FDJ functionary. 'He was in charge and all eyes were on him.'[12] In the last stretch, as sharp coils of barbed wire were spread out across a few remaining road junctions, Honecker returned to police headquarters, retiring to his hideaway on the second floor. At 04.00, before most Berliners were awake, he heard RIAS radio's first reports that GDR police had shut off sectors of the border and, at the same time, traffic between the two parts of Berlin had ground to a halt.[13] As the darkness lightened, Hoffman confirmed the provisional border was fully sealed by 06.00. Glancing at his watch, Honecker said proudly, 'now we can go,' and released his staff. 'Operation Rose' had passed without incident. To celebrate, Honecker, Hoffmann and Mielke raised balloons of cognac to their achievement, the atmosphere was festive. 'That morning,' Honecker remembered, 'Comrade Ulbricht made the first inspection tour at the border. The orders had been precisely implemented. Our leaders had shown great organisational skill. Everything went exactly according to plan. Peace in Europe was saved, and the basis for the great ascent of our GDR was established.'[14]

Within just five hours, Berlin – one of the most famous cities in the world – had been sealed tight.

A New Dawn

On 13 August, at the first blush of dawn, Berliners woke up in a city separated by a closely guarded border. In the general confusion – and with rumours swirling around – the public sought answers to the most pressing questions: was the barrier temporary and why were the Americans taking no action? The German people were completely unprepared for what Ulbricht had done. Many reacted initially with shock, upset about friends and family on the other side of the barbed wire. 'I was very shaken when I heard the words "Die Grenze ist Geschlossen" at the Brandenburg Gate in the early hours of that Sunday morning,' says Kellett-Long, who embarked on a sortie of the city. 'After that, there was very little time for contemplation. And it should not be forgotten how often the lying word "temporary" was used in official announcements, none of which mentioned a wall.'

Honecker remained buoyant throughout Sunday, enjoying the sensation of a job well done:

> Even the Allies in West Berlin were taken by surprise. However much one may try to twist things around in retrospect, the irrefutable fact remains that despite the very comprehensive preparations which were necessary to make it a success, the erection of the antifascist defence wall came as a complete surprise to our enemies.[1]

Whether there was an egregious intelligence failure on the part of the Western allies, or a deliberate lack of interest is still open to debate. For sure, it is known that none of the CIA agents – working in East Berlin under the guise of US diplomats or regular soldiers – predicted events, and, remarkably, after the Wall was built there was no public discussion in the United States about the CIA intelligence failure, nor did any member of the US government complain that the secret service had not received warning of the event. Not even opposition parliamentarians asked why US agents were not privy to any inside information. Moreover, Washington did not receive the first news about the sealing off of West Berlin through official channels, their intelligence arrived instead through flashes from American wire service bulletins. It later transpired that no scrambled calls/tap-proof lines were connected between Berlin and Washington on the night of 12-13 August and, astonishingly, the US

70

government received the first comprehensive information about the situation through ARD's Washington correspondent Lothar Loewe, who received his information from colleagues at SFB TV in West Berlin.[2]

Meanwhile, taking in the unlikely scene unfolding before him, Adam Kellett-Long was astonished at the 'virtual miracle that it had been kept secret in a city alleged to be swarming with spies'.[3] As West Berliners stared vacantly at roadblocks, only the more perceptive gawkers may have realised they were witnessing something momentous.

As this was happening, Khrushchev was kept up with developments via phone from the Soviet HQ in Karlshorst. He seemed satisfied. 'I think this earned Honecker great laurels, especially in Moscow,' says Joachim Jauer, then a ZDF correspondent in East Berlin. 'Moscow, of course, was concerned whether this brazen act of cordoning off Berlin would really take place peacefully, that is, without countermeasures by the West.'

By Monday, as the Western powers remained inactive, GDR newspapers treated the Wall as a cause for celebration. *Neues Deutschland* led with the headline: 'Measures to protect the peace and to secure the German Democratic Republic in force', featuring a photograph of two beaming border guards. What was more, under a sub-heading, 'Normal life in Berlin', the article explained that on Sunday 13 August:

> life was completely ordinary, as on all Sundays. The underground traffic ran smoothly and to plan according to the new regulations. Like every Sunday, thousands of Berliners took the S-Bahn out to the countryside. The usual bustle also prevailed at the pavilion of the German travel agency at the Friedrichstraße S-Bahn station. The excursion lines of the BVG buses were very busy.[4]

An earthier editorial was plastered on the front page of Honecker's former paper *Junge Welt*, which barked that the GDR would not watch passively as the 'mad Bonn warmongers' prepared for armed aggression. 'They took our patience for weakness. It is we who are on the offensive: West Berlin will no longer remain "the thorn in the flesh of the GDR".'[5]

On the other side of the Wall, ARD television news gave it twenty-two minutes – an eternity on a twenty-five-minute evening news programme – and followed up with a second instalment. Meanwhile, special editions of newspapers were rushed out. *BZ*, the local paper for West Berlin, screamed that the date of 13 August 1961 would never be forgotten, because on that day:

> a bunch of people led by Soviet citizen Ulbricht, committed a crime against humanity. These men who call themselves the

leaders of a worker's state, in reality, are nothing but a group of concentration camp supervisors.

They have converted Central Germany into a concentration camp. And yesterday they blocked the ultimate gate which so far has led to freedom. These blockade measures are solely for the protection of Ulbricht and his accomplices. The ultimate gap in the prison zone was closed so that no cry of excitement of an enslaved nation might penetrate the outside. With the blessing of Khrushchev, Pankow has torn to pieces the four-power agreements binding our city. This action must be answered by the three Western powers.

The barrier was 'barbaric', ran one report from in *The Times* of London. 'Herr Ulbricht's wall in Berlin must be unique in history,' Sir William Hayter, the former British ambassador to Moscow opined. 'Countries had surrounded themselves with defensive walls before, but the object has always been to keep enemies out and not subjects in. This wall is a repulsive thing. It is repulsive to read about and even more repulsive to see in reality.'[6]

Amid the furore, the most balanced early assessment was given by Lord Montgomery, the British hero of the Second World War and former commander of British Forces in Germany. 'To describe Germany as one Germany is just a pious fraud. You cannot have one Germany.' Asked if the situation alarmed him, he took a slightly more hectoring tone:

I do not think the East has any intention of attacking the West and I do not think the West has any intention of attacking the East. I think the whole thing has blown up because of the mistrust and suspicion between the two sides. The East thinks the West is going to attack. The West thinks the East is going to attack. Neither side has any intention of attacking the other.[7]

He was right, and as the dust settled, little happened other than Willy Brandt warning against 'dangerous resistance' and the Western Allies reinforcing their garrisons with a few tanks. 'It turns out nobody was upset by it,' Honecker contended in 1990. 'Some went fishing [a reference to JFK who when informed, remarked: 'A wall is a hell of a lot better than a war']. It brought some relief, so to speak, when this action was taken.' He continued: 'Washington, London, Paris, Moscow and us, we all thought it would de-escalate the situation. We all assumed it would ensure peace.'[8] In his German-language memoirs, he gave a thoroughly romantic justification by asking how could the GDR 'stand by and watch as our republic was bled dry in an economic war like no other?'

We took no different action than any other independent, sovereign state. We merely took our defensible frontiers under control in accordance with the international law enshrined then, as now, by the United Nations. This saved the peace and laid the foundation for the further flourishing of the German Democratic Republic.[9]

West German politicians went into overdrive. Speaking in Bonn on 18 August, Adenauer said the GDR's 'illegal measures' filled the Federal Government with concern and disgust and were in flagrant contradiction to the four-power agreements on the freedom to move about in Berlin. 'I am sorry to state that this act of arbitrariness has taken place with the approval of the USSR, the leading power of the Warsaw Pact. Through this approval, the Soviet Government contradicts its constant protestations that it wants to solve the Germany and Berlin issues through negotiations.'[10] That very same day, 18 August, the Soviet Union sent a note to the United States giving full support for the GDR's 'effective control on the border with West Berlin in order to bar the way for subversive activity being carried out from West Berlin against the GDR'. The note stated that West Berlin had been transformed into a centre of 'subversive activity, diversion and espionage, into a centre of political and economic provocations against the GDR, the Soviet Union, and other socialist countries'. Furthermore:

> Former and present West Berlin municipal leaders have cynically called West Berlin an 'arrow in the living body of the German Democratic Republic', a 'front city', a 'violator of tranquillity', the 'cheapest atom bomb put in the centre of a socialist state'. The gates of West Berlin have been opened to international criminals and provocateurs of all kinds, if only to sharpen international tension and widen the dimensions of the provocations and subversive acts against the countries of the socialist community.

'The GDR,' the note concluded, had displayed, over the course of many years, 'great tolerance in the face of such a completely disgraceful and impermissible situation', and by implementing its 'peace-loving and democratic policy', it had borne 'enormous sacrifices'.[11]

Plugging the Gaps

With the border secure, Honecker applied the same enthusiasm to shoring up the Wall, which reshaped the contours of Berlin for 165 kilometres, following old Prussian district boundaries. As well as vast amounts of materials, the other requirement to maintain progress was, of course, money. And there was no constraint on the amount available. Of the total costs of DDM1.822 billion incurred by the GDR between 1961 and 1964 for the operation of national border installations, DDM400 million (22 per cent) was channelled into the construction and upkeep of the Berlin Wall.

On a normal day, around 2,300 soldiers were deployed directly at the border. In addition to the staff in Berlin-Karlshorst, the border command – made up of seven regiments – had garrisons in Treptow, Pankow, Rummelsburg, Hennigsdorf, Gross-Glienicke, Babelsberg, Kleinmachnow, Wilhelmshagen and Oranienburg. Each regiment had five companies, as well as an engineer, intelligence officers, transport unit, grenade launchers, artillery battery, reconnaissance platoon and a flamethrower platoon, as well as a squadron of 990 guard dogs.

As time went on, the flimsy barbed wire was replaced with a 10ft-high concrete barrier, jagged steel girder tank traps, anti-tank ditches, nail traps and watch towers.[1] At the Brandenburg Gate sufficient funds were made available to build a second wall behind the original using concrete slabs weighing three tons, while on Wilhelmstraße – where the barrier cut across the road – a huge poster was hung up, reading: 'Whoever attacks us will be destroyed.' To deter 'irresponsible and annoying' West Germans from pelting border guards with rocks, Honecker approved the deployment of several water cannon trucks,[2] the drenching's caused many protestors to avoid engaging in demonstrations at the Wall.[3]

Looking back, Honecker's exhilaration about this period was palpable. 'We stopped the bloodletting of the GDR that way. It was in the interests of peace, security and socialist construction. We were bound, duty-bound, to carry through the security measures. It was right'.

Not everybody, of course, was content to be walled in and cracks began showing almost right away. The Wall bought Cold War stability at a horrifying human price. Over the next twenty-eight years, hundreds of people would be shot dead; others drowned, suffered fatal accidents, or killed themselves when caught. Many experienced horrible injuries from shrapnel-spraying firing devices that padded the 'death strip'. The bloodletting began on 22 August 1961, when 58-year-old housewife Ida Siekmann became the first person to die while attempting to escape West. That morning, she tossed her bedding down onto the street from the fourth floor of a building on Bernauer Straße – adjacent to the Wall – then jumped out of the window crashing on the paving stones below, dying shortly afterward. Two days later, Günter Litfin, a 24-year-old tailor, was shot dead when attempting to escape by swimming from Humboldthafen to the West, not far from the main Lehrter Railway station. In an interview for this book, Litfin's brother, Jurgen, welled up as he described how Günter was cut down by machine-gun fire – the family found out about the incident on West German television. 'We were forced by the Stasi to say that Günter had been involved in an accident – my brother wasn't a troublemaker – just a modest tailor that wanted freedom. We all tolerated these communists, but, after this, secretly despised them.' Five days after Litfin's death, 27-year-old Roland Hof was shot in the Teltow Canal during an escape attempt.

On 21 November, builders ceased work on concrete barricades along the border, prompting Dennis Martin, the Berlin correspondent of the *Daily Mirror* to report that before leaving, builders tidied up. 'They even swept the top of the new wall at the Brandenburg Gate.' Within a few hours, the cranes, lorries and pneumatic drills – which had rumbled and hammered away for months – disappeared, leaving behind an eerie peace.

Keen to draw a veil over events at the Wall, Honecker turned his attention to other pressing issues, including preparing the so-called 'honorary service' laws, designed to draft 18–25-year-olds into the NVA, riot police, or military units of the state security for eighteen months' compulsory service. From this point, the NVA became an all-encompassing force made up of career officers, regular soldiers and conscripts. But as the post-war generation came of age, 'pacifist views were still widely held,' Honecker remembered. 'This was an understandable reaction after the Second World War with its enormous devastation, losses and the crimes committed by the Nazi army.' Although he insisted it was a peacetime army, training in the NVA was based on Prussian traditions with goose-stepping and endless drilling.

Touring army bases in his shirtsleeves, Honecker endured several testy encounters with unhappy young conscripts. Defending the call-up, he argued that military measures were essentially defensive and 'all guns were not the same' – what was most important, he insisted, was who possessed them and for what purpose. 'We explained the Marxist-Leninist view of wars and armies, the attitude of the working class to the military issue, and the nature of just and unjust wars. We pointed out that the German people and the German working class too had their progressive military traditions.'

Though his opinion did not command unanimous support, he defended a decision to acquire modern armaments including tanks, air defence units with improved anti-aircraft guns, radio equipment and MiG-21 interceptors. This arms bonanza provided an occasion to celebrate on 2 March, when Honecker marked the sixth anniversary of the National People's Army. Standing rigid on a reviewing stand, he beamed at a tattoo featuring the NVA Music Corps – flanked by torchbearers – marching along Karl-Marx-Allee. In a detailed article, *Neues Deutschland* witnessed 'thunderously appreciative' Berliners enjoy a performance of the international workers' song 'Brüder zur Sonne zur Freiheit'. Not everyone was so complimentary. Predictably, Honecker was stung by FRG television commentators who turned a quick, appraising eye at his arms collection and conscription measures. The reports broadcast on the main station, ARD, could be received almost everywhere in the GDR (except in eastern Saxony, which became known as the 'Tal der Ahnungslesen', or 'Valley of the Clueless', as only state media was available). With the advent of television, night after night, East Germans virtually crossed the border into West Germany eager for information that their own media did not offer, but above all, they sought entertainment and escapism. In response to this nightly defection, authorities launched the so-called 'Ochsenkopf' campaign which asked (not ordered) the population to remove devices in television sets that enabled reception from the West (the construction and alignment of roof antennas 'gave away' those tuning into FRG TV). As there was never a legal ban on watching West German programmes, Honecker manoeuvred at periscope depth to secretly encourage groups of FDJers to remove offending TV antennas. While some kids stole aerials, others were snapped, turned eastwards, bent or had their cables severed. However, none of this vandalism seemed to do any good, and instead of creating an information monopoly, it caused resentment and led to criminal charges against several FDJ members.[4]

Honecker had more success giving speeches on the economy, where he worked the crowds across the GDR, telling them it was important to solve economic tasks 'as precisely as the security measures of 13 August in Berlin were solved'.[5] Indeed, by mid-1962, with the flight of citizens stalled, the discord about the Wall had become a mere side-show in Honecker's eyes. Across the GDR, the economy was exhibiting the first signs of recovery, leading to improved living standards. There was an increase in the availability of consumer goods, with official figures showing for every 1,000 households there were 56 cars, 160 motorcycles, 122 refrigerators, 134 washing machines and 327 television sets. Deutsche Post recorded an increase of 33,300 telephone subscriptions to about 670,200 connections.[6] Furthermore, production of the Trabant P60 motorcar began in Zwickau (Saxony) at the VEB Sachsenring Automobilwerke, with the promise of making the country more mobile.

American journalist Arthur J. Olsen noted that people had a little more money to spend, a few more things to buy, and a new sense of individual opportunity. 'All these are reflected in a moderate rise of public morale.'[7]

An additional source of hard currency was found with the establishment of 'Intershop', a trading organisation designed to be used by foreigners. The GDR was ready to stain its ideological purity by targeting transit travellers and visitors from 'non-socialist economic areas' at a Friedrichstraße station kiosk, selling cut-price cigarettes for dollars and all West European currencies, West German marks were especially welcome (GDR citizens were officially forbidden to own Western currency). Gradually, as the scheme blossomed, the kiosk began selling Scotch whisky, Strasbourg goose-liver pate, French champagne, Swiss chocolate, clothing, toys, jewellery, cosmetics – and almost anything else hard currency could buy. East Germans could only press their noses against the window and curse their Ostmark, which was hard-earned and yet worth little. Over time, more kiosks were set up at border crossing points, hotels, rest areas on the transit routes between the Federal Republic of Germany and West Berlin and at train stations, airports and ferry ports.

The SED Sixth Congress, from 15–21 January, launched the start of a momentous year in GDR politics. The carefully choreographed event saw delegates from more than thirty countries, including China, arrive in East Berlin. Yet even before unpacking, Khrushchev stole the headlines after lumbering off a train at Berlin's Ostbahnhof and bellowing at a group of Western journalists: 'you people in the West … we are just waiting for you to disappear from the face of the earth. The future belongs to us. Your times are over. I shall shout a loud 'Hurrah' when capitalism is buried.' Speaking in front of a red curtain bearing the party's insignia, and flanked by SED grandees, including Honecker, his tirade continued:

> We will not have a war to bring the socialist system of society to another country because we think that is an internal matter for each country. A lot of nonsense is talked about our personal relations with Herr Ulbricht. Let me tell you that this is just so much speculation. Herr Ulbricht is the model carpenter, and I am the locksmith.[8]

Looking back on that day, Honecker recounted how, strangely enough, Khrushchev was more popular in the GDR than with his fellow countrymen. 'He had a very graphic turn of phrase and was very clever.' He remembered:

> Khrushchev first called out: 'Long live the world revolution!' Of course, he fanned the enthusiasm of the Berliners with that. He

wanted to spur us on. Anyway, the international press was not so enamoured by the spontaneous – and even, perhaps, uncontrolled utterance, because he was a statesman.[9]

The next morning, as the congress commenced, Walter Ulbricht strode out before 4,500 delegates to deliver a six-hour speech, crafted to please his Russian masters. He opened with a stinging attack on 'dogmatists and sectarians' in China, directed at Beijing's chief delegate Wu Hseu Chwan, who 'sat poker-faced as the applause of the Khrushchev line mounted'. Such rhetoric was common since Khrushchev's explosive secret speech. Differences in ideologies about communism had seen the once healthy Sino-Soviet alliance begin to crack, revealing serious conflicts beneath the veneer of solidarity. It ended with a breakdown in relations between the world's two largest communist powers. From here on, China was often on the receiving end of spikey comments in GDR and Soviet propaganda and political speeches.

None of Ulbricht's brusqueness was lost when he snapped at 'narrow-minded' Albanian leaders, whom he described as 'enemies of Marx and Lenin' (the Albanians didn't bother to attend the congress). However, the focus of the gathering, from a domestic point of view, was Ulbricht's preview of economic reforms. Though Honecker largely remained in the shadows, he emerged to deliver a speech on leadership issues in which he snapped at lower party functionaries for acting 'like little kings'. His voice low and precise, he regaled the story of Heinz Chill, the first party secretary of the Stralsund district, who told a veterinarian it was 'up to her' to have chicks hatched in June and laying eggs by New Year. 'Even with the best ideological training, that is impossible for the chicks,' he joked. On the SED's role in the production process, he outlined new principles which demanded a complete rethink of existing norms:

1. The leading party organisations must radically improve their work 'with people'; perfect their system of drawing up, supervising and implementing resolutions; eliminate 'old, outdated bureaucratic working methods'; and concentrate on solving the major problems.

2. According to the new statute, the members of the party must 'take the lead in planning the most advanced production techniques' and show respect and consideration for their co-workers'.

3. The battle 'on the Western Front of the European socialist world system makes it essential to devote special attention to ideological work'.

4. No one should believe 'that socialist consciousness can be promoted by authoritarianism, paternalism and the callous treatment of others. On the contrary, it is necessary to eliminate inflexible routine, impersonal, bureaucratic administration, dogmatism and the habit of talking over people's heads.' What is needed is 'intelligent, patient work to convince others and responsiveness to 'suggestions from the people'.

5. The evolutionary law of criticism and self-criticism must be applied more rigorously and 'the suppression of criticism in any form must be vigorously opposed'.

After the congress, the reins on the economy were tightened by Ulbricht's hand. He abandoned political objectives, including the question of Berlin, to create a more efficient economy, patterned after Khrushchev's decentralisation policies. His goal was to cut raw material waste, boost mechanisation and create a system where quality rather than quantity took priority. This model had been sketched out by professor Yevsej Liberman in *Pravda* in 1962 under the heading: 'Plan, Premium, Profit,' detailing how a socialist economy could function without subsidies if profit was used as an objective criterion for performance. On 11 February – one month after the Sixth Congress – the Council of Ministers passed a decree on the planning and management of the national economy. Ulbricht retained central control, while weight was laid on profit, worker incentives and quality output. A few months later, on 24 June, the 'Neues Ökonomisches System' (New Economic System or NES) was officially born. It turned over to industrial executives a measure of decision-making once reserved for SED apparatchiks and proved much more daring than anything Honecker or other 'old hands' could have ever imagined. New flexibility gave managers the liberty to set production schedules, determine the range of items manufactured and adjust their firms to market conditions. To help craft and implement the scheme, Ulbricht cultivated the support of intellectuals like Dr Erich Apel and Dr Günter Mittag, two young economists who worked with zeal.

Born in Thuringia in 1917, Apel trained as a tool fitter and mechanical engineer. During the war, he worked alongside Wernher von Braun on Nazi doodlebugs and later turned down an offer from Braun to accompany him to the USA. Instead, he was interned by the Soviets and became involved in their missile programme as chief engineer until 1952. After returning to the GDR, he was appointed Minister of Mechanical Engineering at the age of 35. Günter Mittag, a boundlessly vain, pathologically ambitious diabetic, was slightly younger. Born in Szczecin in 1926, he trained at the Reichsbahn and then studied economics before rising in the ranks of the SED.

Once the NES fuse was lit, Ulbricht dissolved the National Economic Council (in which individual areas dominated entire branches of industry) and formed the State Planning Commission headed by Apel, who promised better living standards and expressed his intention to buy more machinery from the West. At the same time, Ulbricht created a plethora of new ministries for industry, headed by men between 35 and 45 years old. In Berlin, a 'Central Institute for Socialist Economic Management' was founded, which morphed into a kind of communist business school. The SED discovered hitherto neglected topics such as sociology. Speaking to the press about the reforms, Apel said 'energetic and purposeful' methods were needed to deal with 'lazy bones and shirkers' in state-run industries.[10]

Despite giving his public approval, Honecker began wondering how this excessive transformation of industry would end up. He was disturbed to see Ulbricht draw on advice from young intellectuals – a development that created a new balance of power at the highest level. To make matters worse, Ulbricht began stressing that education in managerial and technical sciences was the route to social advancement and material rewards.

That summer, Honecker was equally unsettled when, following the cultural-political thaw in Moscow, Ulbricht introduced a less constipated approach to youth issues. For the first time, Western dance music was allowed to be played on the radio and, as if that wasn't bad enough, it was no longer forbidden to dance the 'twist', and even an LP and two singles by the Beatles were released in the GDR. To justify the move, the youth magazine *Neues Leben*, explained how the four working-class boys from Liverpool were 'protesting against capitalism with their music' – thus, the Beatles fitted snugly into the ideological world of the SED (the Rolling Stones remained banned). For the first time, GDR television gained the ability to buy and broadcast Western films and critical young writers such as Wolf Biermann were allowed to read from their works to packed auditoriums. Publishers brought new releases by Western authors onto the market. Works by Carl Zuckmayer, Ingeborg Bachmann, Max Frisch and other authors who were previously unknown in the GDR were published, and theatres presented productions by modern Western playwrights. At the same time, films such as *The Divided Heaven* based on the novel by Christa Wolf attracted international attention. Eager for new ideas, Ulbricht even suggested West German newspapers such as *Die Zeit* or the *Süddeutsche Zeitung* be distributed in the GDR if there was a guarantee that *Neues Deutschland* would be sold in the FRG; the idea failed due to reservations in Bonn.

Around this time, more than one political journalist, including Klaus Tauber, detected a new Honecker-Old Guard axis. 'To their regret, it was not the Party apparatchiks who were responsible for implementing the reforms, but rather young, decisive, independent managers,' Taubert recounted. 'During this time, Apel and Mittag became a danger for the disgruntled hardliners who were unwilling to reform, their hope for self-preservation lay with the "Crown Prince" Erich Honecker.' Well placed as the head of the SED Party organisation, Honecker had systematically consolidated his position and was able to hear the latest gossip, research intrigues, and use the insights gained when dealing with the SED's provincial satraps. This detailed knowledge, primarily of the weaknesses of his co-functionaries, was filed in an up-to-date card index – a resource that gave him a dominant position in the Politburo.

He was frank when meeting the salt of the Party but had enough nous to publicly support Ulbricht's line. Later, though not at the time, there would be intense interest from Bonn in Honecker's place in the GDR hierarchy. Incoming despatches to the West German intelligence agency, BND, recorded:

> Opinions differ on Honecker's personality and abilities. On the one hand, he is characterised as an 'apparatchik' and a 'record player' who is not very intelligent but is always compliant due to his ambition, which makes him appear primarily suitable for control functions and would thus stamp him as the 'number two' in the regime. On the other hand, however, there is talk of Honecker's instinct for political connections which paired with considerable ruthlessness enables him to appear with an air of unsophisticated self-assurance.[11]

Interestingly, during 1963 the Berlin pro-opposition newspaper *Telegraf* speculated that SED key officials were discussing a replacement for Ulbricht. Honecker, according to the paper, was no longer mentioned as a possible successor but Paul Verner was. The Soviets, on their part, brought Paul Wandel into the discussion. Wandel, a former GDR ambassador to China, was regarded as a special confidant of Khrushchev. According to the *Telegraf*, the discussion of such possibilities showed the extent of insecurity within the SED. 'Ulbricht will disappear as soon as Khrushchev deems it appropriate within the framework of lessening international tensions which he also desires,' the paper concluded.[12]

As it happened, Erich Honecker was assured enough to spend the summer of 1963 out of the limelight. He withheld comment on US President John F. Kennedy's tour of Berlin and Konrad Adenauer's resignation. However, he did make a series of speeches before the Volkskammer elections on 20 October which, predictably saw 99.25 per cent participation and 99.9 per cent 'yes' votes for the SED-backed unified list – an indication that reforms did not spill over into the democratic process.

During those long hot summer months, Honecker had been involved in drafting a new 'border pass agreement', which when implemented, allowed West Berliners to visit relatives in the GDR during Christmas 1963. The scheme led to more than 700,000 people taking advantage of this chance to see their loved ones – in all, 1.2 million people crossed over to the East between 19 December and 5 January and generated some much-needed welcome press in the West.[13] It was at this time that the MfS took over passport control at border crossings to the FRG, West Berlin, Poland and Czechoslovakia. In a country that only allowed its citizens to travel abroad under exceptional circumstances, controls over who travels where and when, was of strategic importance.

At the beginning of 1964, the focus of Erich Honecker's activity seems to have been in the economic area and on the defence front, where he helped to establish 'construction soldier' units which gave conscientious objectors the option of serving 'with a spade' instead of a gun. His work diary shows he was present at the opening of several of Ulbricht's prestige building projects, including the new State Council headquarters on Berlin's Marx-Engels-Platz and the House of Teachers on Alexanderplatz.

During May, he was with Ulbricht in Budapest, where, to everyone's surprise, the GDR failed to reverse Hungary's decision to exchange trade missions with Bonn. Hungarian leader Janos Kadar explained, 'My government seeks good relationships and mutually advantageous contact with the capitalist States.' A month later, Honecker accompanied Ulbricht to Moscow for the signing of a treaty of cooperation and mutual assistance which, despite the fanfare, changed none of the realities of the German and Berlin situations. Its strategic significance was negligible, though Moscow pledged to defend East German borders, meaning it didn't hand the GDR control of the important air and land access routes to West Berlin from the FRG, nor limit Western rights in West Berlin or the city's free political system. Unusually, the Soviets notified Washington and London in advance, assuring the treaty was not designed to spark a new international crisis. Typically, Ulbricht extolled the accord as 'an example of how socialist states can regulate their relations for the maximum benefit of both sides and at the same time for the benefit of international peace'.

During that trip to Moscow, Honecker could scarcely have missed increasing signs of disenchantment with Khrushchev, especially after the humiliating Cuban missile debacle. As many within the Russian Communist Party tired with their boisterous leader, a plot to oust him was hatched by Leonid Brezhnev, the 57-year-old president of the Supreme Soviet, along with the KGB and the military. After years of contact, Honecker enjoyed a friendly relationship with Brezhnev, a burly, bushy-browed, alpha male with the shoulders of a scrum-half (his eyebrows earned him the moniker 'brovenosets,' meaning 'brow cruiser'). He had wide experience in industry and agriculture, loved womanising, pigeon breeding, dominoes, cold-water swimming and most importantly, hunting. It remains unclear, though, if Erich was informed of the impending coup during this period.

In Berlin, meanwhile, Prime Minister Otto Grotewohl was gravely ill. His death in early September left Ulbricht as the surviving member of the triumvirate which founded East Germany. At Grotewohl's funeral, Honecker stood in the first guard of honour, alongside Kurt Hager, Alfred Neumann, Paul Verner and Erich Apel. The *Berliner Zeitung* was suitably poetic, reporting how:

> coming straight from their jobs, women, men and young people paid their last respects to our late Prime Minister ... Great is the sadness that moves them. But their determination to continue the life and struggle of Otto Grotewohl for the victory of socialism in our republic is also great.

Grotewohl's replacement, Willi Stoph – described by Honecker's bodyguard as taciturn, sour, and permanently grumpy – was on hand to greet Leonid Brezhnev's delegation to Berlin for the fifteenth anniversary of the GDR on 7 October 1964. In his first public engagement, Stoph stood rigid alongside Ulbricht and Brezhnev, saluting as a new 'Frog' ground-to-ground missile rolled passed the reviewing stand in a special parade. That evening, unaware of the continued plotting against Khrushchev, Ulbricht entertained Brezhnev at his Döllnsee lakeside residence, where he treated the Russian to a schoolmasterly lecture on economics (these conversations were translated at five-minute intervals). After half an hour of listening to the First Secretary's squeaking, Brezhnev was ushered into a waiting limousine, feigning illness. He had sufficiently 'recovered' by dawn to gear up in boots, duffle coat and stalker to go stag hunting with Honecker, who derived considerable pleasure from their friendship.

Remarkably, amid all this activity, problems at the Berlin Wall kept bubbling back up. In one incident, thirty students from West Berlin had managed to dig one of the most impressive tunnels in the sandy subsoil stretching between Bernauer Straße in the West and Strelitzer Straße in the East. When discovered by border guards a few days after its completion, fifty-seven men, women and children had already crawled out to the West, but many more were still awaiting their turn when GDR troops showed up.

In the fight that followed between the tunnellers and soldiers, border guard Sergeant Egon Schultz was killed when a fellow soldier accidentally shot him. But for propaganda purposes, Honecker claimed Schultz was 'treacherously murdered by shots fired by West Berlin agents', and used his death as part of a campaign against escape attempts and West Germany. Giving the highest visibility to Schultz's funeral, a tearful Honecker provided the graveside eulogy, portraying the young conscript as a heroic martyr:

> Dear parents, dear brother Armin, esteemed mourning guests, dear friends and comrades: Deeply moved we stand at the bier of our friend and comrade Egon Schultz. On 5 October he was insidiously murdered on GDR territory by bandits who came from West Berlin, now we must take leave of you, comrade NCO Egon Schultz. You were a genuine child of our republic, and you gave your best – your young prospering life – to the GDR, to your socialist homeland. Your life was short, but nevertheless very rich and happy.

Glorified as a martyr to socialism, dozens of collectives, schools and institutions were named after Egon Schultz.[14]

Meanwhile, over in Moscow, drama of a different sort was unfolding as Brezhnev finalised details of the Politburo meeting on 15 October which would oust Khrushchev into official oblivion. It was a day full of rumour and excitement. In his private notes when preparing the indictment, Brezhnev outlined the reasons. 'Why it all happened – because of a Khrushchev cult, developed with the direct and most active support of Khrushchev. I get the strong impression that clouded your awareness … the poison of unlimited power spoilt you.'

Just after 08.00, French wire agencies flashed that big news was about to break. Nobody guessed yet, including Ulbricht, that Khrushchev was on the way out. At four in the afternoon, Reuters flashed that an important announcement 'may be in preparation'. Finally, a dramatic bulletin on Radio Moscow, confirmed Khrushchev had retired 'in view of his age and the deterioration of his health'. By this point, the Politburo had offered the post of General Secretary to Brezhnev, who quickly established full command over Party structures.

The following morning, 16 October, Ulbricht congratulated Brezhnev in the warmest possible terms, but according to Vladimir Semichastny, the head of the KGB, his bitterness at being kept in the dark was palpable. He was not alone. Poland's General Secretary Wladyslaw Gomulka and Czech leader Antonín Novotný were also seething at not being informed. However, the blow was all the more painful to Khrushchev, who was wheeled into retirement, his humiliation cemented when *Pravda* accused him of making 'hare-brained schemes' and 'hasty decisions'.

One of the most remarkable aspects of the Khrushchev legacy was the abruptness and completeness with which it disappeared. Almost immediately,

Brezhnev embarked on dismantling his predecessor's reforms in favour of a more orthodox political path. In his inaugural speech, he said that under Stalin people had feared repression, while under Khrushchev they had feared reorganisations and shake-ups, 'the Soviet people deserve a quiet life'. As he terminated Khrushchev's de-Stalinisation programme, the principal victim of events in the GDR would, over time, be Ulbricht's NES process. 'It is not unreasonable to assume that the Khrushchev thaw for the GDR, which the old Stalinist Ulbricht was uncomfortable with, was called off,' Günter Schabowski surmised.

However, nothing in the Eastern bloc happened quickly. As Brezhnev settled into office, Ulbricht ploughed on with reforms; significantly, though, Honecker cozied up to Brezhnev by lamenting Khrushchev's 'tendency towards permanent reorganisation'. Such a comment was typical, says Schabowski, as Honecker 'always and unflinchingly pursued the same goal. He was committed to the Stalinist ideas of the party and socialism. And he had an iron will.'[15]

A Restless Soul

In the second half of the sixties, the German Democratic Republic's search for international acceptance took on new momentum. In February 1965, Ulbricht scored a notable propaganda success in Egypt when greeted with a 21-gun salute and – much to his delight – paraded slowly through Cairo in an open limousine to the cheers of thousands. After a magnificent state dinner, lubricated by fine Egyptian liquors, the First Secretary was awarded the Great Collar of the Order of the Nile by Egyptian President Gamal Abdel Nasser. In foreign policy, Ulbricht attempted to strengthen the GDR's global presence by establishing contact with international organisations and setting up new trade missions. He donated DDM16 million to Castro's regime in Cuba (which recognised the GDR a year later), as well as exchanging general consulates with Iraq. At the same time, preparations were made to accept 1,200 students from countries including Nigeria, India, Iraq and Syria at vocational training schools in Berlin and Leipzig. The GDR was also busily preparing to apply for UN membership which, when submitted in early 1966, was rejected, proving the road to international recognition was rockier than expected.

Meanwhile, the new winds from the Kremlin started to affect Soviet policies in East Berlin. Brezhnev thought little of Ulbricht's reforms and rejected any socialist experiments in his sphere of influence. At a dramatic SED politburo session during July at the Baltic islet of Vilm, old hands lamented the loss of personal ambitions and mourned for the scores of long-serving lesser-rank party officials pensioned off and replaced with younger educated men. Experts at the Institute for Marxism-Leninism, for example, where SED party ideology was formed, had been sent packing and those lucky enough to keep their jobs carped that the Party's absolute claim to authority was in danger, a view shared by Honecker who embarked on a course of confrontation with Ulbricht that was initially covert but later increasingly visible. From here on, he opposed his boss in three policy areas: on German-German relations, on cultural matters and on economic policy. It is certain his opposition didn't spring from any lofty inner conviction, but out of a simple desire for power. (This later became obvious when he was at the helm. Between 1971–9, Honecker expressed willingness to talk to the Bonn government, worked for the liberalisation of art and opened the market economy). For his part, Ulbricht had publicly snubbed his disciple on several occasions, and according to his adopted daughter, Beate Ulbricht, her father complained that Honecker had 'fallen on his head as a roofer and suffered permanent damage'. A few years earlier, in July 1963, Ulbricht had used Honecker's vacation-related absence to weaken his power base by removing his confidant Paul Verner as the new head of the youth commission and replaced him with an old rival Kurt Turba (who had been fired by Honecker in 1953).

Meanwhile, Brezhnev's growing distaste for the NES was demonstrated in September 1965 when Erich Apel – the man entrusted to coordinate economic reforms – was snubbed during trade negotiations in Moscow when his interlocutors fell far short of his requests for crude oil and steel. Thereafter, he was excluded from further GDR-Soviet trade talks after expressing horror at plans for the GDR to pay for Russian coal with high-quality equipment, textile machines, diesel engines, locomotives and ships. Furthermore, the Soviets openly criticized Apel's efforts to orientate the GDR economy toward Western technology rather than Russian experience, defeating his efforts to look outside the socialist bloc for research, technology and science. Alexander Schalck-Golodkowski, who later became a key figure in GDR economics, said Ulbricht's NES was the 'proclamation of an independent path for the GDR', and meant 'a certain departure from the rigid model of the planned economy in the Soviet Union'.[1]

As the NES problem simmered, Brezhnev's stance helped open a new front for disenchanted old hands. Brimming with confidence, the anti-reform majority in the Politburo expanded attacks on the work of the State Planning Commission, prompting Ulbricht – sensing which way the wind was blowing – to drop his support for Apel, a stunning betrayal. Then, at a meeting of the Politburo on 2 December, the sense of conflict grew when Willi Stoph led the charge by calling for state planning to be recentralised and criticised the 'inept' work of Apel who was panned, if not derided, from all sides. Having lost his reputation in the SED and weary of signing the Soviet trade deal, Apel returned to his office at the House of Ministries and shot himself. A 7.65 mm bullet from his service pistol lay at his feet.

In the hours and days that followed, wild rumours abounded about the death, some suspected Apel had been murdered in a power struggle between Politburo members, while Günther Wyschofsky, one of his deputies, later revealed seeing several bullet holes in the office. The clues prompted little action during a three-day MfS probe, described as being 'uncharacteristically sloppy'. Inevitably, within a couple of days, Willy Brandt – who liked to blow on the coals – made his feelings known, telling West German radio there was no doubt that Apel's death had been a suicide, performed in protest over Moscow's continuing exploitation of the GDR. East Berlin tried to grab back the microphone by issuing a furious rebuttal on air and in *Neues Deutschland*, in a piece almost certainly hastily penned by Honecker:

> Brandt's attempt to misuse the death of Comrade Apel for anti-Soviet propaganda is condemned to failure since all GDR citizens are well-informed on the results of the most recent trip of our party-government delegation to the USSR and on the contents of the great long-term USSR-GDR trade agreement. Everyone is aware that Comrade Apel had a great share in the grandiose results of our delegation and in the conclusion of the trade agreement.
>
> Is it not deeply humiliating for Brandt, who pretends to be a politician, to make himself the hawker of the lies of those scribblers who have always behaved like political vultures?[2]

Although it could be speculated that Honecker had a vested interest in Apel's demise given his growing influence and proximity to Ulbricht, his explanation about the death was self-serving. He deflected blame away from where it belonged – SED hardliners, by insisting the New Economic System had not proved itself.[3] 'Apel failed in practice in the working out of a seven-year plan,' he asserted. 'He did not manage to perform the task as formulated.'[4]

One of his pet theories was that Apel's death may have stemmed from his personal life, but did not elaborate, 'the fact that he committed suicide has never been cleared up to this day'.[5] Remarkably, Günter Mittag, co-inventor of the NES, continued his career and became a full member of the Politburo in September 1966, and remained a key figure in the GDR economy. In fact, he was one of the few men – perhaps the only man – that Honecker could call a true confidant.

The story of Apel's reforms is frustrating for what might have been. Some economists contend that, given a chance, the NES would have led to a flourishing economy by the 1970s.

True to form, the morning after Apel's suicide, all GDR media brimmed with condolences. A three-paragraph announcement in *Neue Zeit* claimed the economist had been suffering from circulatory ailments and suffered signs of 'nervous overload' which, despite all medical efforts, led to a sudden breakdown. 'Comrade Dr Erich Apel,' it added, 'suddenly and unexpectedly left us at the age of 48. His tragic death ends his fruitful and creative work. Comrade Apel made particularly great contributions to the planning and management of the GDR's economy.'[6] Never one to play on the keyboard of a guilty conscience, the warmest praise came from Willi Stoph who spoke admiringly of Apel at his state funeral, saying his 'determined and conscientious work' won the respect and trust of Soviet comrades, 'his demise has left a painful void in our ranks'.[7]

And yet, at this grim time, a meeting of the eleventh Session of the Central Committee from 15 to 18 December 1965 finally put Ulbricht's New Economic System on a dead-end path. Once Apel's successor Gerhard Schürer was named, Honecker put down a marker against economists who had yet to 'overcome their tendency to adopt Western standards', before exploring how things stood in the USSR. He also took aim at liberal artists and creatives, worsening a simmering spat with Ulbricht about youth policy. Upset by a wave of unrest by so-called 'rowdies' and 'beatniks', Honecker opened a campaign against beat music played on the youth radio station DT64 and the 'cynical' compositions of songwriter Wolf Biermann for mocking the 'old men' of the SED who, he said, were corrupt and distant, hidden away in Wandlitz. For his efforts, the singer was expelled from the SED and banned from performing. Concern was expressed too at the FDJ for neglecting to teach members in traditional Marxist-Leninist thinking, while Honecker also rallied against hooliganism, long-haired 'bums', wayward teenagers and 'harmful tendencies' in films, plays, literary works and television programmes.

> In the name of 'abstract truth' these artists concentrate on the representation of alleged shortcomings and mistakes in the German Democratic Republic. Some writers believe that socialist education can only be successful through the summed-up presentation of shortcomings and mistakes. They do not notice that the effect of their works of art is dragging backwards and inhibiting the development of the socialist consciousness of the working people.[8]

Reflecting widespread views shared among the old salt, he called for a 'clean screen' to protect the viewers from scepticism and immorality. 'Our GDR is a clean state,' he explained. 'In it there are unalterable standards of ethics and morals.' From here on, before all-important DEFA film projects were approved, Honecker insisted on vetting and approving the script. As West German journalist Dieter Borkowski noted, his 'artistic judgment was modest'. For example, he raved over a dull biopic of Karl Liebknecht, describing it as 'exciting as a crime novel!'[9] (The narrative of any committed German communist required Liebknecht's revolution be marked as *the* defining moment of the twentieth century). As Klaus Taubert recalled, Honecker embarked on banning the entire annual production of DEFA films and vilified critical art as decadent and pro-capitalist. 'But the confrontation with art and culture was only the pretext to act against the liberalisation in the area of the economy and to reverse the dwindling influence of the party apparatus.' By the end of 1965, most of the liberalisation tendencies initiated in 1963 were undone.

Unsurprisingly, with so much upheaval, the Western press speculated about the future of Walter Ulbricht. In 1966, the *Atlantic Monthly* magazine forecast East Germany's leadership would easily survive Ulbricht's departure from the political stage and would continue to operate under 'his two ableist lieutenants: 53-year-old Socialist Unity Party chieftain Erich Honecker and 53-year-old administrator Willi Stoph'. In fact, despite the acrimony, it was Honecker, not the stiff and prissy Stoph, who became more and more important in the smooth running of Ulbricht's life. In 1966, he oversaw details of celebrations marking the twentieth anniversary of the founding of the SED and the fifth anniversary of the Berlin Wall with a military parade, designed to demonstrate the strength of socialism.

Together with Ulbricht, he ate his way through buffets at the inauguration of the first nuclear power plant in East Germany, a gala opening at the new Interhotel 'Unter den Linden' and the 'Lindencorso', a modern new Western-styled restaurant. Relations were still warm enough for the two to holiday together on the Black Sea for several weeks, while on the home front, he enjoyed time with his father Wilhelm who moved into Wandlitz for three months every year after becoming a widower (Erich did not attend his mother's funeral in 1963). Although these holidays were quiet and almost unnoticed, the old man shunned the spotlight whenever possible and had no desire to abandon his home in the Saarland and move permanently to the GDR, nor did Erich's surviving sisters. In an unguarded comment to a reporter from *Der Spiegel* at his home in Wiebelskirchen, Wilhelm confessed that his son and daughter-in-law 'have so little time. I'd rather stay here.'[10]

At the border, Erich Honecker showed his most monstrous side. By 1967, the signs of an authoritarian state were there for everyone to see. That year, guards were told that border violators were to be 'arrested or annihilated'.[11] The regulations on 'illegal border crossings', was clearly laid out in paragraph 213[12] of the criminal code, which stated that in severe cases, perpetrators would be sentenced to between one and five years, and preparations and attempts were also punishable:

> Whoever illegally trespasses or stays within the territory of the German Democratic Republic; does not adhere to the legal provisions or imposed constraints regarding entry and exit, travel methods, or length of stay; uses false information to obtain permission for themselves or others to leave or enter the territory of the German Democratic Republic; or leaves the territory of the German Democratic Republic without the State's permission or does not return will be punished with a prison sentence of up to two years, or probation, fines, or public censure.

In paragraph 105, the issue of 'subversive human trafficking', decreed that 'whoever undertook to entice citizens of the German Democratic Republic to territories or countries outside of their homeland; to transport, transfer, or hinder their return, will be punished with a prison sentence of no less than two years'. By 1970, a reminder in the 'Handbook for Border Guards' included the horrifying line: 'The preliminary arrest must be made by any means (for example using a well-aimed bullet)', thus implying the death of individuals trying to flee was accepted as a possible consequence of the regulations.

From time to time, the Wall featured in the international press, as did news from wider society, where there were some notable successes for the SED regime. During 1967, GDR citizens celebrated the introduction of the five-day working week, while every other Eastern Bloc country continued with the six-day model. Also striking were figures showing the high proportion of female workers; on a world scale, East Germany sat in second place with 47 per cent of women in employment, next to the Soviet Union with 51.7 per cent. There was occasional reportage of German-German relations, such as Ulbricht's proposal that West German Chancellor Dr Kurt Klesinger and Willi Stoph should meet to discuss steps toward cooperation between the two countries. He embellished these ideas at the opening session of the seventh SED Party Congress in April 1967, where he said the two men should be accompanied by experts to formulate agreements. However, his insistence that such a meeting be tied to discussion of his long-demanded objectives such as the recognition of existing borders, disarmament of both Germanys, and the mutual renunciation of nuclear weapons, led nowhere.

In contrast, Honecker's performance at the conference looked narrow-minded and inflammatory. In a twenty-five-page speech, he delivered a stinging attack on China's leaders, accusing them of poisonous nationalism and fostering a personality cult around Mao Tse Tung. Then he took a swipe at West German prosperity by posing the question as to what might have become of the 'capitalist gentlemen' if in 1945 the Eastern sector of Germany had had 120 blast furnaces and the West had only four instead of vice versa? 'The truth is,' he cried, 'that our people by their own strength and with active support, mainly from our Soviet friends, cleared away the rubble left by the Second World War, overcame squalor and chaos and created a modern socialist industrial state.'[13] Such comments sat uneasily alongside Ulbricht's 'overture' to Chancellor Klesinger. But here the unhappiness ran deeper, Honecker – like Brezhnev – was troubled by Ulbricht's approaches to Bonn. As he continued his sharp speeches, the demarcation of the GDR and closer ties with Moscow became a running theme. In a reference to the West's desire for reunification, Honecker barked that 'no matter how much our adversaries in West Germany clamour, they can no longer turn back the wheel of history'.

> We stand firmly by our socialist fatherland, our GDR. And let it be clearly said from this rostrum of the seventh congress to all those who advance or follow Bonn's claim to sole, representation: Socialism in the GDR is final and irrevocable, and anyone who casts doubts on our frontiers, casts doubts on his own existence![14]

In the years of his decline, Ulbricht was absorbed by improving relations with the FRG. However, off and on throughout 1967, he had been unwell. In that period, he tweaked the constitution to declare, 'The German Democratic Republic is a socialist state of the German nation. It is the political organisation of the workers in the cities and in the countryside, who jointly under the leadership of the working class and their Marxist-Leninist Party will realise Socialism.' While the old document made no mention of the SED, the new constitution unequivocally professed 'the leadership of the state is to be exercised through the working class and its Marxist-Leninist Party – the SED'.

As the winter of 1967 drew in, Honecker was invited to the Soviet Union to mark the fiftieth anniversary of the October Revolution and deliver several speeches about 'fraternal socialist cooperation'. Eager to be seen as a statesman, he took centre stage through three days of pomp and pageants. Speaking at the Novovoronezh power station, where preparatory work for the GDR's second nuclear power plant, the Atomkraftwerk Nord, was being carried out, he returned to the issue of the Berlin Wall. He spoke thoughtfully, saying until 13 August 1961, the GDR was forced to pursue socialist development under the conditions dictated by an open frontier, but 'we succeeded, with the fraternal support of the Soviet Union in making the German Democratic Republic a stable, socialist state in which the ideas of Lenin are triumphant'.[15] He made sure the GDR saw his performance by arranging taped recordings to be sent back to Berlin via Interflug, enabling millions of East Germans to watch the Red Army orchestra play the GDR anthem, *Auferstanden aus Ruinen*, at a sumptuous gala dinner, where Honecker gave a stiff salute.

His profile remained in focus during a consultative meeting of delegations from sixty-five communist and workers' parties in Budapest on 28 February 1968, where he proclaimed solidarity with the 'most profoundly just struggle' for freedom by the Vietnamese people. 'The events in Vietnam, Korea, the Near East, Yemen and Greece and the renazification in West Germany, disclose the plans of the main imperialist powers to achieve their aggressive aims with the help of numerous so-called 'limited' wars.'[16] When the applause died down, he railed against the FRG's 'revanchist and expansionist policy of providing the natural breeding ground for renazification, which has now become crassly apparent'.[17]

Against this background, Honecker's attention was firmly focused on Czechoslovakia, where, a week earlier, Alexander Dubček, the youthful new Communist Party leader, had loosened government control and expanded individual rights, giving hope to Czechs, and angering the USSR.

The Problem Neighbour

In 1968, Czechoslovakia became a unique communist oasis of freedom when Alexander Dubček attempted to bring democratic change to the country, promising 'socialism with a human face' by the 'widest possible democratisation', the correction of past mistakes and the rehabilitation of victims persecuted during the Stalinist era.

In this excited atmosphere, it was hardly surprising events in Prague were followed by disquiet in Moscow, where there were fears the reforms would weaken the communist bloc. The situation worsened when Dubček removed media censorship, allowing newspapers to criticise high-ranking officials and call for multi-party democracy– for Brezhnev, it was all too much.

To placate the Soviet leader, Dubček – who was by now reaching new heights of fame and reputation in the West – reaffirmed his support for the alliance with the USSR. But as spring turned to summer, Czechs continued to enjoy the freedom of expression unprecedented in the Eastern bloc. In East Berlin, Ulbricht declared Dubček's reforms as counter-revolutionary and warned of possible 'contagion' to other socialist countries if not nipped in the bud. At the same time, he complained of Czechoslovakia's increasing ties with West Germany. Sensing the brewing storm, Honecker chipped in his thoughts at the sixth session of the Central Committee in June with a speech emphasising the Party's role as the guiding force in social progress:

> The dictatorship of the proletariat has been equated with erroneous leadership methods, with violations of democracy and legality, and with other subjectively grounded errors. But this is turning things completely upside down. We will not permit the central principle of our ideology to be watered down. We know very well that Marxists and revisionists have differed on the question of power since time immemorial.[1]

Faced with the uncertain situation across the border, Ulbricht and Honecker tried to counter with the modest means at their disposal. Firstly, they prohibited the sale of Czech newspapers and magazines, stopped issuing exit visas for East German tourists seeking to visit Czechoslovakia and reduced bilateral scientific and cultural exchanges. Soon after, the GDR largely sealed off its border with Czechoslovakia.

Meanwhile, with Dubček stubbornly refusing to pare back reforms, Soviet plans to oust him with military action began to take concrete shape. On 31 July, Ulbricht (with Honecker), along with several other Eastern bloc leaders, arrived at the Kremlin to hear Brezhnev lay out exactly how the Prague situation would unfold. However, before the bayonet was thrust, the unlikely negotiating team of Ulbricht and Honecker were dispatched to Karlovy Vary in Czechoslovakia for one last attempt at twisting Dubček's arm. Rather worryingly, after seven hours of coaxing and cajoling, their attempts to talk the Czech into going slow on reforms failed, prompting a Western reporter to cynically remark, 'Ulbricht senses in the Czechoslovak reform programme the death knell of his own brand of regime.'[2]

Patience exhausted, Brezhnev gave the green light to the joint invasion of Czechoslovakia by soldiers from four Warsaw Pact countries – USSR, Poland, Bulgaria and Hungary – on the night of 20-21 August 1968. For all the historic significance of this moment, not a single NVA troop marched over the border, given the sensitivities of Hitler's invasion thirty years earlier. The Germans, according to Brezhnev, 'were bitter about their exclusion from the invasion force'.[3] Relegated to spectator status, Ulbricht and Honecker could only listen to the largest deployment of military force in Europe since the Second World War over secret shortwave military communications. Honecker's beloved NVA was limited to providing intelligence and logistical support, which, in reality, meant securing the Czech-East German border. (An East German tank and rifle division were assigned to the reserves of the Soviet High Command but remained in barracks.)

With devastating zeal, a series of swift land and air movements crushed Czechoslovakia's defiance under the tracks of Russian tanks. Humiliated, Dubček was kicked out of office and reduced in rank to a low-level bureaucrat; while others purged from power were forced to eke out a living with tiring menial jobs.

As nations across the world denounced the invasion as a 'shameless act' of aggression, Honecker was horrified to discover that 1,189 East Germans had rallied in sympathy for Czechoslovakia. According to Stasi figures, 75 per cent of them were aged between 12 and 30 years old. In some areas, demonstrators were yanked away, then kicked, punched and beaten by police officers. In Berlin, when Frank Havemann and Hans Jurgen Uszkoreit – both 18 years old – painted the name Dubček on the facade of the central library, they, like many other youths, were sent to prison, followed by years of 'probation in socialist production'. Honecker gave the most forthright – and pointed – defence of the GDR's part in the Prague operation before the ninth plenary session of the Central Committee, where he trumpeted that 'revisionist and counter-revolutionaries' in Czechoslovakia had progressed so far that political means were not sufficient to protect the country from the grip of imperialism: 'International socialist solidarity had to be supported by military means.'[4] He also turned the needle on suggestions that 'building bridges' and 'change through rapprochement' could have solved the Prague dilemma.[5]

The following year, economics took a more severe and direct grip on Erich Honecker's life. The long winter of 1968-69 – the coldest in years – demanded a considerable effort on the part of cooperative farmers, while there was a noticeable shortage of electrical power, gas and solid fuels – a disaster for any government, especially one working on strict planning.

At the tenth conference of the SED Central Committee, Honecker poured out his frustration by demanding comrades in the power and transportation industry draw the proper conclusions from the winter. 'Besides, there was a shortage of metallurgical products and other important raw materials in many areas. Several enterprises and combines had to restrict their electric power supply during peak times; in city gas supply systems there were break-downs and failures as well as quality reductions'.[6] He stressed the need for more scientists in the production of top-level products. 'This requires engineering economists get together with other specialists and accurately figure the costs of every part of the product, on the basis of world top-level standards.' He demanded higher goals be set in productivity and effectivity, particularly in electronics, the chemical industry and machine-building. 'We need at the same time an uncompromising struggle against smug self-satisfaction, overbearing attitudes, and mediocrity in work, on all levels.'

On one-point Honecker was particularly specific: the complete build-up and remodelling of the centres of Berlin, as well as the downtown sections of Dresden, Gera, Suhl, Jena and Schwedt. In the cultural sphere, he expressed satisfaction with GDR TV which, he said, had captured the hearts and minds of millions of people by producing a series of socialist plays by authors including Bernhard Seeger, Helmut Sakowski, Benito Wogatzki and Karl-Georg Egel.

> The achievements of the collectives participating in these television plays have the task of drawing worthy portraits of socialist heroes of our time and have been able to clarify through them – in a surrogate fashion for many people – the revolutionary change in social conditions and in people, here in our German Democratic Republic.

That summer, Honecker was constantly and restlessly on the move. He led a party-government delegation to Moscow, Leningrad and Kyiv, to learn about the work of industrial enterprises, scientific research institutions, metal works, collective farms and cultural workers.

Meanwhile, in the FRG, Willy Brandt's Social Democrats scored a victory in the September elections, opening a new era in West Germany's foreign policy. Suddenly, adherence to the Hallstein Doctrine was abandoned, paving the way for a period of rapprochement with the GDR and Moscow. His election spelt the end of the Christian Democrats' twenty-three-year dominance of the party that had been keen to work with the Western allies, align government policy with the United States and snub any overtures from the German Democratic Republic.

Brandt's process of understanding and reconciliation – or 'Ostpolitik' – was unbearably painful for some West German conservatives who screamed that money sent to Ulbricht to help the population, actually 'propped up his regime'. Others charged that GDR concessions promised on human rights were routinely ignored. After a decade in which FRG diplomacy had focused on snubbing the GDR's desire for recognition, Brandt let it be known that he was prepared to recognise the existence of two German States 'within the German nation'.

However, unlike Ulbricht who viewed 'Ostpolitik' as an opportunity for German-German negotiations, many in the SED Politburo united in scorn, fearing a warming relationship with Bonn. Honecker, of course, was also sceptical – and thus surfaced a new variant of antipathy with Ulbricht. At the twelfth session of the Central Committee in December 1969, Honecker set out a vision that was anything but unifying:

> What they really want is to get a foot in the other fellow's door. One could dictate pages and pages on these gentlemen's ideas on the subject of infiltrating socialist countries according to their notorious 'grey plans' … First, they want to make themselves look open-minded and objective, then they want 'contacts' below what they call the threshold of international recognition to lull our political vigilance, and on top of that, they want the expertise of our specialists to help them close their own scientific gaps.[7]

Without speaking out against Ulbricht, Erich Mielke also took a clear position at the twelfth session of the Central Committee. In siding with Honecker, he accused Brandt's government of failing to provide proof that it was 'honestly interested' in ensuring European security, peace and cooperation with the socialist states. 'On the contrary, under the cloak of willingness to reach an understanding […] it strives to find new and dangerous ways of penetrating the socialist states politically and ideologically.'

As it happened, Brandt's social-liberal coalition turned into an energetic force in West Germany. It expanded civil liberties, improved the welfare state and invested in education. Other important reforms included the protection of the environment, healthcare, an overhaul of the penal system and the pursuit of 'quality of life', which sought to combine the humanisation of the workplace with environmental and health protection. 'We want to become a nation of good neighbours,' Brandt explained, when outlining the core elements of his foreign policy as securing of peace through dialogue.

Relations with Moscow warmed when Brandt signed the nuclear non-proliferation Treaty in November 1969, which Kurt Georg Kiesinger's outgoing administration had declined to endorse. More was to follow. In treaties with the USSR and Poland in 1970, the FRG recognised the existing borders in Europe as inviolable, ending a long period of strain between the two countries. Brezhnev later observed that 'the normalisation of relations between the Soviet Union and the Federal Republic of Germany is one of the most important developments in Europe's post-war history'. Over time, systematic meetings at the summit level became a significant form of Soviet-West German cooperation. 'Experience shows,' Brezhnev said at a dinner in honour of Brandt,[8] 'that when top political leaders join competent experts in various fields in developing relations between two countries, this acts as a stimulant for all concerned to work more effectively and promptly'.[9]

After receiving Brandt in Moscow in 1970, and in Crimea in 1971, Brezhnev eventually visited Bonn in May 1973, paving the way for regular political consultations, broader economic ties and intensive scientific, cultural and tourist exchanges.

Et Tu Honecker

Relations with West Germany, meanwhile, had also taken a more urgent and direct grip on Honecker's life. As the Soviet Union and West Germany improved ties, Ulbricht permitted a meeting between the head of the GDR's Council of Ministers, Willi Stoph, and Willy Brandt. The East German town of Erfurt became the unlikely scene of the meeting on 19 March 1970, which marked the first-ever face-to-face talks between senior government figures of the FRG and GDR. 'The meeting,' TASS noted, was held at the initiative of the East German government which 'thus demonstrated once more its desire to normalise relations with Western Germany'.[1] In a commentary, *Neues Deutschland* added: 'We have shown this initiative and accommodating attitude because we are earnest in our endeavour to make a contribution to the peace and security of Europe. Now everything depends on the West German Chancellor's adopting a realistic and reasonable attitude.'[2] The two sides sought to 'establish normal relations by treaty' and find common interests in areas including road, railway and waterway communications, postal services, simpler trading facilities and financial arrangements. For his part, Stoph would demand recognition for the GDR and reparations payments for the talent lost to the FRG through the exodus of refugees prior to 1961. 'This is a difficult terrain with many obstacles,'[3] Brandt explained. He also revealed he had formed a mental picture of Stoph as a man with rigid views, 'I have the impression that he is a man who quite deliberately keeps his own person in the background, far behind the cause he represents ... and is therefore a difficult partner in such talks.'[4]

Desperate to sour the event, it is probable that Honecker helped to arrange for a crowd of East Germans to give Brandt a hero's welcome in front of the Erfurter Hof, an old-style hotel across the square from the railway station. Press reports described folks standing on the sidewalks shouting for 'Willy' – not Willi Stoph, but for Willy Brandt.[5] 'For a moment,' Brandt recalled in his memoirs, 'they felt free enough to show their feelings. I was moved.' Political observers shrewdly pondered whether events were staged by a 'conservative faction' in the SED to demonstrate how dangerously attractive Brandt was to East Germans.

Egon Krenz was never sure about the extent of Honecker's involvement but was certain that Moscow had a hand in events. 'You had to be very naive to assume that the applause for the West German guest would have been spontaneous and the crowd gathered there voluntarily.'[6] According to Krenz, our 'friends from Karlshorst' – the seat of the Soviet secret service in the GDR – orchestrated the incident to warn Ulbricht of the dangers of acting on his own authority and getting too close to Brandt.[7]

Typically, ADN and TASS published a twisted version of events by reporting that hundreds of residents chanted 'their full support for the policy of the GDR aimed at peace and security in Europe'.[8] GDR Defence Minister Heinz Hoffman later admitted that the Erfurt kerfuffle 'certainly strengthened Honecker's conviction to force a policy of radical separation'.[9]

In the final analysis, not much was achieved in Erfurt, although Brandt named two positive developments. Firstly, a second discussion with Stoph would be held in Kassel on 21 May, and, moreover, the 'argumentation of each side became more comprehensible to the other'.[10] In the event, the Kassel meeting went smoothly but unproductively, bringing the sides no closer together.

Meanwhile, as Honecker resumed undermining Ulbricht's rapprochement with the West, he received a sympathetic ear from Brezhnev, who was becoming weary of West German intentions toward the GDR.[11] As references to his patron became more vinegary in flavour, Honecker continued to recycle a familiar litany of hate toward the FRG by claiming in Europe there were two worlds, 'two diametrically opposed social systems ... the peaceful strategy of socialism and the aggressive, expansionist strategy of imperialism'. He continued:

> Playing the role of the spearhead of American global strategy in Europe, West German imperialism is particularly striving to acquire influence in the political, military and also ideological fields. West Germany's ruling circles are stubbornly resisting the conduction of a treaty on the establishment of equitable relations between the GDR and the FRG on the basis of international law: Such a policy contradicts the requirements for genuine guarantees of peace and European security.[12]

According to Günter Schabowski, these endless rants were hardly conducive to rapprochement and caused irreparable damage to Honecker's fragile relationship with Ulbricht. 'Against the dialogue in Kassel and Erfurt promoted by Ulbricht, against the associated danger of change in the GDR through rapprochement, Honecker advanced his thesis: the recognition of the GDR by demarcation from the Federal Republic.'[13] Ulbricht deplored Honecker's needling and remained unenthusiastic about demarcation, especially the renaming of institutions and organisations containing the word 'German'. For example, Deutschlandsender – the national radio station – was rechristened the 'Voice of the GDR', the state television channel was retitled 'GDR TV', and dozens of other associations and organisations were given the predicate GDR, with the exceptions of the SED, the FDGB and the FDJ. From then on, the German Academy of Sciences was called the 'Academy of Sciences of the GDR', and the National Front of Democratic Germany became the 'National Front of the GDR'. (A constitutional amendment in 1974, finally abandoned the concept of German nationhood and redefined the German Democratic Republic as a 'socialist state of workers and farmers'.) In her role as Education Minister, Margot Honecker joined in the demarcation process by banning schools from teaching the text of the national anthem, she left only the melody of Hanns Eisler's hymn untouched. (A line that mentioned a 'united fatherland' did not sit well with the dream of a 'proletarian nation').

By this point, aware that his days in power were numbered unless he acted against his ambitious protégé, Ulbricht stunned the Politburo on 1 July by sacking his heir and ordering him back to Party school for 'further education'. Ever the master tactician, the old man struck while the Soviet ambassador Abrasimov – an ally of Honecker – was in Moscow. For a brief, tantalising moment, it looked like Honecker was finished. Reportedly, none of the Politburo uttered a sound either during or after Ulbricht's speech.

After he'd hurried out of the room, a flummoxed Honecker appeared at the Soviet Embassy on Unter den Linden. His voice choked and broke as he pleaded with Abrasimov's personal assistant to place a long-distance call to his boss in Moscow. The transcript of that torturous conversation, reads in part:

> Yes, you know, Pyotr Andreyevich, Honecker is sitting in your study at the moment. He is completely desperate and depressed. He says that there was a meeting of the Politburo at which it was decided to relieve him of the post of second secretary of the SED and to send him to party school. Honecker asks you, Pyotr Andreyevich, to inform the leadership of our party about this.[14]

That evening, by all accounts, there was a great deal of toing and froing of messages before Brezhnev dispatched Abrasimov back to Germany. On arriving at Ulbricht's summerhouse, red-eyed from staying up all night, he was treated to a lecture on Honecker's morally wayward conduct and poverty of imagination. His arguments fell on stony ground and after being continually interrupted by Abrasimov, Ulbricht was told to reinstate his deputy in what proved a watershed moment for SED politics. The action strengthened an emerging anti-Ulbricht faction that included Kurt Hager, Horst Sindermann and Willi Stoph.

Honecker now delighted in mocking Ulbricht. Having recovered from his ordeal, he received encouragement from Brezhnev on 28 July during a brief meeting in Moscow. Speaking off the cuff, the Russian complained of Ulbricht's 'ill-considered steps against you (Honecker) and other comrades in the Politburo'. Interestingly, he also asserted that 'there shouldn't be a process of reconciliation between the FRG and the GDR'. While Brezhnev recognised Honecker's zeal and energy, he was reluctant to intervene in the SED power struggle, given some in the higher levels of the Soviet government considered Honecker distinctly suspect and 'even more unpredictable and unreliable than Ulbricht'. With that in mind, Brezhnev continued to explore whether there was an alternative to Honecker. (Abrasimov was sent as a type of roving envoy to gauge opinion among SED old hands. Remarkably, even Willi Stoph, albeit grudgingly, recommended Honecker).[15] Meanwhile, during their discussions, Brezhnev took pains to stress he was 'not in favour of simply pushing Walter aside, even considering the new situation in the Politburo of the SED'. His message was clear: Honecker needed to garner more support within the Politburo before he would act.[16] According to Klaus Taubert, a reporter for the state news agency ADN, Honecker's future was already decided. 'His qualities were obvious. He was a staunch Stalinist. If he'd had an order, he'd obey, uncompromising. He'd stop at nothing.'[17]

Though outwardly united, throughout the summer of 1970, Honecker's contempt towards Ulbricht bubbled furiously. He did, nevertheless, smile for the cameras in Moscow during August when the First Secretary won a cheery public reception, but in a whispered conversation on 19 August, Brezhnev privately expressed concerns to Honecker about both Ulbricht and Willy Brandt. The latter, he said, was 'penetrating socialist countries, including the GDR' through the economy,[18] with the aim of 'shaking' the German Democratic Republic. 'Neither we nor you,' he warned, 'can remain indifferent to such a danger.'[19] It was useful, of course, to also know that Brezhnev deplored Ulbricht's boasting that East Germany would outdo the FRG's economy, saying his oft-used slogan of 'overtaking the West' was wrong. 'Our social order is of a different, higher type. We put the principles of humanism into practice.'[20] It became evident that Brezhnev was clearly behind Honecker for the first time. As if briefing a statesman-in-the-making, Brezhnev insisted the future of the GDR lay in the socialist community. 'We have our troops there. That's a good thing and it will stay that way,' he added fiercely.[21]

> We have no misconceptions about Brandt, about West German social democracy. Illusions are out of place and must not even be allowed. Neither Brandt nor Strauss will introduce socialism in West Germany. There is no process of rapprochement between

the GDR and the FRG, it cannot and must not happen. That's what Brandt wants, that's what Strauss wants, that's what the West German bourgeoisie wants. What is important for us is the strengthening of the position of the GDR, its further positive political and economic development, an improvement in the living conditions of the working class, the peasants, the population of the GDR. It is on this task that we must continue to concentrate. So, concentrate everything on consolidating the socialist GDR. Brandt's goals for the GDR are different from ours.[22]

On the morning of 21 August, Brezhnev and Ulbricht held a private four-hour conversation in which the Russian ignored the First Secretary's request to have his opponent thrown out of the Politburo. The pain was sharpened when Ulbricht was also warned against spreading malicious gossip about Honecker.[23]

Honecker's ebullience in Moscow, once it subsided, led to a long period of waiting. As the weeks slipped by, routine duties took him to Dresden to 'strengthen the ideological work' of the local party on 15 September and, on 8 October, he joined Ulbricht on the eve of the twenty-first anniversary of the GDR to bestow awards on collectives. The following week in Cottbus, he opened the 'Waffenbrüderschaft' exercises, the largest ever joint Warsaw Pact manoeuvres on GDR territory. Addressing the party faithful, he said the drills would 'prove convincingly that the socialist coalition guaranteed its military superiority over imperialism in the 1970s'.[24] A few weeks later, on 24 October, he led an 'inspiring meeting of fraternal friendship' to Bratislava, where alongside Willi Stoph, he addressed the Slovakian National Council.

Amid all this activity, rumours abetted by malicious tittle-tattle about turmoil in Honecker's private life would not go away. In 2016, a former GDR lawyer, Götz Berger, claimed Erich and Margot's marriage was secretly dissolved in the spring of 1970.[25] Although never proven, Berger alleged matters were so serious that the couple sought legal opinion and, equally revealing was an anecdote about Politburo member Alfred Neumann reputedly letting it slip that he had a 'complicated appointment' ahead of him: 'I have to speak to Margot,' he told a friend. 'She wants a divorce! You can't do that in her position.' (He also made the same comment to other confidants.) By this point, it was widely rumoured Margot was embroiled in a relationship with a young actor, four years her junior, engaged at the Deutsches Theater, a canard that later took on the authority of fact among some German tabloid newspapers.[26] Versions of the story percolated around the SED for the next nineteen years. Contrary to Brezhnev's order, there can be little doubt that Ulbricht continued his incessant backbiting and spread unsavoury details about Honecker's private life.

By this time, the First Secretary's mind was quickly distracted by a sudden shortage of consumer goods and foodstuffs which aroused discontent, sparking strikes and unrest. Sniffing an opportunity, Honecker aggravated the problem by engineering an ill-tempered Central Committee meeting in December 1970. He encouraged Hanna Wolf, the rector of the Karl Marx SED party college, to lead the charge by angrily denouncing that gaps in supply – especially in the medical field – had left pharmacies without cough syrup and other medicines. During the discussion, Ulbricht was blamed for the difficulties which left hundreds of companies unable to fulfil goals, despite working overtime. 'Honecker had been working purposefully behind the scenes for some time to establish his power,' Günter Schabowski recounted. 'He had a concept and had people behind it who were just as devoted to it as the Ulbricht team was to their boss.'[27]

The true scale of the challenge to Ulbricht became clear during January when a cabal of thirteen Politburo members and candidates composed a carefully phrased letter to Brezhnev putting down a marker against the First Secretary.[28] Ulbricht, the letter stated, had not been in a position since the middle of 1970 to properly address reality. Furthermore, they castigated him for not adhering to Politburo and Central Committee decisions, but rather of repeatedly questioning them. Moreover, they berated him for advocating his own line vis-à-vis the Federal Republic in contrast to the SED's agreed-upon procedure with Moscow. In chronicling Ulbricht's decline, they charged that as he deviated from the joint resolutions of the brother parties of the Warsaw Pact, it was no longer guaranteed that the forthcoming eighth Party Congress could come to a unified opinion on international issues. As if that wasn't bad enough, the letter decried the fact that Ulbricht increasingly considered himself infallible – on a par with Marx, Engels and Lenin. The conclusion: Ulbricht should be disempowered with Moscow's blessing, but the overthrow must be presented as a 'normal transition' from an older man to a younger man. For half a dozen Politburo members that refused to sign the letter (including Albert Norden and Alfred Neumann), there was sadness at the soiling of Ulbricht's person. And as the First Secretary's edifice of authority began to crumble, it took Brezhnev another three months of procrastinating before acting.

Cometh the Hour

Once he overcame his initial hesitance, the Soviet leader received Ulbricht and Honecker in the Kremlin on 11 April 1971 during the XXIV Party Congress.

Coming quickly to the point, Ulbricht was told to resign as First Secretary, but to relieve his dismay, he would keep the position of Chairman of the State Council and become honorary chairman of the SED, a ceremonial post created to guarantee fraternal amity. Honecker, he was told, was his anointed successor. Wearily, after swallowing this fresh humiliation, Ulbricht left the room.

According to the memoirs of Markus Wolf, the saga didn't end there. Several days later, presumably worried that the old man would continue to exert political influence or even stage a counter-coup, Honecker added intimidation to his lengthening list of antics by turning up at Ulbricht's holiday home seeking to ensure his old mentor would step down (he arrived, according to Wolf, with armed security forces and even cut the telephone lines). After a hot exchange, Ulbricht lost his nerve. Thinking Honecker unstable, unprincipled and unsound, he grudgingly gave way and promised his resignation in writing. (Exact details are not recorded but the conversation allegedly lasted ninety minutes).

In the end, Ulbricht hung on to his office until 3 May when, with ritual insincerity, he chaired his last full meeting of the Politburo. Tired, and possibly still in a state of shock, he mumbled that the years had 'left their marks' and did not allow him to continue such strenuous work: 'I therefore, think the time has come to place these functions into younger hands and I propose to elect comrade Erich Honecker as the new secretary of the Central Committee.'[1]

In a bulletin flashed by ADN, Honecker spoke of the heavy responsibility he had inherited and assured he would 'not spare any strength to prove worthy of this obligation and trust of the members and candidate members of the Central Committee and our whole party'.[2] Later that evening, a congratulatory telegram arrived from Brezhnev, it was sincere and heartfelt:

> Soviet communists view the decision of the plenum of the SED Central Committee to elect you, Comrade Honecker, to the post of First Secretary of the SED Central Committee and Comrade Walter Ulbricht to the post of chairman of the party as an embodiment of the important Leninist principle of the

continuity and collectivity of party leadership, as a pledge of
the firm determination of communists, of all working people
of the GDR to follow the principled course toward creating a
developed social system of socialism in the GDR, toward the
utmost strengthening of the republic as an inalienable part of the
fraternal-community of socialist states, toward ensuring a stable
peace and the strengthening of European security.[3]

In his message of congratulation, Russian ambassador Abrasimov praised
Honecker as an 'outstanding official of the working class' and lauded the SED
for its 'inflexible struggle against West German imperialism, its consistent
course towards the complete demarcation against the imperialist FRG, and the
deep integration of the GDR into the community of socialist states'.[4]

Having victoriously survived fifty years of purges and power struggles,
Walter Ulbricht – a man who had done a great deal to mythologise himself –
slipped quietly into official oblivion. He commandeered the headlines for the
last time on 4 May, when *Neues Deutschland* noted: 'The Central Committee
assured Comrade Ulbricht that, under the leadership of its First Secretary,
Comrade Erich Honecker, the great work of building the socialist order will
continue in a successful manner.'[5] In the same edition, Honecker's biography
sat in the top left corner of page two, it highlighted his 'persistent, selfless
commitment in the interest of the working people'.[6]

When all was said and done, Honecker never returned to an easy relationship
with Ulbricht. His animosity was particularly visible when he renamed the
'Walter Ulbricht Academy for State and Law', and several 'Walter Ulbricht'
factories and pulled two official Ulbricht biographies (described as the 'greatest
German Marxist-Leninist') from bookstores.

Looking back from the perspective of three decades, Margot Honecker
claimed (with a touch of embarrassment) that political differences did not
detract from a 'respectful' relationship with Ulbricht, although, she said,
'Walter did not always make things easy for comrades.'[7] The ignominious
parting for the two men – who had been each other's fortune and misfortune –
haunted the new First Secretary for the rest of his life. In a curious way, Erich
deluded himself by insisting he was not the villain of the piece. In his version
of events, Ulbricht voluntarily resigned, 'and we for our part suggested that he
should remain the chairman of the State Council and honorary chairman of the
party. This was a prime example of how one respects older comrades who have
attained great achievements.'[8]

The Modern Man

On his advent to power, Honecker assembled a tight circle of friends, family, and 'yes-men' advisers to draw personal support and counsel. Access to his orbit fell to Elli Kelm, a short, mousy-haired woman who had served as his gatekeeper since 1952, successfully keeping away whingers and hangers-on. She was considered a formidable presence, or as one security official remarked, 'the Cerberus standing guard outside his office door who stopped everyone except Heinz Hoffmann and Heinz Kessler, and she would have liked to have stopped them too'.

Predictably, Margot's position as Minister of Education was secure, while her brother, Manfred Feist – a man described by Markus Wolf as an 'incompetent functionary' – was elected to the Central Committee. From here on, Honecker's 'core team' consisted of Alfred Neumann, Stoph's deputy; Paul Verner, whom he brought into the Central Committee as secretary for security; Werner Lamberz, who was to lend a hand to the aging Albert Norden; Hermann Axen, responsible for foreign policy within the International Liaison Department; Werner Krolikowski, and Horst Sindermann.

The crafty State Security Minister Erich Mielke and Harry Tisch – who soon advanced to the head of the trade union federation – became candidates for the Politburo. Advice and support also came from Konrad Naumann, Ingeburg Lange, Werner Felfe, Joachim Hermann and Heinz Kessler, all close friends from his FDJ days. 'New faces, that was not his thing,' says Schabowski. 'Once established, they stayed. This also applied to the Politburo. Any change in the group would raise speculation about rivalries.' However, a new appointment came when Egon Krenz was installed as leader of the Ernst Thälmann Pioneer Organisation. Cheekily described as 'horse face' by detractors, Honecker considered Krenz of pleasing appearance and manner – he even had the makings of a successor. 'Honecker's comradely relationship with me impressed me,' Krenz remembered. 'It was heartfelt and productive.'[1]

Meeting Brezhnev on 18 May 1970, Honecker testified the transition of power in East Berlin had been stable. From here on, his relationship with the Soviet leader became psychologically interesting. Honecker's office was adorned by a portrait of Brezhnev with a personal dedication, as was the lobby of the SED building (his office was remodelled by Elli Kelm's husband to his personal specifications). It didn't take long for Honecker to cement his place as a Kremlin favourite by cosying up to the leadership at any given opportunity – he often closely and carefully scoured pages of Brezhnev's writing and speeches for guidance on how to create the most acceptable impression. It is known Brezhnev developed different degrees of closeness with his East European comrades, but according to Brezhnev's bodyguard, V.T. Medvedev, Honecker sought hardest to ingratiate himself, while Romania's Ceauşescu behaved as if he were head of the Warsaw Pact. Travelling as if a Roman Emperor making a world tour, the Romanian always showed up for half a day of talks in the Crimea with his own cooks, food and bottled water. Brezhnev's son-in-law, Yuri Churbanov, confirmed that his father-in-law disliked Ceauşescu and 'all of that Romanian socialism', but remained on good terms with Honecker, Husak and Zhivkov.

For the new First Secretary, portraying the image of a modern man was important. During those early days, he abandoned drab off-the-peg suits for garments cut by the finest 'diplomatic tailors' in Alexanderplatz. From then on, he donned bespoke light grey and blue outfits and colourful silk ties. When the 'new' Honecker took to the podium for the eighth Party Congress in May, he was greeted by a standing ovation after declaring the main task of the five-year plan from 1971 to 1975 was to 'further raise the material and cultural standard of living of the people'.[2] As an expression of gratitude for Brezhnev's benevolence, he declared that consultations with the USSR had 'intensified systematically', and would lead to absolute unanimity on questions of ideology and foreign policy. Across the airwaves, listeners heard his promise of far-reaching changes and a better standard of living. 'We only know one goal that permeates the entire policy of our party: to do everything for the good of man, the happiness of the people, for the interests of the working class and of the working population.' Applause greeted his announcement of a massive building programme that, he said, would see the construction, modernisation and conversion of 500,000 apartments over the next five years. In closing, he again expressed gratitude to the Soviet leadership for their support during the change of power in the SED by vowing to deepen their friendship: 'The GDR was for all time a fixed, immovable part of the socialist community of states.'

Seated beneath him in the hall, Günter Schabowski was 'surprised and relieved' at Honecker's performance. 'We longed for a man at the top who could represent the Hallstein-banned GDR more convincingly ... my scepticism gave way to a commitment to his politics.'[3] If there was one criticism, Schabowski remembered, it was that the new First Secretary seemed decidedly uncharismatic in demeanour and speech. 'He had an awkward manner, strained, high pitched voice, and a monotonous style of delivery.'

Leslie Colitt, the influential *Financial Times* correspondent in East Berlin, tartly remarked that there was no illusion of spontaneity, and any genuinely impromptu moments were isolated. 'Honecker was a callow bureaucrat and terrible speaker, just like his predecessor. He is an apparatchik par excellence.'[4] Even an admirer like interpreter Wolfgang Ghantus thought the obvious solution was to have some coaching, but Honecker shrugged off the suggestion. 'He wasn't a good speaker, he just read and spoke monotonously, without a full-stop or comma. It was terribly difficult to interpret. Margot was much better. She was intelligent and flexible.'[5] Honecker particularly liked organised applause at the start of his speeches before he had done or said anything to merit it.

Another irritation, at least for photographers struggling to capture animated poses, was Honecker's economy of gesture, though he did sometimes fidget and lick his lips. In Honecker's defence, journalist Dieter Borkowski thought the new First Secretary lost his 'inaccessible rigidity' when 'out-and-about meeting the public'. He addressed workers in friendly tones offering the the familiar 'Du', made contacts easily, spoke in simple vernacular, and even cracked jokes.[6] He liked to address shop workers with explicit reference to his working-class origins and, in Borkowski's opinion, his strength came from a 'proletarian tone, chummy sociability in conversation', and a less overbearing manner in dealing with the grassroots.[7]

As the head of the SED, Honecker operated by a mixture of impulse and analysis. His popularity soared when he rolled-out pension increases, rent reductions and a generous credit system for young married couples. Amendments to the social security system extended wage payments in the event of illness, guaranteeing benefits for eighteen months. His overweening authority was also directed at increasing support for the upbringing of children of preschool age; Western pop music was allowed to be played again, long hair and jeans were no longer construed as a symbol of 'Western decadence' or an oppositional attitude. Moreover, previously banned books, for example *Uncertain Friend* by Stefan Heym, were allowed to appear and critical stage plays were performed and achieved great success.

Honecker was genuinely convinced there was a 'great deal of free play' for personal initiative by authors and artists. A writer in socialism, he reckoned, was a conscious, faithful and courageous comrade-in-arms of the working class, discovering and helping to shape the new reality.[8] In one of his most sprightly speeches, he told a mass meeting of the Leipzig Region party organisation that:

> no one is gripped by a mere cliché abstracted from life; what is moving and exciting in books and plays is what experiences can be shared and imagined in them, what gives clearer, more profound access to present, past and future. What is gripping is, as writers

themselves say, the 'whole ensemble' of various characters, all striving forward. Given that, it should not be impossible to find the right mixture of conflicts; and in my opinion while the field between bad and good is certainly not a narrow one, the field between good and better is considerably broader and productive as well. In its cultural policy too, our party is taking Lenin's path, the path by which our writers and artists make a contribution valued by many people because of their closeness to the people and their party commitment, and because of their works' closeness to life, sense of reality and certainty about the future. This is a valued contribution which enriches working people's intellectual world, and which they respect and love.[9]

In that halcyon year, in which Honecker was also elected chairman of the powerful National Defence Council, new routines emerged. Unlike Ulbricht – who generally neglected the Politburo as a decision-making forum – he raised its status. Hans Modrow, the First Secretary of the SED in Dresden, remembered a much friendlier atmosphere at the Tuesday sessions. However, while Honecker's style of rule had a capacity of self-limitation, pity those who mistook his mildness for weakness, or his quiet for lack of calculation.

During these early days, he attached importance to expert opinion and, according to Heinz Lippmann – who spoke generously about his ability to grasp details and enforce decisions – Honecker could confidently compete with the 'managers of big Western concerns'.[10]

From the outset, he perfected and systematized routines. Archived agendas show Tuesdays were always busy with the Politburo meeting, followed by a talk with Erich Mielke. Security issues, according to Schabowski, were never discussed in the Politburo: 'From the eight years that I was a member of the Politburo, I don't remember any decision on the work of the State Security. The only thing that required our approval each year was the appointment and promotion of generals.' After meeting Mielke, Honecker discussed the content and sequence of the evening's *Aktuelle Kamera* TV news. Fancying himself an editor, the new First Secretary routinely infuriated newspaper staff by huffing and puffing over headlines, photographs and features. On some occasions, he involved himself in story conferences through to the final editing.[11] In 1976, millions of newspapers were reportedly destroyed an hour after publication when Honecker decided to withdraw his own comments about East Germany spying in West Germany.[12] (All editors-in-chief of GDR newspapers had to appear every Wednesday when they were told how the party wished to see the big events and topics of the week covered).

Abroad, Honecker was perceived as pursuing a 'more open' course. In a country all too often characterised by strife, dullness and regimentation, the foreign press now warmed to Honecker's GDR. 'The people are getting richer and the whole atmosphere is much happier,' wrote British journalist Stuart Gardner. He saw well and colourfully dressed people (orange, he noted, seemed to be 1971's colour among the trend-setters). 'They look well-fed and content' – and they are keen to talk to an 'aggressive-imperialist Englishman without having to keep glancing over their shoulders to see who is listening'. Similar praise came from an American reporter, Henry Krisch, who observed that despite the political and ideological differences, 'the GDR in 1972 reminds me of West Germany in 1957'. Even visitors from other socialist countries were impressed. Soviet cardiologist Vladimir Metelitsa described Berlin shops as offering a 'wondrous abundance for us, citizens of the great Soviet Union'. During his trip, he discovered consumer venues whose existence he could not have imagined before – such as a specialised clothing store for expectant mothers.[13]

Throughout this period, geopolitical realities were gradually drawing the GDR out of its splendid isolation. On 1 September 1971, the ambassadors of the four World War Allies signed the 'Four Power Agreement' in which the special political status of Berlin was codified, and the Soviet Union finally accepted the incorporation of West Berlin into the Federal Republic. 'After the four-power agreement came into force the situation became healthier for West Berlin,' Honecker pronounced. 'Détente became a precise trend in international relations.'[14] Interestingly, the US State Department gave credit to the new General Secretary:

> An important obstacle to an agreement was eliminated in May 1971, undoubtedly with Soviet foreknowledge, when Walter Ulbricht, a long-time foe of East-West accommodation in Germany, was succeeded by Erich Honecker as First Secretary of the Central Committee of East Germany's ruling Socialist Unity (Communist) Party.[15]

From then on, Berlin gradually lost its importance on the world stage of East-West confrontation, and within a year tensions eased further with the signing of the so-called 'Transit Agreement', making the passage of goods and travellers from both sides easier. It also represented the first legal 'recognition' of the German Democratic Republic by the FRG. The two signatories, Bonn State Secretary, the cautious Egon Pahr, and his East German counterpart, Dr Michael Kohl, expressed readiness to enter an 'exchange of views' on the establishment of normal relations. The move came after Honecker – displaying a newly found flexibility – stated that 'peaceful coexistence' and 'good neighbourly relations' were possible after the 'Four Power Agreement'. Indeed, the second strand in improved relations was signed in December 1972 with 'The Basic Treaty' which developed relations further. In Article 6, both sides agreed that 'the sovereignty of each of the two states is limited to its national territory. They respect the independence and autonomy of each of the two states in their internal and external affairs.' And, although the FRG didn't recognise the GDR as a separate foreign state under international law, the treaty heralded greater international recognition for East Germany and proved a boon as exceptionally favourable West German credits and new trade flooded forth, yielding valuable hard currency.

Meanwhile, in West Germany, an early Bundestag election was called after a vote of no confidence against Willy Brandt. After surviving, Brandt embarked on an ambitious reform policy by lowering the voting age to 18, promoting the emancipation and equality of women and strengthening the right to sexual determination. Other important reforms included environmental protection laws, a revamp of health care, family law, and an overhaul of the penal system. Brandt also contrasted the pursuit of economic growth with the new concept of 'quality of life', which sought to combine the humanisation of the workplace with environmental and health protection.

In stark contrast to Brandt's freer society, the climate of open expression that blossomed during the summer of 1971 and developed throughout the fall in East Germany began to chill. By this time, Honecker was deeply immersed in a new pet project. Having departed from the relative moderation of his first year in office, he showed more of his true colours when railing against artists and writers churning out over-critical books, films and plays. He despised 'depressing authors' penning 'private agonies, profanity, self-hatred and grief'. Works imposing 'one's own sorrows on society' were a particular bugbear which, he said, showed 'the basic attitude of such works is in contradiction to the demands socialism makes of art and literature'.

While some artists had spoken of a 'Berlin Cultural Springtime', the new First Secretary set about dismantling any such illusions. He yammered on about a play by the young writer Volker Braun which supposedly described the GDR as 'the most boring land in the world'. At the same time, he took aim at the DEFA film *The Legend of Paul and Paula* which depicted the life of an unskilled bottle washer and her affair with a state official. He also had caustic words for *The New Sorrows of Young W*, a short work of fiction based on a novel by Goethe. From here on, Honecker was quite incapable of grasping criticism and would only offer his hand to authors showing obeisance to the socialist way of life, whose works inevitably became treasures.[16]

In the course of 1972, Erich Honecker's bullying of writers was matched in ferocity by his offensive on the dwindling private sector. During the spring, he pushed through a forced nationalisation of remaining family businesses, which astonishingly, even in the face of government harassment and high taxes, had held their own by producing niche products that were an integral part of everyday life.

As private shops, factories and workshops were seized, owners received feeble compensation, and the chance to continue working as state-paid employees. It was no fair reckoning, especially given compensation payments were taxed and paid into blocked accounts, leaving many former owners bitterly angry.

Worse still, the corrosive effects of nationalisation soon became visible as the '1,000 little things' for everyday needs produced by small enterprises began disappearing from shops, creating a so-called 'grey market'. This entailed procuring, through contacts, consumer goods or materials which the GDR did not produce in sufficient quantities or which – as quite often happened – it produced for export. Items ranged from nails, pins and screws, to porcelain and pens. From here on, the public spent an incredible amount of time hunting for goods that appeared irregularly on the market and always in totally insufficient quantities.

Before too much time passed, Honecker reported to Brezhnev that 11,000 new state-owned enterprises had emerged, keeping more than half-a-million people in gainful employment.[17]

> Dear Comrade Leonid Ilyich,
> We are pleased to discover time and again that, in spite of your many duties as General Secretary of the Central Committee of the CPSU, you have always taken a great interest in the development of Socialism in the German Democratic Republic. It is a pleasure for me to inform you on behalf of the Politburo of the Central Committee of our Party that the measures for the transformation of joint enterprises and craftsmen's production cooperatives into people's own enterprises have recently been carried out with success. Yours fraternally, E. Honecker.[18]

Honecker was also able to furnish Brezhnev with plans of a hastily contrived GDR–Czech plan to produce a new 'peoples' car' at two plants in East Germany and the Skoda works in Prague. Although the project was dropped, production of the infamous two-stroke Trabant – one of the greatest polluters ever to hit the road – was stepped up.

In a population of one million in East Berlin, there were just 100,000 cars, or one to every ten inhabitants in 1970. That figure is unsurprising, given prospective Trabant owners needed saintly patience as waiting lists for cars ranged from three to seven years. Made from plastic sheets in place of steel for the doors, bonnet, boot and roof, Trabants were a virtual death trap. Add to that the fact that the brakes were weak, there was no petrol gauge or cooling system, and the consumption meter was useless. (A popular joke went thus: what do you call four Trabis at a crossroads? A Tupperware party!).

Strangely enough, Wartburg, the other famed GDR car, could be obtained without much trouble, while there was no waiting list for the unreliable Russian Moskvitch because so few people wanted to buy it. Paradoxically, the car famine led to a booming trade in second-hand motors, which – because of instant delivery – were often more expensive than new vehicles.

Jetsetter

In all, twenty-four countries established diplomatic relations with the GDR in the course of 1972. Switzerland was the first Western nation to open contacts, followed by Sweden, Austria, Australia and Belgium. The United Kingdom, France and the Netherlands followed in February 1973 and the United States in December 1974.

Honecker's mood was exultant; as well it might be having achieved a personal triumph such as Ulbricht could never have matched. Thus it happened that, for the first time, as Markus Wolf noted, Honecker was able to 'explore parts of the globe hitherto closed to us', which he discovered with 'childlike enthusiasm'.

In Latin America, a close relationship was quickly forged with Chile, which was experimenting, albeit unsuccessfully, with its own socialist project. Writing from Santiago on 27 January 1972, Chilean President Salvador G. Allendes accepted Honecker's invitation to visit East Berlin, noting it 'would contribute to further strengthening the already existing ties of solidarity between Chile and the GDR'. In fact, Allende had already announced in 1969 that he would recognise the GDR under international law if he won the election (which he did in 1970. In April 1971, he made good on his promise). Since then, credits in the millions were flowing between the two countries, trade relations were close, and a lively cultural exchange programme was inaugurated. At the same time, the GDR became a member of UNESCO and set up a 'Permanent Observer Mission' at the UN headquarters and was admitted to the UN Economic Commission for Europe (ECE). 'Psychologically', it was easy to understand Honecker's drive to involve the GDR in the affairs of the wider world, according to Wolf.[1] Indeed, he worked industriously at strengthening ties with other socialist countries, resulting in passport and visa-free travel with Poland, Czechoslovakia and Romania. He even proceeded in developing relations with the Palestine Liberation Organisation (PLO), despite the murder of eleven Israeli athletes at the Munich Olympics, an atrocity organised by Abu Daoud, a leader of the Black September group, collaborating with the PLO. Although the GDR condemned the Munich murders, the PLO's charismatic leader Yasser Arafat sought to soothe nerves in a letter to Honecker sent eleven days after the massacre. In it, he urged 'understanding of the action in Munich from the viewpoint of the general problem and its historical events with all of their political, national and human dimensions'.[2]

Arafat found a sympathetic ear. In his reply, Honecker expressed enthusiasm for the Arab-Palestinian people and riled at Israeli 'acts of aggression' against Lebanon and Syria. Remarkably, as the shadows cast by Arab terror darkened Europe's security situation, Honecker's links with Libya, Syria and the PLO were strengthened. Arafat received an impressive reception in Berlin the following year when installed at the stucco Schönhausen Palace as a VIP state guest, where he spent afternoons strolling in the stately garden. As it turned out, the Palestinian was impressed by Honecker's grasp of the Middle East conflict and later claimed all PLO accomplishments were 'achieved with the help of the GDR, thanks to its influence in the world'.[3]

Soon, everything was in place for the PLO to open a consular office in East Berlin. On 29 March 1973, two years after their first encounter, Honecker graciously accepted more words of homage from Arafat, who wrote:

> We are proud of your attitude, which is an expression of the indivisibility of the struggle our people are waging against imperialism, Zionism, racial hatred, occupation and colonialism in all its forms. I assure you and all comrades that we will continue the fight until the freedom and independence of our people and all peoples has become a reality.[4]

Interestingly, after the East German state archives were opened in 1990, we learned of agreements between the Stasi and PLO, including a pact allowing East Germany to become a base for training PLO operatives planning operations against Israel. To facilitate training, Erich Mielke opened a 'Department for International Relations' at a highly guarded compound in the countryside at Kallinchen near Potsdam, on the outskirts of Berlin. Over time, a small but growing flow of PLO militants – including Arafat's own praetorian guard – took intensive courses in intelligence and counterintelligence operations. 'These people already know how to fight. They can probably teach us a thing or two about explosives,' Mielke quipped.[5] A former instructor recounted that students were required to undergo single combat training, a course in automatic weapons and learn techniques for interrupting connection systems and radio monitoring. Furthermore, recruits were taught to drive at high speeds, turning manoeuvres, and conditions that would cause hydroplaning.

> Punctually at 8 o'clock in the morning, the training started for the Palestinians. The training in the use of weapons and explosives was comprehensive. Soviet products were used including

Kalashnikovs and Makarovs. Smaller automatic weapons were also used such as the Scorpion.[6]

For obvious reasons, the Palestinians did not enter the GDR in the usual way, instead they arrived via neighbouring countries. Border guards waved them through, leaving no traces of their arrival or departure. Throughout the 1970s and 80s, Arafat kept up a healthy flow of correspondence with Honecker, and in return for help received, assisted GDR intelligence officers in Syria and Yemen to discover the extent of undercover CIA and West German activities in the region, although Markus Wolf later admitted that his department had little material to give the Palestinians in exchange.

By the early 80s, solidarity aid for the PLO reached DDM6 million, most provided in the form of medication, plasma, tents, hygiene equipment and blankets. As a result of the Israeli attack on Beirut in the summer of 1982, over forty Palestinian paramilitaries were flown to East Berlin for medical care.[7]

Over time, the GDR forged South Yemen into a bridge between the African and the Arab world and, according to Wolf, Aden became a 'playground' for a large corps of East German advisers. Encouraged by Moscow, East Berlin provided Yemen with economic, military and intelligence advisors – and from Aden spread their tentacles to Angola, Ethiopia and Mozambique, where the MfS taught locals about counterespionage and the deterrence of smuggling.

By 1981, East German military and civilian advisors were spread out across Congo, Guinea, Mali, Tanzania, Algeria, Iraq, North Yemen, South Yemen and Syria.[8] Especially strong relations were secured with Libya which purchased military technology on a cash basis, while colonel Ghaddafi's personal guard received intensive training at the Kallinchen facility near Berlin. At the same time, advisers from the MfS organised Libya's internal security system and paid particular attention to protecting Ghaddafi.[9]

Throughout the 70s, the Stasi also had murky dealings with members of the infamous Red Army Faction (RAF) terrorist group by providing them with safe passage via Schönefeld Airport to other countries or training camps in the Middle East. From 1970 to 78, it was estimated that the RAF and other organisations committed to violence, were responsible for over thirty bank robberies and the deaths of twenty-eight people, the wounding of eighty others and the taking of over 160 hostages. RAF members received training in the use of firearms and hand grenades, and some former members even moved to East Germany because they wanted to give up the armed struggle and rebuild their lives. Honecker – according to testimony from Minister Peter-Michael Diestel in the late 1980s – offered terrorists a new identity, work, accommodation and privileges of the communist elite, such as diplomatic passports.[10]

Only a few MfS employees, in addition to Stasi boss Erich Mielke, were privy to such dark shenanigans, though Honecker later denied any knowledge (a former Stasi Major involved asserted Honecker 'most certainly' knew).[11]

Interestingly, Bettina Röhl, the daughter of Urlike Meinhof – one of the leaders of the RAF – says that even in the 60s, Erich Honecker arranged secret funding for her parents' avant-garde leftist magazine *Konkret*, published in West Germany. According to Rohl, the contents and character of the magazine were so important, that Honecker injected funds equating to the equivalent of 20,000 euros from GDR coffers to finance each issue.

With the fall of the Berlin Wall in 1989, it was revealed that twenty-four secret meetings between the MfS and RAF took place in the period 1978–84. RAF cadres were able to enter the GDR at practically any time, also after deadly attacks were committed in the West.[12] There are numerous interpretations of why the SED welcomed terrorists with open arms. In 1990, Hans Ludwig Zachert, the president of the FRG Federal Office of Investigation, provided several theories.

> Some people say that there were the 'early experiences' of Mielke and Honecker – that is, sympathy for these desperadoes – which is a sentimental interpretation that is hard to believe. Another says that East Berlin believed it would get information on the plans of international terrorism, and that in the FRG, from the persons concerned. In addition, there is the idea of secretly leading the 'class enemy' up the garden path, and I think the SED leaders are capable of so much wickedness that the aspect that all this can be turned into money might have also played a role. Maybe an idea like that of the ransoming of agents prevailed – that is, extradition against payment.[13]

The Refined Hunter

All his life, Honecker was drawn to the forests. With his power base secure, more time was devoted to pleasurable pursuits such as hunting – a pastime he indulged with pathological devotion.

A former Nazi-hunting lodge built in the Schorfheide – a vast terrain of lake and oak forest northeast of Berlin – became ever more the focus of his attention. Although outwardly modest, the retreat, known as Wildfang, sat on 10,000 square meters of land and included, utility rooms, a hall for storing the game, a stone fireplace, a boathouse, quarters for guards and servants – and a miniature-sized marble bust of Lenin.

The powerful had been hunting these forests since the twelfth century. First the Brandenburg princes, then Prussian kings and German emperors, finally democrats of the Weimar Republic and then the trigger-happy Nazi minister, Herman Göring who christened his estate 'Carinhall', in tribute to his deceased first wife.

When out in the forests, Honecker dressed for the part, complete with knee-high boots and feathered deerstalker. His greatest triumph was to 'bag a stag', a creature known for its majesty and courage. Over time, he amassed a collection of thirty guns, including elegant Berettas and Brownings, but his favourite was a rifle gifted by Klement Gottwald, the leader of the Communist Party of Czechoslovakia. 'But first I had to learn how to use such a rifle,' Honecker recounted. 'It's not like you have a rifle and then you hit something. I had to learn that first. And then over time, it became a real hobby.' Since other SED Politburo members sought relaxation when killing animals (especially Willi Stoph and Günter Mittag), male friendships developed and alliances were forged. Accounts suggest momentous decisions were made on boozy hunting trips and ideas for policy often began as small talk around a campfire. (Ulbricht preferred to go skiing. It was only when he noticed that Honecker and Brezhnev kept disappearing to hunt that the elderly head of state received training on the weapon but was a miserable shot.)

'When hunting, Honecker was a different person. Here he could laugh – even if he was due to sign a death warrant,' Dieter Wlost, one of his former woodland rangers, once said.[1]

For deep forest expeditions, Honecker commissioned several souped-up four-wheel-drive vehicles, including a Land Rover converted by the West-Berlin company, Karosserie Friedrich Rometsch. Modifications – plush interior, collapsible roof, gun racks and extension for carrying animal carcasses – cost the East German taxpayer DM150,000, or four times the original value of the car. The First Secretary approved every detail and personally designed a variable gun-support for the rear door.

Like a country squire, he polished his hound skills and on one occasion – in a saga that had some elements of a French farce – he instructed his underlings to scour the country to find a suitable hunting dog. Funnily enough, the search was picked up by agents from the FRG: 'A 3½-year-old short-haired pointer had been found in Erfurt, but the owner wanted DDM3,800 but only received DDM2,500, along with a 7x65, caliber 12, block gun and the return of his confiscated gun licence.'[2]

Every year, Honecker bagged around 100 deer, plus hundreds of hares. On one September evening in the 1980s, according to hunting logs, he shot five deer in a row. In order to satisfy his passion, neither expense nor effort was spared in fencing the entire Schorfheide to contain the game, while dozens of forest wardens maintained the animal population. 'Honecker's addiction to hunting even led him to demand that the game population be improved through imports,' recalls forester Horst Mildner. 'And so, animals were introduced, such as red deer from Hungary.' Bodyguard Bernd Brückner remembered 'trophies' were measured, photographed and certified in the presence of the General Secretary. 'That was a ritual,' he recounted, 'you could feel a real joy, even exuberance from Honecker.' What was particularly remarkable was that Honecker 'ate nothing, absolutely nothing from the forest. He did not eat mushrooms and he certainly did not eat game.'

In later years, US Ambassador to East Berlin, Richard C. Barkley, recalled one of the 'more interesting things' was the so-called diplomatic hunt where the entire politburo and members of the local establishment went out to shoot rabbits in the outback. 'It was a tradition, an old German, almost pagan, tradition in that you blow horns for the hunt, and you sing the songs of the hunt,' Barkley explained. He remembered one such trip near Erfurt:

> They took us in, and they gave us boots and everything. Everything was courtesy of the East German army. The East Germans actually, had developed one of the best shotgun industries in the world at that time. So, we were all given shotguns etc, and we had a 'minder', a hunter who had dogs and all. It started out the previous night with a big banquet. It was a social event; it was not a political event. But obviously at the same time, you could

Honecker's childhood home in Wiebelskirchen. The region was once part of the French Lorraine district which came to France in the eighteenth century then back to Germany since its annexation after Waterloo. (Wikipedia, EPei)

Honecker found modest lodgings on Brusseler Strasse and, still relatively lean and fit, was able to make covert handovers of clandestine material and even smuggle a small printing press into the heart of the Nazi capital. (Nathan Morley)

Communists take to the streets of Berlin in 1930 calling for Socialism like that in the Soviet Union to be formed.

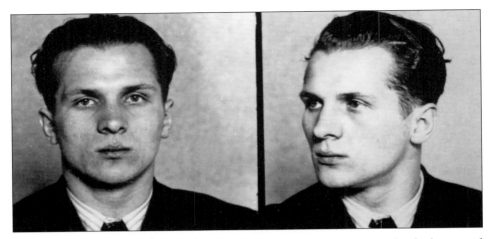

Honecker's police mugshot. Nothing in his experience or imagination had prepared him for the merciless, degrading misery of prison.

Walter Ulbricht leader of German communists in exile who had been preparing in the Soviet Union for the establishment of a (communist) post-war Germany.

Honecker first met Ulbricht in this building at Prinzenallee 80 (now Einbecker Strasse 41). The encounter would change his life. (Nathan Morley)

Honecker cast his net far and wide to enlist recruits to the FDJ adopting the posture of a young go-getter, full of gung-ho spirit and vitality.

Honecker frequently mixed with Wilhelm Pieck, widely regarded to be the most charismatic figure in the KPD movement. (SED archives)

Charlotte was moved to the St. Joseph's hospital where she died on 6 June 1947, physicians said her passing was due to 'degeneration of the brain tissue'. (Nathan Morley)

Above left: Margot Feist (foreground) found a powerful supporter in Wilhelm Pieck when she began an affair with Erich Honecker.

Above right: Erich Honecker in 1950.

The SED Politburo elected in 1950. Centre front row: Walter Ulbricht, Wilhelm Pieck and Otto Grotewohl. Honecker is in the back row, far right.

The FDJ Boss. Honecker wrote the foreword to countless FDJ pamphlets. This one from 1949.

On June 16, 1953, workers in East Berlin rose in protest against government demands to increase productivity. Violence unfolded with such extraordinary speed that the Russians declared martial law and sent in T-34 tanks, the same machines that had ploughed through Berlin in 1945.

As the Central Committee secretary for security issues, he held responsibility for the police, the state security service and the 'National People's Army'.

The entire SED apparatus – including Honecker – worked from the Central Committee building on Werderscher Markt in the former Reichsbank for which Adolf Hitler had personally laid the foundation stone in 1934. This concrete behemoth became the supreme centre of power in the German Democratic Republic. (Nathan Morley)

Pankow. Honecker's lived in spacious home on Majakowskiring in Pankow, a leafy cul-de-sac with century-old trees, a pristine park, and gilded-age mansions. (Nathan Morley)

At Wandlitz, the Honecker house had just seven rooms – 180 square meters of living space – and a small private garden and patio. (Nathan Morley)

By summer 1961, Honecker was installed at an operations centre on the second floor of the Police Presidium on Keibelstrasse near Alexanderplatz. (Nathan Morley)

To deter West Germans from throwing stones at border guards, Honecker approved the deployment of several water cannon trucks, the drenching's caused many protestors to avoid engaging in demonstrations at the Wall.

Above left: JFK takes a peek over the Berlin Wall. (U.S. federal government)

Above right: October 7, 1961. Four-year-old Michael Finder of East Germany is tossed by his father into a net held by residents across the border in West Berlin. The father, Willy Finder, then prepares to make the jump himself. From the booklet "A City Torn Apart: Building of the Berlin Wall." (CIA)

Above: Walter Ulbricht and his young protégé in the mid-1960s.

Left: Erich Mielke: A tiny man with a pudgy babyish face and a constant smile that gave him the look of a mischievous, overweight kid.

Above: To satisfy the perennial quest of appearing engaged in seeking better relations with Bonn, Willi Stoph met Willy Brandt to try and 'establish normal relations by treaty' and find common interests between their states.

Right: The cover of the West German BZ newspaper notes the departure of Ulbricht in 1971.

Honecker meeting the public. His strength came from a 'proletarian tone, chummy sociability in conversation' and a less overbearing manner in dealing with the grassroots.

Honecker with Queen Beatrix of the Netherlands, June 1987. (Dutch National Archive)

Right: Applause greeted Honecker's 1971 announcement of a massive building programme that, he said, would see the construction, modernization, and conversion of five hundred thousand apartments over the next five years.

Below: Federal chancellor Helmut Schmidt and Honecker shaking hands on 1st August 1975 in Helsinki.

Above left: Cheekily described as 'horse face' by detractors, Honecker considered Ego Krenz (pictured) of pleasing appearance and manner – he even had the makings of a successor.

Above right: Set in the midst of warming relations, authorities in Bonn discovered that Gunter Guillaume – one of Willy Brandt's intimate advisers and personal assistant – was, in fact, spying for the East German Stasi. The scandal caused the resignation of Brandt and soured Bonn-East Berlin relations.

Left: US Ambassador to East Berlin, John Sherman Cooper, kept Washington posted on developments in the GDR.

Honecker's Official Portrait. A photo which defined a generation. Honecker's official portrait which hung in schools, government offices, and embassies from 1971 onwards. (Nathan Morley)

All his life, Honecker was drawn to the forests. With his power base secure, more time was devoted to pleasurable pursuits such as hunting – a pastime he indulged with pathological devotion. Here pictured with Brezhnev.

Although never friends, Honecker and Ceausescu became increasingly close in the late 1980s.

Pyotr Abrassimov, the Soviet Ambassador, Erich Honecker and Konstantin Chernenko.

Honecker with Erich Mielke, head of the East German Ministry for State Security.

Honecker's first one-on-one meeting with Gorbachev in May 1985 at the Kremlin was a stiff and distant affair.

Right: Margot Honecker continued to work as Minister of Education until late 1989.

Below: 'Don't feel any pain or weakness,' Honecker noted in his diary before entering room 700 of Moabit criminal court (pictured). After being called over to the dock, he described his trial as a travesty of justice. (Nathan Morley)

Above: After 57 years, Honecker returned to Moabit prison. (Nathan Morley)

Left: Finally, the end for Erich Paul Honecker came at 7 am on 29 May 1994 at 'House G' on Carlos Silva Vildósola in the presence of his wife and daughter.

Leonid Brezhnev and Erich Honecker in a socialist fraternal kiss, as painted on the Berlin Wall. The work is titled: "My God, Help Me to Survive This Deadly Love". (Nathan Morley)

see that there was a political pecking order. Not only in terms of who sat at what tables but where people were. The next day we went out and shot rabbits. Actually, the organisation was quite remarkable. The East Germans were known to be able to do that kind of local organisation. For example, when we got off the train there was a huge crowd cheering the diplomats. It was interesting to watch because diplomats are seldom cheered. There were these rather silly grins on most of these people's faces as we walked along the tarmac and we were cheered heartily. Anyway, the next day, the politburo came out first led by Honecker. He could see a number of them were not enthusiastic hunters, but Honecker was. They were all dressed of course in their hunting gear. I noticed that those with the finest headgear were the highest-ranked in the politburo. Honecker had this sort of sable Russian hat. It turned out they went over to one section, and then sent the diplomats out into the fields as sort of beaters. We would march across the fields and rabbits would take off. They had been breeding rabbits there for a long time, so there were lots of them. They would run over the hill and who was there, over the hill shooting them as they came down the line but Erich Honecker and his troops. We were slogging through the mud. I remember what a really gory day it was. It was unforgettable in the sense that you were thrown together in a sort of ancient ritual and watched these so-called modern people engage in this ritual with great joy. I understand that Honecker of course, this will not surprise you, killed more rabbits than anybody else. I am sure the numbers went down depending on the rank of the politburo member. But seldom did you get them all together to watch any kind of interaction along that line. It was clear that Honecker was the boss.[3]

Auf Wiedersehen Walter

Walter Ulbricht's anger had descended into senility by the time the curtain fell on his life on 1 August 1973, just a month before the GDR was admitted to the UN. Possibly out of guilt – and certainly on the orders of Brezhnev – his passing roused Honecker to one of his most notable displays of magnanimity. He instructed *Neues Deutschland* – still the most deafening SED organ – to run a black-bordered front page with an obituary documenting Ulbricht's contribution to the GDR's founding, painting him as an ornament of an 'old world', who deserved respect for his past services. Predictably, the obituary notice carefully avoided mentioning his policies in the 50s and 60s.

Over in the West, Ulbricht's demise was greeted with a bored yawn. 'Personally, he was cruel, unappealing, and uninspiring,' *The Times* asserted when describing an efficient functionary who wielded immense power in an anonymous manner. His goatee beard and high-pitched voice, the paper added, 'inspired ridicule', and even in his personal relations his 'contempt for all human considerations' was evident'.[1] America ignored his passing. In fact, a State Department cable, instructed ambassadors that, 'since the United States does not have diplomatic relations with the GDR, you should not sign the Ulbricht book'.[2] In a lavish funeral, the former First Secretary was buried alongside the urns of Otto Grotewohl, Wilhelm Pieck and Rosa Luxemburg at the Friedrichsfelde Central Cemetery, (and a stone's throw from Honecker's fiery ex-wife, Edith Baumann, who had been interred nearby after succumbing to cancer a few months earlier). Remarkably, though Brezhnev didn't attend, the Soviet Union's main national television network ran a direct relay from the funeral. In a final gesture of 'goodwill', Honecker permitted the Institute of Marxism-Leninism at the SED Central Committee to publish 'selected works of Comrade Walter Ulbricht'.

Throughout this period, Erich Honecker's gaze had been fixed on the Middle East where tensions between Israel and her neighbours had reached boiling point. The pot finally exploded on 6 October 1973, when, hoping to snatch back territory lost to Israel in 1967, Egyptian and Syrian troops launched a coordinated attack against the Jewish state on Yom Kippur, the holiest day on the Jewish calendar.

Writing on 10 October to Syria's President Hafez al-Assad, Honecker stated that 'for the righteous fight, which your people fight against the aggressor and for the liberation of the territory occupied by Israel, the GDR will always provide active support'.[3] Despite the First Secretary's limitless and affectionate devotion to Assad's cause, the Syrian campaign was a disaster from the outset. While Egyptian troops swept into the Sinai Peninsula, Assad's forces struggled to drive the occupying Israelis out of the Golan Heights, leading to a humiliating ceasefire at the end of October.

Showing solidarity with the deflated Syrian leader, Honecker arranged a vast shipment of military equipment be delivered to Damascus from the GDR. 'The people of the German Democratic Republic, together with the people of the Soviet Union and other countries of the socialist community, support, as always, those countries and peoples who fight for freedom and independence,' Honecker wrote in a personal letter to Assad on 3 November 1973.[4] He then listed a staggering array of military hardware shipped from East Berlin to Damascus, including a squadron of twelve interceptor MiG-21 fighters, sixty-two 'T-54 AM' Soviet battle tanks with ammunition, 720,000 rounds of machine-gun bullets, 3,600 hand grenades, 3,300 bazookas and 30,000 'TM-46' anti-tank mines. 'The government of the German Democratic Republic,' Honecker concluded, 'are convinced that this support will contribute to the success of the righteous fight of the people of the Syrian Arab Republic, fighting for freedom and independence, and assure you, Excellency, of their ongoing solidarity.'[5] Though Assad's cup ranneth over with deadly foreign hardware, it soon became clear his chronically weak army faced an unmitigated disaster. From the beginning, Israeli troops shelled targets in Damascus, including the Defence Ministry, the headquarters of the General Staff, the Air Force command centre and oil refineries and power stations in central Syria. To make matters worse, when the Egyptian-Israeli ceasefire exposed Syria to defeat, Israel snatched even more territory in the Golan Heights.

Despite his misfortune, Assad expressed gratitude for the GDR's support and awarded a contract for the construction of a giant cement factory near Tartus on the Mediterranean coast to an East German concern. Although the factory thrived, it was a poorly evaluated project and created an environmental disaster polluting a long stretch of pristine coastline and destroying thousands of olive trees.

That autumn, the tension and violence in the Middle East was matched decibel for decibel by events in South America, where a military coup d'état deposed the Popular Unity government of President Salvador Allende. Led by General Augusto Pinochet, the rebellion not only seized power but ended in the dramatic suicide of Allende, who shot himself with an AK-47 assault rifle. 'The working people of the German Democratic Republic learned of the outrageous fact that a military coup against the constitutional government of Unidad Popular and the elected President Salvador Allende has been unleashed in Chile,' *Neues Deutschland* raged. The brutal crackdown by the military, backed by the CIA, and Allende's suicide caused a worldwide sensation. During a session of the central committee, Honecker paid tribute to the life and work of Allende saying he was faithful to his people and their struggle for freedom and independence, for democracy and social justice. 'Our party will always, hold in high esteem his memory and the memory of the murdered communists and socialists of Chile, of all those who have given their lives to the cause of the people.'[6]

Offering further proof of their anger, thousands of East Germans took part in rallies in Dresden, Rostock, Leipzig and Halle in what *Neue Zeit* described as a 'genuine declaration of solidarity between the GDR and its brother Chilean people'. Henceforward, at Honecker's urging, the Politburo granted asylum to Chilean communists fearing for their lives, a move which led to about 2,000 refugees relocating to East Germany.

Remarkably, their integration was a largely un-bureaucratic affair. Chileans were aided by the Free German Trade Union Confederation (FDGB) and the 'Solidarity Committee of the GDR' which provided funds to finance accommodation and clothing. Each emigrant family received a transitional allowance of DDM2,500 to bridge the time until a job was found. (Stasi files reveal Chilean emigrants were primarily members of the intelligentsia, students, employees, educators, officials and artists.)

Amid the carnage in Santiago, Honecker managed to have Leo Yanez Betancourt plucked from the notorious Dawson's Island prison in Chile. Betancourt, a young communist activist, had been dating Sonja Honecker while studying in Dresden in 1972 but had returned home to help in the forthcoming elections. Having been briefly detained by Pinochet's henchmen, Honecker – at the insistence of his sobbing daughter – successfully secured his release.

By way of reply, the GDR agreed to continue business ties with the new Pinochet regime, and eight employees of East Germany's Ministry of Foreign Trade remained in Santiago. As for Betancourt, he was spirited to East Berlin to resume his romance with Sonja. The following year, the couple presented Erich and Margot with a grandson, Roberto.

From then on, the bond between father and daughter grew closer. The Yanez family was installed on the thirteenth floor of a tower block at Leipziger Straße 55 in the centre of Berlin, and Sonja's career blossomed modestly[7] as a secretary for agitation and propaganda in the FDJ Berlin district leadership.[8] Thoroughly spoiled, Honecker gave his daughter everything he never had. According to Heinz Lippmann's anecdotal evidence, Sonja had enjoyed a privileged childhood, pampered and sheltered from everyday hardships. For example, during her studies at an institute in Halle specialising in preparing students for study abroad, her father sent an official chauffeured car to whisk her home every weekend, although her fellow students were only allowed leave once a month.[9]

Sonja's marriage though was a difficult union; Leo was calm and even-tempered, while she could be restless and nervous – she never adapted to the cultural differences between Germany and Chile.[10]

As for Erica, Honecker's first daughter with Edith Baumann, she married SED functionary Karl Wildau, a future GDR ambassador to the Netherlands.

Friends Afar

The First Secretary made his first sally out of the East European socialist stronghold when, in answer to an invitation from Cuba's Fidel Castro, he led a high-level delegation to Havana in February 1974.

In the excitement of the moment, Honecker displayed a touch of the theatricals by sending a telegram to British Prime Minister Edward Heath while flying over the United Kingdom. He wrote:

> Your Excellency, allow me to convey to you and to the British people my best wishes as I fly over the territory of your country on my way to the Republic of Cuba. I should like to combine this wish with the hope that the relations between the German Democratic Republic and the United Kingdom may develop for the benefit and happiness of our peoples and in the interests of peace, security and cooperation in Europe.[1]

Eight hours later, the theatricals continued when, squinting against the bright sunlight, the German delegation arrived to a celebrity welcome in Havana, where cheers of 'Long Live the First Secretary' could be heard as they disembarked from a gleaming Interflug jetliner. Across the Cuban capital, workers had been given time off in order to line the streets and wave GDR flags. 'Now,' Honecker recounted, 'Castro, together with his vivacious people, welcomed our delegation on the island of freedom.'[2] Dressed not in a suit but in a white jacket and a Canotier, Honecker played the part of the exultant guest, smiling deeply before the public and shaking hands. Over the coming days, he held stage centre, during one effusive solidarity demonstration after another. Front page coverage was awarded to his visit to Santiago de Cuba where the uprisings against foreign rule had erupted in the 50s. 'This is where it began,' *Neues Deutschland* noted.[3] 'The armed struggle against Batista's dictatorship with the attack on Santiago's Moncada barracks by the daring revolutionaries led by Fidel Castro.' It was observed by an excitable commentator on Cuban television that a loud chorus could be heard: 'Long live the friendship between Cuba and the GDR', and 'Long live Comrade Erich Honecker.'

Amid the cheers, Honecker avoided outright condemnation of the United States by demanding only that Guantanamo be returned to Cuba; while, for his part, Castro sidestepped any frontal criticism of China. A joint declaration, however, took an indirect swipe at Beijing by condemning 'anti-Communism, anti-Sovietism, revisionism and chauvinism,' wherever it occurred.[4] Behind closed doors, Honecker held a string of frank and heated discussions with Castro. The Cuban successfully pushed the General Secretary to pay higher prices for Cuban sugar and gave an overview of the recent coup in Chile. 'There were in our embassy,' he disclosed, 'enough weapons for a battalion, automatic weapons, armour-piercing weapons, and there was also a force of special troops.'[5] However, despite his offer of practical help, Castro revealed the late President Allende did not want the Cubans to get engaged in fighting.

Once back from Cuba, Honecker made immediate plans to publish a new German volume of Fidel Castro's speeches in addition to commissioning a film about the 'friendship visit'.[6] Undoubtedly, the success of the trip added to the sense that a renewal was underway, which accrued directly to Honecker's benefit. Soon after, special praise came when the GDR and FRG happily agreed to establish missions, which although did not have the diplomatic status of embassies, performed similar functions. During May, West Germany's 'Permanent Representation' office opened at Hannoversche Straße 28–30 in East Berlin under the direction of Günter Gaus, while the GDR mission in Bonn was accredited to Willy Brandt's office, not to the Foreign Ministry. However, at virtually the same moment the new delegations were unpacking, a spy saga in the West German government wiped the good news from the headlines.

Set in the midst of warming relations, authorities in Bonn discovered that Günter Guillaume – one of Willy Brandt's intimate advisers and personal assistant – was, in fact, spying for the East German Stasi.

The bizarre sequence of events, which ended with Guillaume's widely publicised arrest, had begun decades earlier. In a case of straightforward espionage, Guillaume had been dispatched by the Stasi to the FRG in 1956 as a sleeper agent. The pace was sedate. He joined the SPD in Frankfurt and began working his way up the party ranks and by 1969 when Brandt was appointed Chancellor; the young spy – reserved, cool and a good organiser – was awarded responsibility for government liaison with the labour unions.

While Guillaume betrayed every secret that passed across his desk, he was unable to provide any really sensitive information. Nevertheless, the scandal was enough for Brandt to bite the bullet for negligence. At 23.34 on 6 May, radio and television stations across West Germany interrupted programmes to make a brief announcement. 'According to our Bonn studio, Federal Chancellor Willy Brandt has tendered his resignation. Our Bonn correspondent adds that

Brandt accepted full responsibility for acts of negligence in connection with the Guillaume spy case. That is the end of the news'.[7]

The resignation topped-off a torrid period that had seen Brandt's chancellorship face currency turbulence, rocketing inflation, record unemployment, industrial strikes and a slump in the economy. Detractors also charged his 'Ostpolitik', too, had fallen short of expectations, and even party colleagues expressed sharp criticism of his leadership style.

Though tangled and dangerous, the Guillaume incident also embarrassed the GDR, prompting Honecker to wash his hands of any blame. In 1991, he attributed the stupidity of Markus Wolf for the debacle, saying he 'did not have the courage to inform me in time that a traitor to Brandt, Guillaume, was sitting close to him'. How much of the affair Honecker knew about is impossible to tell, but it is known he lost patience with the Stasi, and avoided reading MfS intelligence reports, which, he thought, contained the same 'gloom-and-doom information' as *Bild*, the West German tabloid known for its pungent celebrity coverage.[8]

At a routine session of the Politburo after Brandt's resignation, harsh criticism was voiced against the Ministry of State Security. According to *Der Spiegel*, 'people in the know in East Berlin' claimed that Erich Mielke was 'called on the carpet',[9] and Horst Sindermann, the pallid premier, complained he would face a barrage of 'unpleasant words' on an upcoming trip to Moscow. In the final reckoning, the Guillaume affair entailed no personnel consequences for the MfS but Soviet thoughts about the debacle took on a less trusting edge. The KGB was never quite sure whether the SED leadership used Guillaume as a suitable lever for toppling Brandt, who remained extremely popular in the GDR. After all, according to *Der Spiegel*, SED public opinion polls showed nearly 80 per cent of East Germans regarded Brandt as having genuine peace intentions and sought good relations. With Brandt in the wilderness, Brezhnev was livid at the loss of a reliable détente partner and forced Honecker to stop intelligence agents from causing trouble for politicians that had rendered 'excellent service for inter-German relationships.'

Despite a bitter aftertaste, Bonn's investigations into Guillaume's activities revealed no startling revelations. For his part, Markus Wolf admitted the affair was one of the biggest mistakes of the East German secret service. 'Our role in bringing down Brandt was equivalent to kicking a football into our own net,' he lamented. 'We never desired, planned nor welcomed his political demise.' Completely unrepentant, Guillaume was sentenced to thirteen years in prison and released in 1981 as part of an exchange of agents in the GDR. With Honecker's wholehearted backing, he was promoted, awarded medals and an honorary doctorate.

Meanwhile, Willy Brandt was succeeded by 55-year-old Helmut Schmidt, the former Finance Minister – who, despite his pose of tired-weariness – was a man of immense charisma. Hoping to open relations quickly, Honecker declared: 'We are ready now, as before, to continue our constructive policy of peace and lessening of tension that in the future will have a positive influence on the relations between the German Democratic Republic and the Federal Republic of Germany.'[10] Evidence suggests, however, that Schmidt was in no hurry to engage with the GDR.

Regardless of having been 'called on the carpet', Erich Mielke continued to plough resources into infiltrating foreign organisations 'bent upon attacking the GDR from within'. He talked about the need to discover enemy plans in order to blunt any such attacks by using spies, subversion and industrial espionage. Writing in 'Einheit', a journal dedicated to socialist theory, Mielke claimed such activity was necessary to preserve the unity of the socialist society.[11] The article caught the eye of the US Ambassador to East Berlin, John Sherman Cooper, who sent a revealing cable to Washington:

> The state security organisation remains an enigma wrapped up in a mystery in that the members of the Organisation are not listed publicly nor is any budget for the ministry published along with the government's budget. Members of the state security organisation carry military rank as members of the Police forces inside East Germany. The organisation is controlled and run by the central committee of the SED and, in the last analysis, by the twenty-three members of the Politburo.[12]

In stark contrast to the hugely funded MfS, West German intelligence efforts to monitor the East German leadership were clumsy, given the difficult operating environment. In fact, they did not have a single source within the MfS, the SED Politburo, the government, or anywhere else. Over a period of four decades, not one of the at least 15,000 spies from the BND, Military Counterintelligence Service, or the Federal Office for the Protection of the Constitution, ventured into the GDR, which was only snooped on from a distance and not up close, meaning intelligence was sketchy at best. Instead, agents used various sources, including *Neues Deutschland*, to gather morsels about Honecker's schedule. Based on the gaps, conclusions were drawn about his vacation, sick days or private engagements. The SED Party bulletin also served as a source of information about his political activities and travels.

Western newspaper reports and diplomats provided the BND with additional scraps of information, while agents amassed a wealth of anecdotal evidence. Although BND reports were cobbled together chronologically without evaluation or analysis, they create a diverse picture of Honecker's political activities and colourful trivialities. The information was divided into different categories: spa stays, vacations, official trips, award ceremonies, personal and political activities. As mentioned earlier, the so-called 'Honi' file also detailed his hunting habits, which proved a constant source of fascination for counterintelligence officials. Although brief, one cable even laid out details of Honecker buying ski boots for his grandson and confusing two pairs, resulting in him gift-wrapping two left-footed boots in a Christmas box. Interestingly, the BND devoted considerable attention to Sonja and her son, Roberto. One note records that Roberto looked like the 'younger version of Margot' (in brackets: 'Actually very pretty'). There was also intelligence about Honecker's taste, including a note detailing how during a vacation in Baabe, the First Secretary took a fancy to a green velvet armchair in a room utilised for his office. According to the report, he found it so beautiful that he wanted it for his Berlin office. His request was granted. Curiously though, the BND files omit to mention that 1974 ended with the death of Honecker's sister Frieda, leaving just Gertrud, who still lived in the parental home in the Saarland, and Erich as the only surviving members of the original family.

For Erich Honecker, one of the great successes of 1974 was pushing through a constitutional amendment that finally abandoned the concept of German nationhood and redefined the German Democratic Republic as a 'socialist state of workers and farmers'. The changes took effect on 7 October, the twenty-fifth anniversary of the foundation of the GDR.

Honecker explained the reasons for the changes by saying that the Constitution must consider the 'new qualitative progress in shaping the developed socialist society in the communist future'. Turning to the new Constitution preamble, he asserted that it was doing justice to the historic change. 'Today the GDR is an internationally recognised sovereign state which had linked its present and future indissolubly and forever with the country of Lenin and the other states of the socialist community.'

The new preamble stated:

> In pursuance of the revolutionary traditions of the German working class and based on the liberation from fascism, the people of the GDR have, in agreement with the process of the historical development of our epoch, realised its right to socioeconomic, state and national self-determination and is shaping the developed socialist society.

The preamble had previously said that the people of the GDR, 'led by the responsibility to show the entire German nation the road to a future of peace and socialism', had given itself this socialist Constitution. The newly formulated passage that the GDR is a socialist state of workers and peasants, previously read that the GDR was a 'socialist state of the German nation'.

In clause 8, a passage was deleted that spoke of the 'overcoming of the division of Germany forced by imperialism upon the German nation', as well as of the 'bringing together step by step of the two German states until their unification on the basis of democracy and socialism'. In the new sections, it was underlined that the GDR was 'an inseparable component of the socialist community of states'. Furthermore, the status of the State Council, the Council of Ministers and the Presidium of the People's Chamber was defined and partially strengthened through the amendment of the Constitution.

The Statesman

Though Honecker's enthusiasm for international politics overtook his interest in domestic issues, he still travelled extensively throughout the GDR. April found him at a series of anniversaries commemorating the end of the Second World War, including an appearance at Brandenburg-Görden prison, an occasion which marked the re-emergence Pyotr Abrasimov – the Russian envoy who had helped reinstate him in 1970 – as the new Soviet Ambassador.

In his address, Abrasimov praised the courage and strong convictions of KPD members who 'served as an example to those inside Germany in the battle against Nazism'. He praised the First Secretary and others like him who had been jailed for their 'heroic' opposition to fascism. In spite of such fervent words, however, a perceptible frost was settling over his relations with Honecker.

For the next eight years, Abrasimov would reside inside the elegant 334-room Soviet Embassy on Unter den Linden. His scowling face topped by a tinted mane became a fixture at high-level functions. Associates remembered he could be distant, short-tempered, icy and occasionally charming. And although there is no reliable evidence of him interfering in the day-to-day administration of East Germany, he was viewed – especially by foreign observers – as a 'little governor'. The West German magazine *Der Spiegel* sarcastically reported talks between Abrasimov and SED leadership were always referred to by *Neues Deutschland* as 'friendly and cordial'. However, over time, they became 'cordial and sincere,' which, according to diplomatic parlance, spelt differences of opinion.[1]

However, Abrasimov's diplomatic experience was genuinely useful in the spring of 1975 when he helped Honecker prepare to take his first step onto the world stage at the signing of the historic Helsinki Accords. Officially known as 'The Conference on Security and Cooperation in Europe', the process had begun some years earlier at the behest of Brezhnev with the aim of securing the territorial integrity of his satellite states. The Helsinki Accords, according to its own description, were motivated by the 'political will, in the interest of peoples, to improve and intensify their relations and to contribute in Europe to peace, security, justice and cooperation as well as to rapprochement among themselves and with the other States of the world'.

Ready to play his part, Honecker spent April and May putting out cautious feelers to fix a 'private encounter' with US President Gerald Ford who would be present in the Finnish capital. 'Honecker speaks highly of you, and Secretary Kissinger,' US ambassador to Berlin, John Sherman Cooper told Ford before the Finland gathering. 'They never mention Vietnam or economics, except trade. He said you were the biggest moral influence since Eisenhower. We should make the greatest efforts we can with them.'[2] Despite flattering overtures, the unofficial response was not encouraging. In a short telex to Cooper, Secretary of State Henry Kissinger sent the President's regrets but noted:

> in giving our reply, you might also note that assuming the seating arrangement is based on the French alphabetical order, the President and the First Secretary will be sitting next to each other during the conference sessions, and they will undoubtedly have the opportunity to exchange informal greetings.[3]

Besides Honecker and his party, a brigade of GDR journalists accompanied the delegation to Helsinki where the Finns had prepared a stunning ceremony, complete with appropriate pomp and ceremony. The Treaty, unveiled at Finlandia House, a vast white marble building in central Helsinki, was followed closely in East Germany. In the first speech, British Prime Minister Harold Wilson described the meeting as a turning point in history:

> Détente means little if it is not reflected in the daily lives of our people. There is no reason why, in 1975, Europeans should not be allowed to marry whom they want, hear and read what they want, travel abroad when and where they want, meet whom they want.

The signatories guaranteed the inviolability of frontiers; territorial integrity of states; peaceful settlement of disputes; non-intervention in internal affairs, avoidance of threat or use of force; sovereign equality; equal rights and self-determination of peoples; and respect for human rights and fundamental freedoms, including the freedom of thought, conscience, religion, or belief. For the first time since the end of the Second World War, the Western states accepted the borders on the continent.

It was hardly surprising that citizens in the GDR took a special interest in clauses on human rights and personal freedoms, given the Accords specifically stated:

> Within this framework the participating States will recognise and respect the freedom of the individual to profess and practice, alone

or in community with others, religion or belief acting in accordance with the dictates of his own conscience. The participating States on whose territory national minorities exist will respect the right of persons belonging to such minorities to equality before the law, will afford them the full opportunity for the actual enjoyment of human rights and fundamental freedoms and will, in this manner, protect their legitimate interests in this sphere ... By virtue of the principle of equal rights and self-determination of peoples, all peoples always have the right, in full freedom, to determine, when and as they wish, their internal and external political status, without external interference, and to pursue as they wish their political, economic, social, and cultural development.

Throughout the gathering, it was clear that Honecker had the wind at his back. Wearing a natty grey suit and striped tie, he told delegates that the occasion confirmed the turn from 'Cold War' to détente in Europe: 'Peace and security are deeply in harmony with the character of the socialist order of society.' However, he noted 'with concern', that the gathering was not the final point but a prelude to new initiatives. 'It is our objective to banish aggression and war forever from the lives of Europe's peoples and States. Military detente was falling short of progressing political détente.'[4]

Honecker rejoiced when the French alphabetical seating arrangements provided his desired encounter with Gerald Ford during a dinner given by Finland's president, Urho Kekkonen. In his golden recollections, Honecker proudly recounted congratulating Ford on the results of the Apollo-Soyuz mission, 'He replied with congratulations on the successes of the GDR swimmers at the world championships.' However, despite the pleasantries, archives reveal that both Ford and Chancellor Schmidt privately complained about the 'unfortunate seating arrangements'.

> *President Ford remarked that he spent virtually all his time talking to Erich Honecker and Archbishop Makarios. Chancellor Schmidt also complained about his delegation being seated next to the GDR which left him no choice but to converse with Mr Honecker. Secretary Kissinger commented that the long talk Makarios had with the President was ironic inasmuch as the United States Government had not previously agreed to a meeting between the two.*[5]

Although still reeling from the Guillaume affair, Honecker held a session of official talks with Schmidt which took on a 'business-like and relaxed atmosphere'.⁶ Turning to grand strategy, the Chancellor noted that he, like his predecessor, was interested in continuing the policy which had been introduced in 1969. For his part, Honecker expressed interest in expanding trade, though Schmidt said it was 'up to the GDR to work harder to increase its sales to the FRG market'. Pushing the subject, Honecker asked that West Germany do everything possible to expand its purchases from the GDR, which had decreased, to which Schmidt – bolder than his predecessor – sarcastically replied that 'the federal government was not able to act as a buyer'.⁷

Honecker returned to Berlin with an increased passion for foreign affairs and with first-hand knowledge of leading statesmen. It gave him satisfaction to chat with politicians such as French President Giscard d'Estaing, Finnish President Urho Kekkonen and the leaders of Italy, Norway, Denmark, Belgium and Sweden in the presence of the thirty-five signatories to the Final Act. His memoirs betrayed pride at the recognition gained at his first appearance on the world stage. 'Most of these encounters were my first personal contacts,' he recounted. 'This opportunity of getting to know each other was doubtless in our mutual interests and conducive to trust and better understanding.'⁸

Funnily enough, Ford's complaints about the seating in Helsinki had dimmed by early 1976, as a brief exchange regarding Honecker at the White House with Ambassador Cooper reveals, when the President remarked:

> **President**: Tell me about things in East Germany. I had a couple of good talks with Honecker.
>
> **Cooper**: He can't stop talking about it. He had the pictures on the first page. He told me he felt as if you had been friends for twenty years. You're telling him you and I were friends has helped me. He has really never gotten over it. May I tell him I saw you and you sent best wishes?
>
> **President**: You certainly may.⁹

While Honecker received all the professional accolades he could have hoped for, life at the matrimonial home also seems to have stabilised. That summer, he took Margot and the family to Poland for a month's vacation, their first together in several years. Twice a week, however, he slipped quietly away for hunting jaunts in the Polish countryside while Margot, wearing a bandana around her hair, played the simple hausfrau by doting on the children and preparing family meals. She remained an earthy, practical woman, capable of domestic toil.

Under cotton awnings protecting him from the blazing sun, Erich fussed over grandson Roberto, who was nearing his first birthday. 'He was a real grandpa, he really enjoyed this role,' says bodyguard, Bernd Bruckner. Over time his relationship with Roberto flourished and he was an exceptionally devoted grandfather and even taught his grandson to ride a pint-size bicycle. Besotted as he was, nothing was too much trouble. 'If Roberto wanted a toy from the West, he would get it,' recalled Lothar Herzog, the butler. 'There was a big dining room at the hunting lodge. At Christmas, half of the room was full of toys, and they were all for Roberto.'

On one occasion, he even took his grandson hunting and allowed him to take aim from the back of his souped-up Range Rover. Roberto bagged his first and only deer. On hearing of the adventure, Margot berated her husband for his irresponsibility in letting the child near a gun. 'When Grandma banned something,' Roberto recounted, 'it was final. Grandfather never took me with him again.'[10] There was no argument, 'grandfather was a withdrawn loner, a shy person who never raised his voice in conversation and kept calm in every situation'.[11]

Back from holiday, Honecker headed to Moscow to sign the third treaty on friendship, cooperation and mutual assistance with the USSR, which, unlike the two previous accords, omitted references to German reunification and Allied special rights in Germany. By this point, Leonid Brezhnev – ashen-faced, overweight and prone to severe sleeplessness – presented a vision of decrepitude. Suffering from a disorder restricting blood flow within the brain; his ability to focus on tasks was failing, meaning big decisions and policy was left in the hands of his inner circle, namely Dmitry Ustinov of the Soviet Army, Yuri Andropov of the KGB and Foreign Minister Andrei Gromyko, the consummate diplomat and a man that irritated Honecker the most. His condition was even more fragile when Honecker returned to Moscow for the twenty-fifth CPSU in February 1976, when Brezhnev gave the impression of a sick, elderly man who was only kept functioning with the help of medication. Although slowed by a cocktail of tranquilisers and sleeping pills, he did, though, have a few lucid moments and delivered a speech on the normalisation of relations between the Soviet Union and West Germany.[12]

For his part, Honecker gave one of the five speeches by the heads of socialist delegations on the second day of the congress. Although lavish in his praise of ties with the Soviet Union, trade links with Moscow were on the decline as the GDR continued to take out massive, short, medium and long-term loans in the West.[13] Nevertheless, with growth slowing and the country increasingly reliant on imports, East Germany was encountering economic turbulence by early 1976.

After examining reams of data, economic experts Günter Mittag and Gerhard Schürer sent Honecker a devastating five-page report warning that eastern Germany would drift towards 'ungovernability' if the debt burden was increased (Schürer became the most direct and honest source on the failures of the economy but was also the most ignored). Willi Stoph – the harshest of economic hawks – was equally uncomfortable, as was Russian diplomat and economist Juli Alexandrovich Kwizinski. He remembered Honecker was impervious to the alarm signals being registered in diplomatic circles and recounted concerns about East Germany consuming more than it was able to produce, resulting in massive foreign debt, which under Ulbricht's administration, had remained serviceable. 'Soon, however, it turned out that almost the entire export growth of the GDR was used up to service the loans that had already been taken up,' Kwizinski noted. 'Many of the GDR's economists sounded the alarm but no one in the Central Committee of the SED seemed to value their opinion.'[14] A graphic illustration of the GDR's trading patterns was revealed in *Deutschen Aussenpolitik* – a semi-state publication – which asserted that East German traffic with Comecon, the organisation facilitating trade and economic development of Eastern European countries belonging to the Soviet bloc, had slipped from 61 per cent in 1970 to 56 per cent in 1976.[15]

Simultaneously, however, Honecker laboured under the hope that new trade links with the United States, especially in agricultural products, would keep the economy moving. He was also heartened by a fisheries agreement opening American ports to GDR ships, and a visit from the British Trade Secretary Edmund Dell seeking new opportunities marked the first trip to East Berlin by a British Cabinet Minister since the Second World War. On top of that, 'Intershop', the burgeoning chain of hard-currency stores, recorded 9.5 million visitors annually, bringing dollars, Sterling and Deutsche Marks. Also, vast foreign reserves continued to arrive via Genex, East Germany's official trading company in the West, an outfit aimed at securing Western currency by selling products ranging from self-assembly kitchens to textiles at prices set to undercut the Western market. In competing on the global market with the low-wage countries from the Third World and with China, the GDR dumped its merchandise at cheap rates while people at home paid dearly. For example, as exports always had the foremost priority, the high-quality East German Wernesgrüner beer could be found on sale in West Berlin supermarkets but not in the Eastern part of the city; likewise, fine woodwork from the Ore Mountains was unavailable in nearby Dresden but obtainable in Hamburg. With quality goods earmarked for export, what remained in the country was often only junk or of second-rate quality. For instance, one particular model of a cassette recorder priced DDM650 was of such miserable quality that it conked out after just a few minutes of operation. Jokers with testy complaints had already concocted a gag: 'Erich Honecker, during an inspection tour of a factory, asks about the rejects in the ratio to production. The answer: 8 per cent. The SED boss: "Is this enough to supply the people in the GDR?"'

A murkier source of income was secured by the thriving trade in political prisoners. Between 1963 and 1989, the FRG made ransom payments to free over 30,000 political prisoners from East Germany in exchange for around DM3 billion. Additionally, Wolfgang Vogel, a Honecker confidant, negotiated much-desired exit visas to the West for many East German families and was later said to have blackmailed several GDR citizens in the process. But Vogel had other motivations, too. It emerged in 1993 that over 200 people seeking to leave the GDR were forced to give their land to officials, Stasi officers and other SED beneficiaries, via Vogel's mediation. In sixteen specific cases, Vogel was accused of coercing people wishing to leave into making cash payments of up to DM250,000.[16] The case, in all its tawdry detail, showed how the whole bureaucracy of extortion worked.

Additionally, vast reserves of money were secured by wheeler-dealer Alexander Schalck Golodkowski, the head of 'Commercial Coordination' (KoKo), a department assigned to procure foreign exchange. Once described as the 'eminence behind Erich Honecker', Schalck was one of the GDR's most powerful men – more powerful, at any rate, than most of the members of the Politburo. Although he wasn't a member of the inner circle, Honecker trusted him completely and relied entirely on him when it came to acquiring currency. As a foreign trade specialist, his position placed him in charge of the Party and government war chest – much of it in cheap eastern money but, above all, a lot of hard currency.

Upon first reflection, it appears many KoKo companies participated in dubious business: dealing in arms and art, freeing prisoners, and supplying luxury goods to Wandlitz, yet taken together, the vast majority of KoKo activities were ordinary deals, including the trade of blood plasma, fuel, food, building materials and the disposal of Western waste at GDR landfills. 'From 1972–89 we transferred DM27billion to fixed assets,' Schalck later revealed. 'In addition, during the same period, revenues amounting to DM23 billion were acquired through agreements with the FRG.' These sums were used in the GDR national economy on the instructions of the responsible Politburo member Günter Mittag, or in individual cases based on special decisions by Honecker. Perhaps, not surprisingly, Schalck divulged that Honecker held the purse strings to an account amounting to DM100 million. 'The general secretary,' he revealed, 'knew that he was able to use the money immediately in case of unusual events, such as particular bottlenecks in supplies for the population.' Willi Stoph held a similar account, containing DM250 million.[17] And thanks to his enthusiastic leadership, during the course of his twenty-two years on the job, Schalck:

- circumvented NATO embargoes by bringing 10 billion marks worth of electronic equipment into the GDR, i.e. the arsenal of the Ministry for State Security (MfS) for the surveillance of the country's population;
- provided the HVA or Main Administration for Intelligence Collection, the Stasi espionage division, with hard currency for 'operational purposes';
- transferred DM50 billion into the GDR, by his own admission although intelligence sources estimate the figure was closer to DM100 billion;
- opened some 1,000 accounts in the East and West.

Veneer of Stability

During the blistering summer of 1976, Honecker declared that the GDR had achieved its past objectives. Greeted by a prolonged ovation, he prattled through a 45,000-word speech at the ninth SED Party Congress, where he stated East Germany would continue its policy of détente and meet its 1975–80 goals. The special significance of the congress lay in the fact that it discussed and adopted a new programme setting the historically significant task of further building a developed socialist society and thereby creating the basic prerequisites for the gradual transition to communism.

The Party programme also mapped out the long-term outline of SED policy regarding relations with the FRG, by declaring it should be developed as relations between sovereign states with different social systems on the basis of the principles of peaceful coexistence and the norms of international law. 'This orientation is based on the realities,' Honecker insisted.[1] In a private conversation with the US Ambassador, he spoke matter-of-factly when declaring housing for every family would be achieved by 1990, and perhaps by 1985. The congress was also interesting for unveiling plans for the promotion of television and radio in the directives for the Five-Year Plan:

> The effect of radio and television is to be raised by programme improvements in order to promote more strongly the development of socialist consciousness and to satisfy better the growing demand for information, education and entertainment. Television for schools is to be expanded. Investment in radio and television is to be concentrated on the further expansion and modernisation of studios and the improvement of reception.[2]

For East Germans, the appeal of West German television, with its glamorous dramas, *Heimat* films, uncensored news and Western soaps, was obvious. The two GDR state channels were bereft of modern programming and even ceased running commercials in 1976 after a Honecker-inspired purge on the advertising industry. Tuning to the West, East Germans were especially fond of *Dalli Dalli*, a lively knockabout quiz aired on ZDF. With mischievous casualness, host Hans Rosenthal announced the broadcast dates on the first show of every season, especially for East German viewers with no access to TV guide magazines. By the same token, the BBC attracted scores of teenage fans in the GDR with their *Records al la Carte* show, in which full-length songs were played so listeners could record them on cassette and build a personal collection of Western hits. AFN, the American Forces Network in West Berlin out-foxed other channels by playing popular music through the night, long after the GDR network had signed-off air.

The ninth Congress also highlighted the urgent need to upgrade newspapers which remained poor in both terms of language and content, though given most were organs of SED opinion rather than newspapers, this is not surprising. Though articles were rarely signed, the style of each feature was almost identical. (On one occasion, *Neues Deutschland* printed Honecker's official portrait forty times in a single edition).

A notable success for East German state TV was when it held millions of viewers spellbound during the summer of 1976 with live coverage of the thrilling exploits of the GDR Olympic squad. In all, the team won a scoop of medals at the Montreal Games, including forty golds, second only to the Soviet Union. 'The miracle that you hear about in the face of the success of our athletes in every corner of the world is no secret. It is called socialism,' Honecker beamed. As was his wont, he became very absorbed in the drama, rarely missing the TV coverage.

Only with the fall of the GDR was the widely held suspicion confirmed that East Germany's success in international athletics and swimming was fuelled by one of the most elaborate – and successful – doping schemes in history. Between 1964 and 1990, Manfred Ewald, a close friend of Honecker, served as president of the DTSB, the East German sports ministry. During his tenure, the Stasi took control of drugs in sports, and – swollen with each international 'triumph' – doping became official policy in 1975. It seems that in the politics of sport, Honecker was the hammer, not the anvil, and approved a systematic approach to doping – through the 'state plan 14.25' making it policy to administer muscle-building anabolic steroids to young athletes. In terms of producing medal winners, the project was a complete success. In a dark-of-night operation, neither athletes nor their parents were advised of the practice.

Throughout the Montreal Games, a clandestine medical facility outside the Olympic Village was set up where athletes were given performance-enhancing steroids ranging from testosterone to epitestosterone – administered at scientifically determined intervals to avoid drug tests. At the close of the Games, after undermining the integrity of one of the world's most prestigious sporting events, Stasi agents dumped ten suitcases of drugs and hypodermic syringes into Montreal's St Lawrence River.

Back in Germany, the glorious Olympic team was trotted about before the local press like prize cattle. Honecker paid tribute to the medal winners and expressed to the sportsmen, coaches and officials 'thanks and recognition for their exemplary actions, high fighting morale and outstanding sports performances with which they represented their socialist fatherland so well'.[3] Asked what he thought was the reason for the fact that East German athletes, although the GDR population was only one-tenth of that of the United States, won more medals than the latter's athletes, Honecker replied:

> The reasons for the successes of our athletes are manifold. Essentially, they are derived from the fact that in our country numerous talents are being promoted with the help of children's and youth associations. I believe that this is the main reason for our athletes' success.[4]

The GDR's doping scheme would be repeated at other international events, including the 1988 Olympics, where Kristin Otto and other members of the record-shattering women's teams were pumped with performance-enhancing drugs. (Otto, winner of six gold medals, had steroid levels almost three times the limit needed to trigger a positive result. Finally, in the year 2000, Ewald and director of sports medicine, Manfred Hoeppner, received suspended sentences after being charged with causing bodily harm to 142 women through doping).

During the 70s, Honecker was also turning a blind eye to the unrestricted flow of narcotics passing into West Berlin from the GDR. Curiously enough, one of the attractions for the international trafficker, was the 'open-door' policy which meant West Berlin's large population of Turks could fly with Interflug into East Berlin's Schönefeld Airport carrying drugs and enter the West without customs controls.[5]

The trade – described by media as causing a 'heroin epidemic' – was serviced by many independent small sellers supplied in modest individual quantities via an army of go-betweens travelling to East Berlin from Turkey and the Middle East. In the early 1970s, overdose deaths were practically unknown in West Berlin, but by 1976, fifty-four people had died; in 1977, eighty-four overdosed. Over thirty victims were found dead in public places, in parks, public toilets, or the underground. As the alarming situation worsened, the US embassy delivered a stark warning to Washington of 'evidence that East Berlin is a transit point, but East German cooperation has not been forthcoming. Berlin has the potential of becoming another Amsterdam with concomitant political and security implications.' In a cable to Washington, the embassy noted:

An FRG ministry of health official raised the issue with his GDR counterpart in their last meeting. In a later response, the GDR expressed 'astonishment' that the FRG would speak for Berlin on a purely Berlin matter. Given this GDR attitude, our FRG contacts have little hope or expectation that East Germany will respond any further to the West German request.[6]

The US brief was correct, the GDR – which had no major drug problem – displayed no interest in attempting to apprehend couriers. Furthermore, those same couriers had no desire to sell drugs for non-convertible DDM and did not linger in East Berlin. They presented no threat to GDR security, health, or morals, and contributed to the economy by purchasing Interflug tickets with hard currency. Some suspected that the GDR disinterest was also sustained by a desire not to do anything which might alleviate a serious West Berlin social problem – at least not with exacting a high price.

By the late 70s, it was calculated that there were around 6,000 drug addicts in West Berlin, many would gather in the Zoo and the Kurfürstendamm underground stations waiting to buy their 'fix' of heroin.[7]

Meanwhile, as the glow of Montreal Olympic triumphs faded, Honecker found distraction in a pet building project opposite the Berlin Cathedral at the lower end of Unter den Linden, a street that traded on its illustrious past. At the site of the old Hohenzollern palace, he oversaw the development of the new 'Palace of the Republic', a vast glass and steel structure housing a 5,000-seat congress hall, theatre, disco, art gallery and sauna-gymnasium. All that splendour wasn't cheap, with the government pouring more than US$300million into it, along with the wage bill for 3,100 workers and conscripts labouring on the site. Flooded with sunlight on clear days, the palace was full of jaw-dropping vistas from windows facing out to the neo-Baroque cathedral across the street and the vast television tower.

Illuminated by hundreds of lamps, the ornate ground level floor was crafted from marble imported from Karelia and Yugoslavia. 'Here,' noted the *Berliner Zeitung*, 'visitors can find numerous facilities such as a post office, telephones, newspapers and bookstores as well as souvenir shops.'[8] The second floor, replete with three lively restaurants, a pub and an ultra-modern cocktail bar, boasted a combined capacity of 800 indoor and terrace seats. There was even gold-rimmed crockery, but it was quickly discovered that the plates weren't dishwasher-safe, so they ended up in the basement and were only taken out for special events.

When opening day arrived after thirty-two months of construction, Honecker celebrated 'a house of the people' which, he said, testified to the GDR's socialist national culture. 'The Palace of the Republic will become a venue of living political, spiritual and cultural life, both for the citizens of the capital and for all the working people of our Socialist Republic'.[9]

With this auspicious start, Honecker also forged ahead with other major town planning projects for Berlin, including completing Marx-Engels Platz; and transforming Friedrichstraße into a bustling shopping district. Work also started on renovating the Platz der Akademie to its historic form, the restoration of Charité University and work on Karl-Liebknecht-Straße, Rathausstraße and the wide, windy intersection at Alexanderplatz. 'These objectives,' Honecker stated, 'aimed at raising cultural and material living standards,' and would spur Berliners to 'greater efforts to strengthen their fatherland, our socialist GDR.'[10] Over time, in contrast to Ulbricht's efforts at sweeping away Berlin's imperial past, renovation projects expanded. 'Literally rising from the ruins, Berlin today is increasingly becoming a symbol of the triumphant advance of socialism on German soil,' Honecker gushed, as work started on restoring the Zughaus, Gendarmenmarkt, Konzerthaus and neighbouring stone and granite churches, which returned to their pre-war grandeur.[11] 'The fine restorations,' observed British writer Anthony Read, 'stood out like new teeth in a mouth full of decay. Between and around them the ugly gaps of bombed sites remained, flanked by buildings still bearing the scars of war, their facades pot marked and cratered by thousands of bullets, shells and shrapnel fragments.'[12]

Among the greatest pleasures of Honecker's duties were the opportunities to welcome foreign dignitaries to Berlin. When Indian Prime Minister Indira Gandhi became the first world leader to enjoy the splendour of the new Palace of the Republic at a lavish banquet in July 1976, the American Ambassador remembered 'the biggest publicity splash in recent memory'. He reported how Indian flags and banners were nailed-up throughout East Berlin with slogans of friendship and photographs of Gandhi side-by-side with those of Honecker.

Her presence offered the East Germans an opportunity to promote stronger ties with Delhi and other non-aligned nations, and seek greater economic cooperation, especially in the area of coal mining. Already by this time the relationship between the First Secretary and Gandhi was better than cordial. The previous year, when India declared an emergency to control an 'internal disturbance', Gandhi thanked Honecker for his 'understanding and sympathy'.[13] For Gandhi, the Berlin visit evoked many personal memories. 'Forty years ago, I came here with my mother,' she recounted. 'It was a time when dark clouds were gathering over Germany and its neighbours. We took a deep interest in this struggle between freedom and fascism. With growing dismay, we found that appeasement was mistaken for peace.' Honecker lapped up her laudations of friendship, and was positively beaming when she proclaimed the '[relationship] between [them] was an excellent example of cooperation between countries with different systems, which is a fact of contemporary international life'.

In gratitude, Gandhi received a 21-gun salute farewell. Dressed in a long-sleeved yellow silk dress, she used her departure to extend an invitation to Honecker to pay an official visit to India. It was a crowning moment for the SED's well-oiled diplomatic machine. 'It will be interesting to see if he stays as far away from the subject of Indo-Pakistan relations as Mrs Gandhi did from East-West German matters,' the US Ambassador in East Berlin, John Sherman Cooper, acidly noted. He also pointedly observed that none of the 'numerous photos' published during Gandhi's visit connected her in any way with the Berlin Wall.

Honecker's status as the darling of the Helsinki process was never going to last for long. By the mid-1970s, the issue of prominent critics came into sharp focus when singer Wolf Biermann was stripped of his citizenship while touring in West Germany, accused of 'speaking against' the GDR during a concert in Cologne. The action left Biermann unable to return to his wife and child in East Berlin. Predictably, however, as his supporters in the West decried the 'inhumane lunacy' of the action, more and more of the GDR's best artistic talent applied to emigrate. Caught completely off guard, Honecker faced a vicious backlash and a barrage of intellectual venom. 'Two months ago, I would never have thought about leaving, but now I am not quite so sure,' one well-known author confessed. Poet Reiner Kunze, actor Manfred Krug and composer Tilo Medek, all highly regarded internationally, were among the first to pack-up. Off too, went scores of creatives and innovators, never to be replaced. Prominent intellectuals previously considered to be in conformity with the system, including Stephan Hermlin and Sarah Kirsch, were left appalled at the Biermann action. In a letter to Honecker, long-time dissident Robert Havemann expressed incomprehension and called for the expatriation to be reversed: 'Accusations and suspicions that he is an enemy of the GDR are simply nonsense,' he wrote.[14]

Watching with disbelief, even Soviet diplomats viewed the Biermann expulsion as an act of gross clumsiness and began questioning Honecker's logic. 'Instead of worrying about more important things, the SED general secretary occupies himself with thousands of details in the party apparatus, for example, which functionary marries whom and when,' one Russian embassy official angrily observed.[15] It was indeed true that even humdrum, squalid business passed the desk of Honecker. For example, he took a close interest when the GDR's Public Prosecutor mulled launching proceedings against actress Marta Rafael, wife of Karl-Eduard von Schnitzler, the chief commentator of GDR TV and host of the virulently anti-Western show *Der Schwarze Kanal*.[16] Rafael was caught shoplifting stockings worth DM16.40 from KaDeWe in West Berlin. Understandably, the incident shook the credibility of her husband, who had shot to fame by demonising the capitalist West by editing together extracts of

ARD and ZDF television footage and recording caustic, sharp and malicious commentary over it. For FRG journalists, it was a story sent from heaven. In the following days, they used Rafael's indiscretion as an opportunity to report in detail about the couple's exit privileges, and visits to West Berlin bars and shopping tours on the Kurfürstendamm (a small and privileged circle was permitted to undertake Western travel. This consisted of people like von Schnitzler, functionaries, academics, famous artists and top athletes. This 'travel cadre' was expected to act as upstanding GDR ambassadors, but the danger of defection was great. Over 600 sports personalities did not return). Regarding Rafael, Politburo member, Paul Verne, recommended that the state should 'rule out further inquiries' but added, 'it is another matter that we instruct a comrade to talk to Karl-Eduard von Schnitzler or his wife about their offence'.

Rafael screamed innocence, saying she knew nothing of the theft, which she claimed was a deliberate provocation by the FRG. Her defence: the stockings had 'been planted' in her bag. She justified this with the fact that she had been interrogated in West Berlin by 'people from the secret service'. Honecker's approach, as you might expect, was to quietly sweep the entire saga under the rug. *Der Schwarze Kanal* continued uninterrupted. (Incidentally, Wolf Biermann's song the *Ballad of the corrupted old men* – put von Schnitzler on a level with GDR hierarchs Honecker, Mielke and Hager.)

As more citizens presented submissions for official emigration, Honecker classed applicants into two groups. One of them, he bluntly stated, was 'ideologically stubborn', wanting to leave at all costs, while the other group applied for exit permits because of 'personal conflicts, irritation and similar reasons'.[17] The latter was by far the biggest group, and Honecker implored officials to 'talk patiently' with such aspirants to 'make them withdraw their application'. He encouraged the establishment of so-called 'coordination groups' comprising of party, state and economic functionaries to handle every individual application.[18]

It was ironic, and yet deeply appropriate that memories of the Biermann debacle remained fresh decades later. 'If one dirties his own nest and thereby favours others … let him stay there,' Honecker huffily reflected in 1991. 'I can still remember the dust was raised at the time. I regretted that in connection with this, so many artists turned their backs on the GDR. But, as I said, sometimes decisions are made in life which arise from necessity.' These haughty and self-complacent remarks seem almost demented in the light of what happened, but Erich was not alone in his musings. Margot had known Biermann and his family since the 1940s. She had kept in contact with his mother for a long time, 'and when Wolf Biermann became involved in the opposition, so-to-speak, I sought him out at his home and he sought me in my office,' she explained, adding that by the mid-1970s, the singer was in the 'kind of situation where he was not approachable with common-sense arguments. I had arranged another discussion between him with the central committee at the time, but it was too late already.'

By this point, Margot's position in the GDR was formidable. On 18 April 1977, her 50th birthday, the Politburo and the Presidium of the Council of Ministers awarded her the Karl-Marx medal in 'appreciation of great services to the construction of socialism'.

Nevertheless, to the wider public, her reputation remained poor. It worsened when she introduced compulsory 'military science lessons', which focused on air rifle and submachine gun practice, map-reading, tackling assault courses, and the promotion of patriotic thinking. Parents' despair at the militarisation of youth was exacerbated with the introduction of weekend physical training at military camps. Speaking during a visit to the 'Pablo Neruda' secondary school in Oranienburg, Margot Honecker saw for herself how facilities were utilised to ensure a 'high-standard of military instruction'. According to *Neues Deutschland*, 'The girls and boys expressed their readiness to protect and defend the gains of socialism.'[19] In a rambling editorial, the paper opined that military instruction offered the best possible prerequisites for acquainting youngsters with the basics of national defence. 'The young people said that they felt fine in the camp and that their stay was marked by many collective experiences.'[20] The church frowned on the scheme, but protests were unsuccessful, thus the arrangement remained compulsory in high schools until 1989.

The Squeeze Begins

As the Honecker era entered its sixth year, there were worrisome perturbations in the country. A world recession was compounded by an international oil crisis, sparking a rise in the price of raw materials and energy imports from the USSR. Compounding matters, farmers recorded a miserable grain harvest. A raft of cost-cutting measures ended Interflug's domestic routes from East Berlin to Erfurt and the Baltic Sea coast, while visitors to the GDR along with embassy officials and journalists were presented with gasoline ration cards.

Honecker gave a startlingly candid presentation on the international economic situation, sketching in stark terms the problem of rising raw material prices, saying the GDR's long-term economic strategy had been affected by these developments. He said prices of manufactured goods had not kept pace with the rise in raw material prices, which had cost the GDR an extra 14 billion 'Valuta Marks' since 1973.

Harder to duck was the problem of coffee prices on the world market, which shot up dramatically, leaving the SED facing a barrage of criticism. Up until the summer of 1977, the GDR had spent around DDM150million on the import of green coffee, but as the crisis worsened, the cost nudged up to almost DDM700million for the same amount. As economy became the watchword, the Politburo replaced some types of coffee with a blend called 'Kaffee-Mix', a stodgy concoction made from inferior raw coffee, roasted peas, rye, barley and sugar beet pulp (51 per cent bean coffee and 49 per cent surrogates). In a letter to Honecker, Politburo member Albert Norden feared 'enormous dissatisfaction' at the coffee situation:

> It is simply unthinkable to me that we want to stop serving real coffee in restaurants altogether and that in future only 20 per cent of the current quantity is to be sold in shops. And a coffee mixture at that, something we have no experience in – neither in its production, taste, nor consumption patterns.[1]

Norden's concerns were valid as soon after, a storm of public criticism broke out. The Stasi reported it was evident that the 'quality and price of the new coffee variety 'Kaffee-Mix' was being rejected by broad sections of the population'.

To make matters worse, the 'mix' could not be percolated in older coffee machines still common in cafés and canteens. And as if that wasn't bad enough, 'Kaffee-Mix' (sarcastically referred to as 'Erich's Krönung') swelled into a thick, sticky goo, clogging filters. Bitterness over the issue was the cause of frequent arguments and anonymous hate mail. Once coined, the term 'Erich's Krönung' – a play on a much-loved Western coffee brand – was to have a long life. In a secret meeting of the SED leadership, Honecker indicated that GDR customs would allow more coffee to come in private parcels from the FRG and in the luggage of visitors than provided for in the regulations. 'The more coffee from the West that comes into the GDR, the less has to be imported,' Honecker concluded.[2]

These parcels, known as *Westpakete*, were sent by West Germans to their friends and families in East Germany and usually contained coffee, food, soap, spirits, confections and other goodies. Although much desired, they were occasionally the subject of jokes:

> Erich Honecker wants to see how popular he is among the population, so he rings people's doorbells. A boy opens one and asks: 'Who are you?' Erich bends down: 'I'm the one who makes sure that you have a TV and always enough to eat!' – 'Mama, hurry, Uncle Frank from Hamburg is here!'

It is estimated that *Westpaket* parcels met about 20 per cent of East German coffee needs. When the heat finally subsided on the 'Kaffee-Mix' debacle, the SED withdrew the concoction from the market. But no sooner had the scandal blown over, than a new embarrassment appeared in early 1978, courtesy of the West German weekly *Der Spiegel*, which announced with glaring headlines that it had obtained an 'opposition manifesto' from a group in the GDR called the 'Bundes Demokratischer Kommunisten Deutschlands' (BDKD).

Although there was plenty of scepticism about this hitherto unknown movement – said to be made up of 'high and mid-level functionaries' – the magazine published the entire manifesto, crammed with bruising allegations and indelicate wording. Over the course of two editions on January 2 and 9, it accused SED leaders of living in 'golden ghettos' built in the forests and guarded like fortresses. Readers were enthralled by accusations that the SED hierarchy were shamelessly corrupted and enriched themselves in special stores with private imports from the West. Leaders were showered with 'decorations, bonuses, special clinics, pensions and presents'. No less startling, it caustically remarked that no ruling class of Germany had ever 'sponged so much as those two dozen families who run our country like a self-service store'.

Spread over thirty pages, the full manifesto presented a formidable list of complaints, including, among other things:

> We ask: did the working-class fight for supporting an immense host of good-for-nothing parasites in the party apparatus? Did it fight to make a life at the expense of the state treasury possible for these ML [Marxism-Leninism] preachers? Did it fight to achieve the fact that despite the Council of Ministers' decision on the reduction of the apparatus, year after year the state administration keeps growing, growing, growing? And all that even though a dozen computers would suffice to set 100,000 administrators free for bitterly needed services?
>
> Honecker himself, repeatedly and loudly, announced better living conditions in the service sector. Waiting periods for repairs of household equipment in some cases have increased threefold. Gas and electric stoves, circulation pumps, washing machines, vacuum cleaners, or refrigerators cannot be repaired for months in the GDR. This is being hushed up in East Berlin.
>
> Under Ulbricht, you had to wait for about four years to get an apartment in the capital. Now you must wait about eight years on average, and that despite the housing construction programme which came twenty years too late!
>
> We demand that party finances be published. The parasitic party bureaucracy has no claim to even one pfennig of the state budget.
>
> Why does the GDR rank at the top of the world record of divorces, suicide rates and alcohol abuse?
>
> Where are the defects of this society to be found?
>
> Let us name another problem that is seriously worrying the entire population. The physicians at the university clinic in Berlin can't operate on patients suffering from cancer before a waiting period of two to four years, unless a patient is able to buy a place in the hospital at the cost of enormous sums of money. The waiting periods for surgery are a death sentence in many cases.
>
> While the clinics of the bigwigs are half empty, there is a shortage of unbelievably underpaid physicians and medical helpers in emergency stations and hospitals. Injured people lie around for hours without first aid being applied. Strong patients must help transport seriously injured people. What medical helper can feed his family on DDM350? Qualified personnel are being moved to special clinics and naturally get better pay there.

We demand that an end must be made to the irresponsible expenditures for performance sports and television amateurs. What is a gold medal worth if it cost DDM25 million marks? Why does a professional soccer player make DDM2,000 while a highly qualified and specialised physician makes only DDM1,500, night shifts included?

We ask: Has the working class fought for the eight-hour workday or the incessant shift system? Families are separated day and night, yet the party raises the finger and says: Bring up your children more socialistically, they are labile! Over the weekend father has to join the works' militia, mother goes to ZV [civil defence], the son to the GSF [an organisation for paramilitary and military sports training], and the daughter to the DRK [German Red Cross] – everything for the protection of the Politburo caste!

We demand that all restricted areas in the GDR must be free again. Our peasants must be able to use the restricted areas, which are the size of Luxembourg, for productive agricultural work. To start with, the minefields can be cleared by those who gave the orders to mine them.

After publication of the document, media coverage was worse than anticipated, and Honecker feared a public relations nightmare when the issue was amplified by Western TV, and beamed into East German homes. As the crisis stewed, he suspected, wrongly, that the story was cooked-up by *Der Spiegel* and the Federal Intelligence Service. After making minor modifications and embellishments to the text, he instructed the GDR Foreign Ministry to take the highly unusual step of shooting-off an angry telegram to *Der Spiegel*'s office in Hamburg:

In the last few months, your paper has maliciously slandered the German Democratic Republic and its allies to an ever-increasing extent and has deliberately attempted to poison relations between the German Democratic Republic and the Federal Republic of Germany through fabricated news and reports.

Eventually, after months of trying to suss out the author of the supposed manifesto, the Stasi arrested Hermann von Berg, a disgruntled professor at the economics section of Berlin's Humboldt University. As a devout Marxist, von Berg was motivated by a hatred of injustice and an ardour for decency in SED affairs. Although he issued a swift denial, von Berg later admitted dictating the manifesto to *Der Spiegel* correspondent Ulrich Schwarz at his apartment.

For his efforts, the professor spent three months in prison, lost his job and was ultimately expelled to the Federal Republic in 1986.

Though embarrassing for Honecker, Chancellor Helmut Schmidt was equally roused, fearing the document would endanger the policy of détente. Once scorned, as he considered he had been, Honecker began planning a campaign against foreign journalists operating within the GDR.

The brutal winter of 1978–9 – one of the worst in living memory – left the GDR shivering in the lowest temperatures for two decades. On 28 December 1978, a 72-hour snowstorm in the north cut-off the Baltic Island of Rügen, leaving ill-equipped and ill-prepared emergency services flummoxed. As the bitter weather tightened its grip, the entire country sank into total darkness on New Year's Eve when lignite opencast mines plunged to minus 20°C, leading to the collapse of the power supply. (One of the main causes of this predicament was a 1976 decision to convert all electricity and heating supplies to lignite-based fuels.)

Amid this turmoil, Erich Honecker jetted off for an official visit to India. Under Asian skies, he was bedazzled by the boisterous reception in New Delhi.[3] The trip got underway with a wreath-laying at the Mahatma Gandhi memorial, followed by a whistle-stop tour of Agra and Bombay to inspect industrial, scientific and merchant shipping concerns. Of immeasurably greater moment was his place on the podium alongside Prime Minister Morarji Desai, who nodded in agreement as Honecker denounced the apartheid policy of South Africa and expressed support for the 'just struggle' against colonial oppression.[4]

On his return to Germany, the US Ambassador to the GDR, David Benjamin Bolen, noted the considerable amusement among diplomatic observers about the presence of the interfering Soviet Ambassador Pyotr Abrasimov, at the airport for both the departure and arrival of Honecker. 'While Abrasimov's presence can be explained, in part, by the fact that Honecker stopped briefly in Tashkent,' a top-secret cable stated, 'the general explanation is that Abrasimov's presence demonstrates, once again, Moscow's dominant role in GDR foreign policy. We have also been told by diplomatic colleagues that their East German contacts were asking, disingenuously, whether it was customary for Abrasimov to be present on such an occasion.'[5]

The following month, as a key figure in the deployment of Soviet strategy in Africa, Honecker embarked on a four-nation tour which began in Libya, where a year earlier his trusted lieutenant and heir apparent[6] Werner Lamberz had been killed in a helicopter crash.[7] From then on, Egon Krenz was groomed for high office and treated as 'crown prince' (more in the media of the Federal Republic than in the GDR), but as Günter Schabowski noted, Krenz 'never heard any confirmation of such an intention' from Honecker.[8]

Exploiting the propaganda potential of the Libya trip, *Neues Deutschland* reported that during the drive from the airport, 'thousands of Tripoli citizens gave the guests from the GDR a spirited welcome'. Ghaddafi said the German Democratic Republic and the Socialist Libyan Arab People's Jamahiriya fought together 'against colonialism, racism and Zionism'. Furthermore, he praised events in Tehran – where Ayatollah Khomeini arrived back from exile in triumph – as a victory of the Iranian people's revolution. Reporting on a banquet given for Honecker, *Neues Deutschland* noted applause and laughter when Ghaddafi gave the First Secretary a 'splendidly crafted Bedouin saddle and equestrian clothing embroidered with folk motifs as a gift'.

The following morning, a beaming Honecker arrived in Angola to sign a twenty-year 'Friendship and Cooperation Treaty' with President Agostinho Neto. Speaking to Luanda's parliament without notes, he condemned 'the devious attack' by Chinese troops on Vietnam and assured the 'brave Vietnamese people' of the full solidarity of the German Democratic Republic. From Luanda, he flew on to Zambia to inspect refugee camps, but ostensibly to meet Joshua Nkomo, leader of the 'Zimbabwe African People's Union', and favourite in the fight to overthrow Rhodesia's white government. Nkomo gave a lengthy briefing on the struggle 'against the racist Smith regime, for independence and the realisation of the right to self-determination'. In a statement carried by ADN, Nkomo looked forward to the day 'when we shall meet again in a free Zimbabwe'. ADN added, 'Such a meeting will not take place in a capital called Salisbury but in a metropolis by the name of Harari. The capital of a liberated country will obviously not retain the name which was given to it by imperialist oppressors.' By lunchtime the following day, the GDR delegation arrived in Mozambique to cut deals on selling machine tools, textiles and chemical products.

Although Honecker had, in fact, no specific programme for Africa, his fevered activity cemented East Berlin as the main Warsaw Pact agency building up strong relations with liberation movements and helping to train and finance pro-Soviet Marxist cadres. During his travels, he succeeded in gaining endorsement for his bitter attacks against China while handing out solidarity 'donations' – such as DDM5 million to the ANC – which was enthusiastically accepted. The money was plucked from a hefty 'solidarity fund' used to bankroll liberation movements[9] and finance periodicals including the monthly *African Communist* journal, the mouthpiece of the exiled South African Communist Party. Money was also directed to *Sechaba*, the official organ of the African National Congress of South Africa (a gesture never forgotten by Nelson Mandela) and to the *South-West African People's Organisation of Namibia*. 'Not surprisingly,' wrote Colin Legum, one of the finest contemporary writers on African politics, 'the East German-financed publications of these liberation movements keep up a campaign of vitriolic denunciation of West Germany whose leaders are accused of seeking to play NATO's imperialistic game in Africa. Their successful propaganda has done considerable damage to Bonn's standing in many African countries.'

Peter Foster, the British Ambassador to the GDR, watched Honecker's unremitting thrust into the Third World, which, as he noted, 'continued unabated with a stream of inward and outward visits and some new friendship agreements as the outward and visible signs of an industrious contribution to the subversion of Western interests and the development of new sources of raw materials'.[10] When asked why such a cordial relationship had developed between the GDR and African states, Honecker said some people may find it hard to understand 'the fact that there are no racial barriers between us'.[11] Elaborating, he believed the peoples of Africa thought 'we are meeting them man to man, on equal terms, and practicing solidarity. That is, if you like, a concrete result of our visits to some African countries. They have opened wide vistas for the development of our relations in the political, economic and cultural field.'

Despite working to a gruelling schedule, Honecker spent any free moments at his hunting lodge, where his daily routine varied little from previous years. Butler Lothar Herzog recalled his discipline was probably one of his greatest strengths:

> When we would return from state visits, which were really all over the world, he would go to his office the following day – regardless of where the journey had taken us, or what the time difference had been. I admired that in him – because we felt the toll of all those trips we took, and yet we weren't under as much stress as he was.[12]

Back home, having assumed the problems of the winter weather response were squarely behind him, Honecker worked himself into a lather when reviewing recordings of Western TV news coverage. His jaw dropped as he watched hours of critical analysis of the poor East German response to the paralyzing storms, played in contrast to gushing reports about the FRG's faultless reaction in dealing with snow, ice and blizzards.

He fumed about ARD, the 'sabre-rattling' West German TV network, which seldom tiptoed around difficult topics. On one occasion, Honecker was incandescent when the channel made disparaging remarks on the costly purchase of new stretch Volvo limousines for high-ranking SED members (seven were bought for politburo members using hard currency). For years, he accused certain West German journalists accredited to the GDR of violating not only the spirit, but also the letter of the Helsinki agreement by 'not contributing to peace and the development of good relations'. In an interview with the Saarbrücker Zeitung, he bemoaned that critical reporting and slander were two different things and that 'GDR-FRG relations cannot be normalised when the truth is cancelled.'[13] Though rarely agitated, he was equally frustrated at the 'chicanery' of dissidents criticising internal developments on FRG TV. He loathed critical 'man-in-the-street' interviews filmed in the GDR and weaved into FRG news reports to add impact and immediacy. 'It's not a happy combination, is it?' Honecker once remarked. In another interview, he snapped: 'You know, FRG mass media constantly publicises incorrect reports about the GDR. If we wanted to deny all of them, we would have very little time to deal with our proper work.'[14]

In the end, *Der Spiegel*'s 'opposition manifesto' story combined with other negative reporting denoted the expiry of many privileges enjoyed by the foreign press corps. Tired of the denigration of the GDR, the government introduced new controls in April 1979 seeking to prevent sidewalk interviews – the move was intended to discourage GDR citizens from giving statements to foreign journalists, as well as dissuading reporters from seeking them. At the same time, West German journalists who had been a persistent thorn in Honecker's side became a particular target.[15] Furthermore, Western correspondents seeking interviews were required to apply to the Ministry of Interior for permission and expected to announce trips outside East Berlin twenty-four hours in advance, stating the purpose of the journey.

It was no coincidence that this sudden crackdown came during the continuing economic malaise. One astute interpretation from the American embassy was that retail prices were set to rise, and criticism of government policy would be amplified by grumbling East Germans pouring their hearts out to Western TV. In fact, as predicted, a series of sharp price rises on consumer goods, textiles, furniture and car parts were introduced as higher quality items were presented at twice the price of the products they replaced.

Despite the credit crunch, Honecker managed to lavishly fund celebrations marking the 30th Anniversary of the GDR. American foreign correspondent John Dornberg witnessed the First Secretary exhort East Germans to 'work harder, produce better quality goods, study more intensely, have more children, tighten their belts, waste less energy, and even brush their teeth more often – all in honour of our nation's birthday'.

To mark the occasion on 5 October, columns of goose-stepping troops marched through East Berlin to open an orchestrated show of worker solidarity and national unity. Television viewers saw live coverage of Brezhnev receiving a 21-gun salute before cruising past flag-waving crowds like a conquering hero in an open-topped limousine with whitewall tires. From a balcony on

Alexanderplatz, a journalist saw the ailing Kremlin chief gripping the side of the car firmly 'and only occasionally raised his free hand to wave'. To add to the festivities, East European leaders were joined by Asian and African representatives, including Joshua Nkomo and the PLO's Arafat. The occasion of the 30th Anniversary was also used to ink an agreement between British editor Robert Maxwell and the SED to publish a Honecker 'autobiography' to be issued by Pergamon Press. When completed, it filled 300 pages of single-spaced typescript and, as the focus was more political than personal, Honecker only penned a few childhood sketches, the rest was 'composed' by fourteen Central Committee departments or, as one commentator put it, 'party official first-person narrators'. Inevitably, the book, *From My Life*, was loaded with self-justification and perfectly captured his vision: Erich Honecker, revolutionary, peacemaker, statesman.

Around this time, Honecker was confronted with more immediate problems when Brezhnev embarked upon an invasion of Afghanistan aimed at bolstering the faltering communist regime in Kabul. In speech after speech, Honecker was publicly an unflinching supporter of the action, but privately believed it had no clear attainable objective, a view also articulated by Bishop Albrecht Schoenherr, chairman of the Evangelical Church Federation in East Germany, who said the invasion was 'not viewed with enthusiasm' by the GDR leadership. Speaking on Radio Free Berlin, Schoenherr added that while the GDR could not escape from the obligations of its alliance, 'an aggravation of the situation is certainly not what East Germans would like to see'.[16] Indeed, several protests took place across the GDR. In one, the words 'Russians out of Afghanistan' were daubed on walls in Rostock, while pamphlets were thrown from a moving car during the rush hour in front of Leipzig's main railway station. On these it was written: 'Now we know what we are arming for; the Russians need weapons and our support.'[17]

While the Soviets were absorbed in battle, international distaste at the aggression prompted President Carter to curtail the export of American grain to the USSR, postpone the ratification of the Salt II treaty, ban the sale of high-tech equipment and reduce the quota of fish Russia was allowed to catch in American territorial waters. As Moscow continued to pour thousands of troops into the country, Honecker declined a demand from Vladimir Kryuchkov, the hawk-eyed KGB chief in Afghanistan. Kryuchkov was desperate for East German officers to join intelligence-gathering missions. Though affable to a fault, Honecker instead articulated social solidarity by sending medical supplies and specialists to help the electrification of Afghanistan and develop college and technical education institutes. Engineers from Radio Berlin International rebuilt Radio Afghanistan's studio, and specialists improved the technical quality of its programmes.

However, even with the distraction of Afghanistan, where the Soviets began facing hit-and-run guerrilla-style combat, the economic crisis was never far away. On 13 December 1979, Honecker delivered a comprehensive Politburo report to the eleventh session of the SED plenum covering a basket of economic policies. He claimed that although planned targets had been met, the necessity for more efficient production was urgent, while at the same time, he criticised government ministries for not making scientific advances quickly enough. Importantly, as will be seen in later chapters, Honecker announced that 1981–5 imports of Soviet energy supplies – a major driver of the economy – would be higher, amounting to a 7.7 per cent increase in oil deliveries. During his presentation, two major economic problems – the balance of trade deficit and inflationary pressure – were blamed on world market fluctuations. To meet these problems, he prescribed a change in the composition of exports and stricter controls on imports, particularly those from non-socialist countries (domestic substitutes would have to be found for the import shortfall, except coffee).

He outlined an official policy to be based on stable prices for staple goods, but cost-based pricing for 'high-quality' goods. As a result of the changing world situation, the GDR, Honecker said, had to deal with 'an important ideological problem', where economic performance could no longer be evaluated solely on the basis of comparison with the previous year's figures. From then on, the essential question was whether or not the economy had kept pace with the demands of the international marketplace. More specifically, he called for a change in the composition of the GDR's export goods in favour of high-quality products, especially for exports to capitalist markets in order to become more profitable.

In a few candid sentences, he complained that the GDR could not meet the demand for some of its high-quality exports, while other goods designated for overseas markets were of such shoddy quality that buyers could be found only with difficulty, or not at all. Importantly, as far as the home front was concerned, he warned exports would take precedence over the local consumer market, in order to draw foreign exchange.

Although the construction programme wasn't the watershed he'd hoped for, he stipulated it must provide for the restoration of older buildings rather than bulldozing them and erecting new structures. This move was partly prompted by a growing chorus of disapproval at the wholesale destruction and neglect of historic buildings across the country, especially in Berlin, Leipzig and Dresden.

At the end of his speech, Honecker was particularly anxious to dwell on the improvement in living standards, paying special attention to advances in worker safety, easy credit for newlyweds, the lengthening of vacations, pension increases and benefits for working mothers. He threw out a torrent of statistics to support his argument that things weren't so bad. For example, he noted that 69 per cent of the population had a net income of over DDM1,200 in 1979, compared to only 30 per cent in 1970. He catalogued the consumer durables purchased as a result of the pay increases: in 1970, 56 per cent of households had refrigerators, in 1979 almost 100 per cent; 54 per cent had washing machines at the beginning of the decade, compared to 80 per cent in 1979; while 69 per cent owned televisions in 1969, 90 per cent did by the end of the 1970s. The figures showed a great increase in family income, most of which was apparently soaked up by purchases of consumer durables, such as white goods, tools and furniture. However, by this time, demand for such products had fallen, as a report compiled by the American embassy in Berlin highlighted:

> Once a family has one refrigerator, there is not much interest in buying a second one. So, the family upgrades its expectations and looks around for some higher-class goods to purchase. The search is frustrated by the non-convertibility of the currency, which discourages the government from selling imported high-quality consumer goods for DDM, and by the inefficiency of a non-market economy that produces long waiting lines for consumer goods [eight years for a Trabant, the standard automobile]. The result is that there is too much money chasing too few goods. If market mechanisms were allowed to take their course, the inability to satisfy consumer demand would lead rapidly to higher prices; if the market mechanisms were suppressed, the results would be shortages of consumer goods and a flourishing black market.[18]

The year 1979 ended with a surprise announcement that West German Chancellor Helmut Schmidt would meet Honecker in early 1980 for the first East-West German summit since 1971. It was an encouraging sign.

The Eighties

Erich Honecker's New Year's message began in familiar fashion with promises for better times ahead in the 'struggle for peace and socialism', and so on. 'We do it responsibly, objectively, and with well-founded optimism.' Even though such addresses typically conveyed an inoffensive message, he touched upon Afghanistan saying, 'the party and state leadership and the people of the GDR support the measures taken by the Soviet Union at the request of the Afghan party and state leadership to guarantee peace and security'. By this point, the debacle in Kabul was severely draining the Soviet Union's economic resources.

On the ground, Babrak Karmal was installed as ruler, backed by Soviet troops, just as Mujahideen rebels – financed by the CIA – launched military operations designed to bog down the Russians. Though never a cause he wished to champion, Honecker defended Moscow in *Pravda* by declaring it:

> laughable that those who are themselves to blame for the deterioration in the international situation are trying to link it to events in Afghanistan. The GDR is in complete solidarity with the Afghan people's struggle and is firmly on the side of the Soviet Union, which is giving them international assistance.[1]

The tense atmosphere over Afghanistan, which was turning into a Vietnam-like quagmire, prompted chancellor Schmidt to call-off his planned meeting with Honecker (rescheduled for August). The news was muted in the GDR media, which focused on several domestic events that winter, including Honecker's attendance at the 30th-anniversary celebrations for the Ministry of State Security. In an address to officers, he praised their 'courageous fighters on the invisible front'. Newspapers respectfully reprinted the speech, together with a picture of pint-sized Mielke, clad in a braided white uniform, beaming from cheek-to-cheek. During this encounter, Honecker and Mielke briefly discussed Brezhnev's increasing senility, which had left him barely able to move. According to former aides, he spoke with difficulty, and his fogginess and confusion could be alarming. On one occasion, convinced that enemy forces were invading Moscow, he refused to retire until reassured that troops were mobilising to stop the imagined attackers. Not long after, he confused a television actor with a Second World War veteran and attempted to have him decorated for bravery.

There was some brief respite from domestic problems in 1980. During a visit to Cuba, Honecker spent time fishing and swimming, and was treated to a monologue from Fidel Castro about a US programme of biological warfare against the island. He accused the US of releasing pests to destroy sugar and tobacco harvests and told Honecker about a series of 'very strange plagues' appearing on the island, which he considered acts of sabotage:

> One of these was a fungus on the tobacco plantations, which destroyed 90 per cent of this year's tobacco production and forced us to import tobacco. It involved blue mould. We also had a very serious plague on the sugar plantations. It caused a loss of roughly a million tonnes of sugar. Then we had the African swine fever. We now have this swine fever virtually under control.

Amid all this, the Kremlin was knocked off balance as communist rulers in Poland grappled with widespread shortages, a symptom of massive foreign debt. Stuck in a tricky spot, the Poles implemented a system of gradual but continuous price rises. But as things worsened, a vocal group of Gdansk shipyard workers staged an illegal strike. Led by a charismatic young electrician named Lech Wałęsa, the workers drew up a list of twenty-one demands and refused to leave the docks until they were met. Soon after, they demanded political concessions, resulting in the 'Danzig Agreement', allowing the creation of a self-governing independent trade union with the right to strike.

The international press, which had been initially slow to react to events in Gdansk, was now overcompensating. Monitoring the situation from Berlin, Honecker rightly worried that 'one could not completely dismiss the possibility that the Polish germ could spread to East Germany'.[2] He looked favourably upon a request from KGB Chairman Yuri Andropov to provide the Stasi's help in monitoring Poland using a network of informers and spies (an East German journalist was also placed among Lech Wałęsa's intimate circle).[3] Soon after, Polish workers were joined by academics and intellectuals to form a new movement: 'Solidarity'. In a combative mood, Honecker told television viewers, 'one thing is clear. Poland is and will remain a socialist country. It belongs inseparably to the world of socialism, and no one can turn back the wheel of history. Together with our friends in the socialist camp, we will see to that.' He exaggerated when arguing that West Germans along with other Western nations had abetted striking Polish workers.[4] 'Poland is our neighbour,' he frostily remarked. 'They want to replace the Soviet shape of socialism with a Polish model. The close alliance and friendship with the Soviet Union forms the sole guarantee for a peaceful future in happiness.'

Shocked as to the extent of the onslaught, *Die Welt*, asserted Honecker – as an 'uncompromising governor of Soviet predominance' – represented Moscow as a satellite as Ulbricht once did. 'He will do everything he can to prevent the formation of a liberal national movement in Poland, or even the development of national anticommunism which could orientate toward the West.'[5] According to BND files, he is even said to have offered to 'take over the main burden with his troops in the event of a possible invasion of Poland in order to free the Soviet Union from this burden'.[6]

Suffering anxiety, the harsh rhetoric forced Chancellor Schmidt to again call-off his much-anticipated meeting with Honecker that August. By his own recollection, fearing the Soviet Union and its allies would invade Poland, Schmidt advised Honecker not to participate but received no clear answer. 'That's why I had postponed my visit.' Commenting on the issue, the *Frankfurter Rundschau* sarcastically noted: 'They just cannot get together, these two Germans, Schmidt and Honecker. Conditions are not right for the second time this year. First, it was Afghanistan, now it is the Poles who do not allow politics to go according to plan.'[7]

Though Honecker seemed confident and self-assured when Schmidt postponed their meeting, he was deeply vexed at the snub and responded by issuing a slew of measures restricting human and political contact between the two Germanys. As the situation changed from day to day, the flow of Western visitors to the East was reduced, currency regulations tightened, and new controls were imposed on cultural visits and church relations.

Although foreign affairs offered some escape from the troublesome Polish problems, Honecker's pent-up anger was unleashed during his first state visit to Austria in November, where he angrily reported to his host, Chancellor Bruno Kreisky, that Helmut Schmidt had not even considered it necessary to have a minister or at least a State Secretary deliver the bad news about cancelling their meeting but had used the telephone. The intense disrespect, according to a Viennese diplomat, 'really hurt him'.[8]

Despite a few dissenting voices, the Austrian press was unfailingly polite about Honecker's visit. Only a commentary in the daily *Vienna Kurier* by analyst Heinz Nussbaumer raised eyebrows. In his 300-word assessment, Nussbaumer questioned whether in the 'present crisis of détente' it was expedient for Honecker, 'a man who could hardly deny his share of responsibility for the development of that crisis', to be greeted with all protocol honours. The author cited two of Honecker's reactions to the Poland crisis. Firstly, the raising of the compulsory Deutsche Mark conversion quota for West German visitors and, secondly, his decision to impose visas on Poles.[9]

As it happened, the trip to Vienna paid dividends. The East Germans secured huge loans along with an Austrian promise to bankroll the development of a new steelworks in Eisenhüttenstadt, a town in the Oder-Spree district of Brandenburg (these loans made a decisive contribution in keeping the GDR economy afloat during the early 1980s).[10] In other ways, too, Honecker was triumphant. During his talks with Kreisky, he touted the prospect of cultural exchanges between the two countries and even held out the possibility of improved tourism for youngsters and teenagers.

After Vienna, Honecker resumed his gaze upon Warsaw by cordoning off the possibility of contagion with a new set of travel restrictions. On 4 November, Brezhnev wrote to Honecker explaining it was essential to provide Poland with extra economic aid, designed to help prop-up the shaky regime in Warsaw. Inevitably, the move caused hardships for other Socialist states, including the GDR.

> Dear Erich!
> After discussing the matter in the Politburo we decided to write to you and Comrades G. Husak, J. Kadar and T. Zhivkov with regard to an important, even extraordinary, matter. Recently, as you well know, we received Cdes. S. Kania and J. Pitikowski in Moscow. The situation in their country is extremely difficult. An acute need arises for all of us to help Poland survive the current crisis. You know very well the political situation in the PPR [Poland]. Counter-revolution is advancing and practically grabbing at the party's throat. At a recent meeting with Polish friends, we shared our considerations about the need to break the tide of events and to launch our own offensive against the forces of counter-revolution. We will inform you further about this meeting. In these conditions the situation in the economy acquires immense importance, and now it is near catastrophic.
>
> Further aggravation of the situation in Poland threatens to inflict grave damage on the entire socialist commonwealth. Therefore, it is our internationalist, I would say our class, duty to do everything in our power not to allow this to happen. I would say right away that we are assuming the main burden in this matter. In spite of our own economic problems, which I have reported to you, we judged it necessary to provide considerable financial and economic assistance to Poland by way of giving resources in freely convertible currency and by way of additional supplies of a number of goods and products.

But one cannot avoid certain contributions from other fraternal countries. When we weighed and discussed this issue, we, of course, understood well that it was not a simple matter. Therefore, we wanted to come up with a solution that would minimally affect the fulfilment of your internal plans, one that you would be able to shoulder. Specifically, we suggest cutting back somewhat on oil supplies to a number of the countries of the socialist commonwealth, the idea being to sell this oil on the capitalist market and to transfer the resulting currency on behalf of certain countries to Poland, in order to allow it to alleviate in part its critical financial situation and purchase some vitally needed foodstuffs and other products.

As for the GDR, if you agree, then the amount of oil supplies from the Soviet Union could be cut back in 1981 by 600–650,000 tons from the agreed level, all this without touching the level of supplies of German products to the Soviet Union. I am asking you, Erich, to treat this suggestion with empathy. I am certain that this manifestation of fraternal solidarity will allow our Polish comrades to weather this difficult hour. With communist greetings,

L. Brezhnev[11]

Although shaken by the economic implications of Brezhnev's note, Honecker's nervousness at the political situation was revealed in his reply in which he requested an urgent meeting of the General and First Secretaries of the Communist Parties:

According to information we have received through various channels, counter-revolutionary forces in the People's Republic of Poland are on the constant offensive, and any delay in acting against them would mean death – the death of socialist Poland. Yesterday our collective efforts may perhaps have been premature; today they are essential; and tomorrow they would already be too late.[12]

When it happened, the emergency meeting of the Warsaw Pact held in Moscow on 5 December, saw Honecker call for extreme measures. Alluding to 1953, he ruefully reminded his audience that:

we also had a difficult situation in the German Democratic Republic in 1953. The imperialists were instigating the fall of the workers-and-peasants' power from outside and counted on counter-revolution from within. We, therefore, had to act quickly. We combined political with administrative measures. We made a public appeal to the party members and functionaries of our party, to all who were committed to the defence and strengthening of the workers-and-peasants' state. Within a short time, we managed to isolate the counter-revolutionary forces from the workers and to defeat them.[13]

In the end, the meeting produced relatively little. Much to Honecker's disgust – Brezhnev led Warsaw Pact leaders to rigorously reject military intervention. But never one to be deterred, Honecker suggested to Stanislaw Kania a list of drastic measures to get workers under control. (Kania did not adopt any of his suggestions.)[14]

To the public, then and since, Honecker appeared in those tense months as an agitated soul, filled with alarm and anger over his unstable neighbour. A secret BND report noted that he had been taciturn and 'occasionally even bitter' since his December meeting with Brezhnev. 'Obviously,' the report noted, 'it is difficult for him to come to terms with the Kremlin's wait-and-see policy towards the still smouldering counter-revolutionary process in Poland.' His mood was also, if the BND is to be believed, affected by his personal domestic arrangements.

The agency reported that according to a 'high SED official', the union between Margot and Erich Honecker was 'still broken'. Furthermore, a source, identified as 'GZ10' reported that while outwardly Margot supported her husband out of duty, the marriage was floundering. Interestingly, the same document contains the curious line: 'Is Margot H. in a relationship with Günter Mittag?' While rumours of an affair were rife, nothing was ever confirmed.

In a relationship punctuated by humiliations, Margot lived unhappily with Erich's wandering eye and unhealthy penchant for Western porn (the VHS porn videos, paradoxically, were allegedly procured by Günter Mittag from sex shops in West Berlin). Over time, Honecker amassed a vast collection – one that the German media covered extensively at the time, particularly titles such as *Lady Diamond* and *The Black Nymphomaniac*, starring Ajita Wilson playing a reporter and nymphomaniac infiltrating a sex gang.[15] Honecker owned two copies of *Black Emanuelle*, which according to *Lexikon des Erotic Films*, tells the story of a dark-skinned photographer 'who is screwed over by a white couple and then by a whole hockey team'. Snugly hidden in the basement of his vacation home in Libbesicke See, *Der Spiegel* magazine later reported, Honecker amassed a total of 4,864 videos at a cost of DM1.3million.[16]

Also, it is true that during periods of strained marital tension, Erich Honecker could be inventive. On one occasion during the summer of 1981, to prevent Margot from accompanying him on a state visit to Japan, he arranged for her to be invited to Yugoslavia (in the capacity of minister of education). It worked: Margot flew to Belgrade and Erich arrived in Tokyo, on what turned out to be a trip full of tragic-comic moments and gaffes. Bodyguard Lothar Herzog never forgot how Horst Bries, the GDR ambassador to Japan, was so excited after leaving an audience at the Imperial Palace with Emperor Hirohito that he accidentally put on Honecker's shoes, even though they were far too small. 'For better or for worse,' Herzog recounted, 'the head of the State Council then had to slip into Bries' worn-out shoes'.[17] On another occasion, he looked awkward when receiving an honorary doctorate from a Japanese university and showed himself ill-adapted to protocol when refusing to wear formal tails. For him, such attire was the 'epitome of bourgeois decadence'. In the end, he was received by Hirohito wearing a dark suit and chestnut coloured tie.

Within the period of eighteen years, Brezhnev had taken a relatively robust Soviet economy and transformed it into one of stagnation and lower industrial production. Compounding matters, the debt-free country he usurped from Khrushchev in 1964 had amassed over U\$20 billion worth of hard currency debt. Herb Meyer, a US specialist in economic warfare and the right-hand man of CIA boss William Casey, reported that the Soviet Union had sold 240 tons of gold on the world market in 1981, compared to only 90 tons in 1980 – an unmistakable sign that the USSR was in great trouble.

Equally disturbing – for the GDR at least – was by the summer of 1981, the situation was having a severe impact on relations with Moscow. During August, Honecker met Brezhnev in Crimea, where he shared illusory ideas about ceasing to take up loans from the USSR from 1982 and achieving a significant reduction of debt to the West by 1985. However, Honecker was stunned to hear Brezhnev reply that the GDR could not count on any Soviet loans to balance bilateral trade in the coming four years and that the agreed volume of oil deliveries – East Germany's most important raw material for its exports – 'was in doubt'. The full extent of that revelation arrived in an explosive letter on 27 August informing Honecker the USSR could no longer supply East Germany the agreed 19 million tons of petroleum per annum.[18] Brezhnev lamented being forced to sell 'considerable amounts of oil and petroleum products to capitalist countries in order to obtain currency for the purchase of grain and foodstuffs which we cannot do without'. He also had to reckon with calamitous weather conditions, meaning the USSR would find itself with a food problem. 'The current year,' he added, 'is also unfavourable'[19] and was exacerbated by a US-EEC grain embargo imposed after the invasion of Afghanistan.[20]

Across the Eastern bloc, signs of malaise were rife: Poland was in default with her economy virtually owned by Western banks and guarantees from Western governments, while Romania was struggling from going belly up and stopped servicing debt.

After agonising over the proposed cuts, Honecker assured the Soviet leader he understood the decision was forced by 'extraordinary circumstances', but emphasised it directly affected the internal plans of the GDR, 'we would like to draw your attention, dear Leonid Ilyich, to the consequences that a reduction in the supply of energy sources from the USSR would have for our republic'.[21] Furthermore, he asserted, if the GDR lost even a part of the supplies of Soviet energy sources, it would 'undermine the pillars of the existence of the German Democratic Republic'.

To back up his argument, Gerhard Schürer was dispatched to Moscow to push his views. During a meeting with Nikolai Baibakov, the chairman of Gosplan, the Soviet State Planning Committee, Schürer brought out the official SED economic plan and, putting it on the end of the conference table, graphically described that cutting oil to the GDR would cause 'enormous losses across the whole of the economy'.[22] While Baibakov argued for understanding, his response of 'nothing can be done', came as a bitter disappointment.

In turn, to soothe the East Germans, Brezhnev sent his Central Committee secretary for international relations, Konstantin Russakow, to Berlin to explain that 'a great disaster has befallen us, something that has not happened since the creation of the Soviet Union. If you don't bear the consequences with us, there is the danger that the Soviet Union cannot maintain its international position.'

For effect, Russakov added that Brezhnev instructed him to: 'tell Erich, I cried when I wrote the letters. We have calculated everything. We cannot expect more from our people.' Unmoved, Honecker said the GDR could not be made liable for Russia's plight and warned of the consequences, saying the shortage would undermine the people's trust in the party and state leadership. 'We are deeply affected by your misfortune, but the GDR must remain stable.' As his emotion battled with judgment, a particularly revealing insight into Honecker's confidence (and deep anxiety) came when he slipped in the threat that the GDR might curtail its own deliveries of uranium to the Soviet Union.[23]

Before long, Honecker was branching out toward the Federal Republic. Subsequently, his twice-postponed meeting with Helmut Schmidt took place in December 1981 and proved, mercifully, free of petty wrangles. In his dealings with Bonn, Honecker secured a six-month extension of an interest-free overdraft, expanding the GDR's financial scope for a few months. However, Schmidt was unable to achieve the abolition of stiff compulsory exchange rates for Western visitors to the GDR, which had increased from DM13 to DM25 per day. Assessing his adversary, Schmidt thought Honecker a 'gifted political tactician', but relatively subdued and lacking in self-assurance.[24] 'It never became clear to me,' Schmidt recounted, 'how this mediocre man was able to stay at the head of the Politburo for so long.'[25]

He listened politely as Honecker rattled-off pre-prepared orations on European security, including the barb: 'Good neighbourliness cannot flourish in the shadow of US atomic missiles.'[26] Schmidt unsuccessfully advocated the GDR joining the International Monetary Fund but 'Honecker,' he said, 'believed in all seriousness that the GDR had achieved a world-class level economy and was one of the most important industrial nations in the world'.[27] At the same time, however, 'he was worried about the low exchange rate of the DDM and the GDR's foreign exchange crisis. The desire for more Western foreign currency loans came up again and again.'[28] Moreover, Schmidt wouldn't budge from prior positions to recognise a separate East German citizenship and to elevate the West German mission in East Germany to an embassy. Schmidt extended an invitation for Honecker to visit Bonn, and other than banal generalities, there was no substantial discussion on Poland, despite the cause being seized by the new US President, Ronald Reagan, who continued his ferocious crusade against communism. During a press conference in June 1981, a UPI journalist asked Reagan if events in Poland constituted the beginning of the end of Soviet domination of Eastern Europe. Reagan answered:

> I just think it is impossible – and history reveals this – for any form of government to completely deny freedom to people and have that go on interminably. There eventually comes an end to it. And I think the things we're seeing, not only in Poland but the reports that are coming out of Russia itself about the younger generation and its resistance to long-time government controls, is an indication that communism is an aberration. It's not a normal way of living for human beings, and I think we are seeing the first cracks, the beginning of the end.[29]

Just before Christmas events in Poland were calming, after a successful coup d'état installed General Wojciech Jaruzelski, a man closer to Brezhnev's heart than any of his predecessors.[30] On 13 December, Jaruzelski imposed martial law and consolidated his hold on the country by detaining scores of workers and freethinkers.

Do svidaniya Brezhnev

On 10 November 1982, Leonid Brezhnev died. Two days later, Yuri Andropov – a grey skinned man who rarely smiled – inherited the mantle of power, along with a dire economy. In many ways, Andropov differed from his predecessor in that he was not a convinced communist in the revolutionary sense. Earlier in his career, he had served as ambassador to Hungary, where he was involved in the suppression of the 1956 uprising. By 1967, he was considered so valuable that Brezhnev named him Chairman of the KGB. Described by Markus Wolf as a closet liberal and even a fan of jazz, Andropov enjoyed an amicable relationship with the SED leadership. He encouraged East Berlin's quest to develop new technology, which Honecker recounted included supporting the GDR's production of new photographic technology. In later years, the First Secretary was keen to point out that a young Soviet politburo member, Mikhail Gorbachev, was also impressed by the GDR's scientific and technical development. 'Our republic was given high marks in all areas,' he recounted, 'including for the new multi-spectral camera and other automatic construction systems, extension of the textile industry, of the glass and plastics industries, of chemistry, shipbuilding and so on.'[1]

Behind the Kremlin walls, rumblings of discontent at Honecker's hubris and confidence became more vocal. In fact, Honecker was cocky enough to grumble to Andropov about the antics of Pyotr Abrasimov, the Soviet ambassador in East Berlin, who he complained, 'it was impossible to conduct political dialogue with' given his authoritarian manner and propensity to meet Western ambassadors without reference to the GDR government. Such antics finally led to Abrasimov's recall.

Meanwhile, on the international scene, Honecker kept up his foreign travels with state visits to Syria, Kuwait and Cyprus, where he was presented with the 'Order of Makarios' in recognition of his efforts for 'détente and peace and for his consistent support for the people of Cyprus'.

A sign of Honecker's mortality came on New Year's Eve 1982, when he was supposedly the target of an unsuccessful attempt on his life.

The drama began at 13.00 on the B109 – a Brandenburg country road – when a 41-year-old heating engineer, Paul Essling, tried to overtake the First Secretary's convoy. As the car neared the village of Klosterfelde, Essling cut in at high speed on Honecker's tail but a State Security vehicle managed to force the attacker's Lada off the road.

As he screeched to a halt, Essling jumped out of his car and fired shots from a 7.65mm Walther pistol, hitting a security official in the breastbone and lung. Seconds later, as two Secret Service agents raised their Kalashnikovs, Essling turned the gun on himself and fired a single shot to his head. Honecker, who was uninjured, remained crouched behind the passenger seat of his black Citroen.

Although it seems unlikely that the incident was a targeted assassination (Essling was drunk and had just had an argument with his girlfriend), FRG media caught wind of the story, prompting *Stern's* East Berlin correspondent, Dieter Bub, to claim the Stasi had instructed friends and relatives of Essling to remain silent; by this point however, half of Klosterfelde was gossiping about the incident. In a later article, *Stern* reported Essling had installed kitchens in Wandlitz and was appalled to discover, 'how members of the government and party officials lived in luxury'. Honecker made no statement after the incident, and the episode went unreported in GDR newspapers.[2] After much speculation about events that day, the public prosecutor's office in Neuruppin concluded in 1995 that it had not been an attempted assassination.

Honecker privately enunciated this theory, never believing he would be the target of an assassin's gun.

That winter, the First Secretary underlined his message that the positioning of new US missiles in Western Europe could spark war on German territory. American nuclear deployment plans involved placing 464 cruise missiles – 160 in the United Kingdom, 112 in Italy, ninety-six in West Germany and forty-eight each in Belgium and Holland. In addition, 108 Pershing-2 weapons were due to be deployed in West Germany. 'Let no one forget: these devilish creations will be installed for a nuclear war, for nuclear suicide,' Honecker warned, adding that the FRG would be transformed into a 'nuclear launching pad for Washington', and exposed to a devastating counterstrike. He pleaded:

> Really, no one can be uncertain about the far-reaching consequences for the future of détente that will result from the implementation of this decision. That these weapons should not be deployed is the forceful demand of all those who support peace and a secure future for Europe, because the prospect of a nuclear war is not acceptable.[3]

Between January and December 1983, the press tallied over thirty Honecker speeches, most dealing with some aspect of the nuclear crisis.

Meanwhile, relations between East Berlin and Bonn took a sudden dive. When a West German citizen, Rudolf Burkert, died suddenly during an interrogation at a border checkpoint, the incident presented problems for Honecker and highlighted the rough treatment meted out to FRG visitors to the East.

'Strangely enough,' noted the daily *Westfalen Blatt*, 'many citizens who take almost casual note of the dramatic incidents along the intra-German death strip, have become sensitive to the situation because of the Burkert case. Could this be because the victim was an FRG citizens this time?'[4] Though there was no indication physical force was applied at the border, the episode inflamed widespread anger in the FRG and prompted Helmut Kohl, the Chancellor who had succeeded Helmut Schmidt, to call for a thorough investigation. 'In truth,' Honecker explained to Kohl during a phone call, Burkert 'had suffered a heart attack', and there was 'no culpable conduct by GDR organs'.[5]

However, to make matters worse, another border death involving 54-year-old West German, Guenter Zoellner, caused widespread fury. Zoellner had died when walking from a railway carriage to a border post to be interrogated. It transpired that GDR guards had hauled him off the train after discovering two pounds of ham in his suitcase that was not entered in his customs declaration. From then on, a chorus of Western travellers piped-up with tales of aggressive treatment by East German border authorities, who enjoyed wide latitude to examine travellers. The fallout even reached the pages of *Pravda* in Moscow, which asserted: 'the West Berlin public is following with increasing alarm the inflammatory propaganda campaign launched by extreme right-wing West German and West Berlin circles against the GDR'.[6]

Given the unfolding of events, Honecker cancelled a trip to West Germany planned for late 1983. However, amid this strained time, he secured a financial loan of DM1billion from a consortium of West German banks in a deal engineered by Bavaria's state prime minister, Franz Josef Strauss (Alexander Schalck-Golodkowski played the role of intermediary and applied a deft negotiating touch from a position of comparative weakness).

In June, the GDR gave Bonn securities for the full amount of the loan along with promises to ease currency exchange requirements for Westerners visiting East Germany and, for the first time, the pledge that GDR citizens would have the legal right to apply for permission to emigrate to join close family members in the West. The expectation thus raised was that the GDR would, sooner or later, embark on border relaxations. In an extraordinary diplomatic enterprise, Strauss was received on a private visit with his wife and son at Honecker's hunting lodge, where they were left impressed by his agility and mental responsiveness. 'It's a shame that he's a communist,' Strauss's wife slyly remarked. 'Even after his first few sentences, I was surprised not to be facing the wooden functionary I had seen on TV. He never stepped out of his role, but the image of mask-like rigidity that one creates of him is wrong.'[7] Moreover, Strauss thought the First Secretary spoke very fluently and thoughtfully:

> Honecker, who had survived the Hitlerite Reich, not in Moscow but in German prison, seems to have a somewhat different personal structure [to Ulbricht]. He expressed his readiness to do everything to stabilise and improve the people's living standard, saying that this is why more cooperation is needed.[8]

In the end, the loan proved a victory for Honecker but cast a spotlight on the dire state of the GDR's monetary affairs. By the summer of 1983, East Germany had racked up debts of DM27 billion in the West – a staggering amount requiring annual interest payments of roughly DM3 billion.

Since 1979, these loans had been repaid solely by incurring new debts, as much as 40 per cent of all arrears were payable and due within a year. This was the principal problem, meaning that the GDR had to raise DM10 billion that summer, DM7 billion for repayment and DM3 billion for interest payments, a task beyond its means. With that dire outlook, Bonn's loan covered its debt service to creditors; otherwise, it faced bankruptcy. Evaluating the situation, economist Werner Obst, told West German TV that predominantly the GDR sought to import modern technology with the help of these credits, but it also imported consumer goods.[9] 'With these huge loans it should have modernised its own economy to a point where the repayment of the credits would have been possible, and this is precisely what did not happen.' The ultimate blame did not go solely to foreign trade, Obst explained, rather, it was necessary to recall that the GDR had a planned economy in which profitability was not the dominant principle:

> As a result, there is careless use of capital, material and labour. We call this an enormous squandering of all resources in the GDR, so that notwithstanding the mass use of labour and despite longer work time, their level of productivity is only about half the FRG's. Measured against the former performance of this part of Germany, this is a situation for which the communist party leadership must take the responsibility.[10]

The bottom line: Honecker's seemingly healthy economy was built on sand.

As often happened after shaky periods in GDR-FRG relations, the climate suddenly improved. In September, Honecker greeted West Berlin's Mayor,

Richard von Weizsäcker, and signalled his willingness to relax money exchange rules for visiting Westerners. During his trip, the mayor met the SED cabinet, including Egon Krenz, whose star was steadily rising. By this point, he had become the youngest member of the Politburo and taken on the role of secretary of the central committee with responsibility for security; the same position Honecker had held until 1971. Within the coming year, Krenz gained supreme prominence when appointed Honecker's deputy on the Council of State, thus making him the second-most powerful man in the country.

Uncertain Times

On 9 February 1984, Yuri Andropov died of a chronic kidney ailment after less than fifteen months in the job. When a four-day period of official mourning ended, he was succeeded by 72-year-old Konstantin Chernenko, a sharp-tongued geriatric, suffering from emphysema and cirrhosis of the liver. Temperamentally, Chernenko was Honecker's opposite, a dour-faced, analytical politician who mastered the detailed complexities of policy, and was never happy to let others lead or influence him. Worse still, he loathed Honecker's arrogance and East Germany's ambitious foreign policy, and was especially critical of the First Secretary's plans for a five-day visit to Bonn, scheduled for late September.

Having watched warming relations between the two Germanys with suspicion, the old Russian fretted about the GDR's increasing financial dependence on the Federal Republic, fearing Helmut Kohl was trying to foster a pan-Germanic national identity to supersede socialist solidarity.

To spook the SED leadership, Chernenko engineered a sharp article in *Pravda* attacking Honecker for accepting credit from West German banks in return for easing restrictions on travel between East and West Germany.[1] Having listened calmly to Moscow's reservations, Honecker stood firmly by his intention to visit Bonn, a move which led *Pravda* to follow-up with a second rebuke, under the banner headline: 'On the wrong path', which accused Bonn of using an economic lever to change the post-war order in Europe and destabilise the GDR. In Bonn, the Chief government spokesman, Peter Boenisch, sharply denied a report in *Bild* claiming FRG Foreign Minister, Hans-Dietrich Genscher, was preparing an 'emergency flight' to Moscow to save the Honecker visit.[2] However, when the West German Minister of State, Philip Jenninger, worriedly picked up the phone to ask Honecker directly about the visit, he reportedly replied: 'The GDR's foreign policy is made in Berlin and not in Moscow.' Despite his bluster, the die was cast in the Kremlin on 17 August, when the Soviet leader delivered Honecker a thorough dressing down.

Flanked by Minister of Agriculture Mikhail Gorbachev and Defence Minister Dmitriy Ustinov – Chernenko charged that the FRG was the 'main executor' of US policy in Europe, while the Bundeswehr had grown from an army that was formed for defence purposes 'into the main force of NATO'.

As Honecker listened in silence, Chernenko gave a sour account of West Germany's offensive military doctrine saying Bonn and Washington acted in full agreement: 'The US supports new missiles in Europe; called a crusade against socialism ... the FRG is the executor of Reagan's politics on our continent.' A grey-faced Ustinov declared the course of the GDR would affect Soviet security interests and the loyalty of the National People's Army and facilitate espionage opportunities for NATO. However, the main problem for the Soviet leadership was 'the financial dependencies of the GDR on the FRG'. Reading from typewritten papers, Chernenko said any hopes Honecker harboured for a visit to Bonn were not desirable. 'You ought to remember,' he warned, 'that the development of relations between East and West Germany must always respect the security interests of the Soviet Union first and foremost.' Along the way, he also expressed concern that GDR foreign policy contacts with Western industrialised countries were intensifying, a reference to a January visit by the Canadian Prime Minister, Pierre Elliot Trudeau to East Berlin, and the Prime Minister of Sweden, Olof Palme's, meeting with Honecker in Stralsund during June. The German delegation was stunned by the Soviet leader's aggression. According to Markus Wolf, the meeting broke up in a frosty atmosphere. 'Honecker, enraged at his humiliation, had indulged in a rare show of temper once he was alone again with his team and mocked Chernenko's school-masterly act.' From then on, Wolf recalled the impasse over the Bonn visit dominated all other questions with Moscow: 'I had never known a period when things were so strained.' East German agents listening in to a phone call between the FRG's Press Spokesman Klaus Bolling, and another senior West German official discussing the Honecker-Chernenko spat transcribed the following brief exchange: 'This is turning into a really big deal,' Bolling observed, 'It's more exciting than Dallas and Dynasty put together!'[3]

Over the next few days, Honecker sulked. He cast around for a way to save his Bonn trip and found support from Romania's Ceausescu, and Janos Kadar, the Hungarian who was highly esteemed by Brezhnev and Andropov. But hard as it was to swallow, the First Secretary acquiesced to Soviet demands and cancelled the trip.

Watching from afar, John Hughes, a spokesman from the US State Department, added to East German discomfort. 'I think you have to look at the motivation of Mr Honecker and look at whatever pressures there may have been on him,' he said. 'Moscow clearly has not had a vested interest in this meeting going ahead.'[4]

Interestingly, remarking on the saga in his secret 'Annual Report on the GDR to London', the British Ambassador in East Berlin, Timothy Everard, observed that Honecker did 'not look much chastened', but 'more like a man biding his time', confident that mutual interests would eventually reassert the importance of inner German relations.[5] 'Meanwhile,' the report added, 'his standing up to the Russians, even if temporarily faced down, has been good for his own public image'. Everard remarked that while Honecker was 'not exactly popular', he was respected by broad sections of the population 'both for his inner-German policies and for his evident concern for their material progress'.[6]

Meanwhile, the ailing Chernenko – literally on his last legs and only kept alive by doctors – struggled to keep up with other troubles, including the international backlash when Soviet forces shot down a South Korean airliner that accidentally strayed into Russian air space, with the loss of 269 lives. Then, in the sabre-rattling spirit of 1983, Ronald Reagan was re-elected US President in November, signalling gloomy implications for already strained relations. This was made worse by Reagan's remark that the Soviet Union was an 'evil empire ... the focus of evil in the modern world'.[7]

Meanwhile, another crisis burst upon Honecker when 150 GDR citizens, desperate to gain passage to the West, began squatting at the FRG embassy in Prague, some even climbed over the gates seeking refuge. At the same time, others sought sanctuary in Western embassies in Warsaw, Budapest and Bucharest. This embarrassing trend even saw the niece of Willi Stoph enter the Prague embassy, she was permitted to emigrate to West Germany soon after. The squatting drama even played-out a few blocks from the SED headquarters when fifty-four East Germans took refuge in the FRG mission in East Berlin and were eventually 'bought out' for a reported US$1.8 million, adding a psychological strain on already delicate ties between the two Germanys.

Despite these embarrassments, an energetic 73-year-old Erich Honecker continued to dominate the SED and Government. By the beginning of 1985, the British ambassador observed how he retained the appearance of running the country flawlessly, noting his 'skilful and realistic management' reduced the conflicting pressures on and within the GDR – 'especially that of people hankering to enjoy the interests and satisfactions of the modern world'. Age, too, had made him gentler in manner, he charmed visitors and flattered colleagues where he could. His self-confidence became even more assured when the decrepit Chernenko died on 11 March and was replaced by Mikhail Gorbachev, the youngest member of the ruling Soviet Politburo. In way of congratulation, Honecker's carefully prepared laudatory message sending 'cordial and fraternal greetings and congratulations' was broadcast twice that same day on GDR state television:

> The CPSU Central Committee elected into this highest function
> of Lenin's party a tested Marxist-Leninst and internationalist, a
> good friend and comrade who enjoys the respect and high esteem
> of the communists and all working people in the GDR. The GDR

and the SED will continue to be a close ally, loyal friend and reliable companion of Lenin's country.

With all their strength, the GDR citizens support the USSR's consistent struggle, rich in initiative, for the ensuring of peace and the prevention of a nuclear catastrophe. Inspired by the 40th anniversary of victory over fascism and our people's liberation by the glorious Soviet Army, the workers in our country attain great achievements for the comprehensive strengthening of the first worker-peasant state on German soil and firm member of the socialist community.

With communist greetings,
Erich Honecker.[8]

Ironically – given his efforts to keep them apart – it was Chernenko's funeral that provided a venue for the first meeting between Honecker and the new Federal Chancellor Helmut Kohl at a guest house in the Lenin Hills above Moscow. On that occasion, Honecker also enjoyed a brief chat with Gorbachev who, at 54, was the first Soviet leader to have grown up after the Second World War and the Stalin era.

To begin with, his assumption was viewed positively in East Berlin, despite his announcement at Chernenko's funeral that the Brezhnev Doctrine (the USSR would intervene to save regimes in Eastern Europe) was no longer Soviet policy. However, Gorbachev did extend the validity of the Warsaw Pact treaty for a further twenty-four years, before embarking on his own reform programme to drag the Soviet Union out of political and economic stagnation.

In contrast, Honecker and his administration had become slightly more easy-going. The SED regime's struggle against the ideological competition of the church was replaced by a kind of truce. Not that the church had become 'harmless', it still provided vocal opposition to a multitude of wrongs, especially on issues of pollution and the environment. In international affairs, Honecker, meanwhile, busied himself with a visit to Italy in April, where he met with Pope John Paul II, marking his first state visit to a NATO country. After flying back to Berlin invigorated, any feelings of pride soon evaporated as he became the butt of a joke when newspapers splashed a photo showing him together with the pope. The gag: 'Karl Marx called religion the "opiate of the people", thus Honi [*sic*] is now in the opium den.'

After a few days at his hunting sanctuary, Honecker was in Athens, then back in Berlin hosting French Prime Minister Laurent Fabius, the first government leader from the three Western Powers to visit the GDR. Honecker also found time to deliver a speech outside the restored Semper Opera in Dresden before 150,000 people, marking the Allied bombing of the city in 1945. 'Forty years ago, everything of German and world cultural value concentrated here in such an impressive and unique way was reduced to rubble and ashes in a matter of hours,' he said. 'The commemoration of this event marks a warning and commitment by us not to allow a third world war.'[9]

Throughout this period, Honecker continued to correspond with Helmut Kohl and, during the frantic pace of change in the Soviet Union, held his first one-on-one meeting with Gorbachev in May 1985 at the Kremlin – it was a stiff and distant affair, but a far cry from the prickly tension he endured with Chernenko. A far more pleasurable encounter came with Willy Brandt's three-day visit to East Berlin in September. Unlike in 1970 – when he was portrayed as a white knight in Erfurt – Brandt's carefully orchestrated itinerary shielded him from public view. Honecker need not have worried, the only hiccup occurred at a news conference where German journalists spared Brandt embarrassment about the Guillaume affair, but a less considerate American asked whether he had 'pardoned Honecker' for 'slipping the spy' into the Bonn Chancellery. After a deathly silence, Brandt said: 'Ten years is a long time in politics. I can't recall that the name you mentioned came up in our talks.'

All in all, 1985 proved an eventful year in Politburo affairs; two old-guard hardliners removed themselves; Defence Minister Heinrich Hoffmann by heart attack and Konrad Naumann – the maladroit Berlin party chief – by a supposed coup attempt which took place in two phases.

In early November, Naumann recklessly misbehaved during a surreal encounter with a group of academics from the Academy of Social Sciences while discussing plans for the 750th anniversary of Berlin. Naumann, who had a decades-long reputation for drinking, was already tipsy when he barked at the scientists: 'Shall I tell you some facts, or do you want to hear the shit printed in *Neues Deutschland*?'

The remark caused a ruffle and one of the professors criticised Naumann saying: 'You are also just working to get a black limousine.' Sarcastically, he replied: 'Do you drive a Trabi?' When the academics burst out laughing, Naumann lost his self-control, launching into an obscenity-laced tirade. He accused the scientists of being an incompetent and 'lazy bunch, eager for money', and claimed things would change 'when he took over' the Central Committee Secretariat for Science and Culture.

Incensed, professors protested to Honecker. A week later, Naumann was confronted and accused in a tense Politburo session but denied everything, complaining he had become the victim of slander. However, when Honecker tartly responded by producing a mini-Dictaphone containing a tape-recording of the academy outburst, Naumann punched back by calling Honecker an 'impotent dwarf'. Like an arsonist firefighter, Naumann went on to say that he enjoyed the support of Berlin construction workers who would tear down the 'Politburo residences in Wandlitz, the ghetto of the prominent people.'

177

Honecker answered tersely: 'He who speaks like that is sick.' Five minutes later Naumann was out of a job.

A slightly different version of events from Professor Herbert Meissner, a Fellow from the Academy of Sciences, added granular detail to the incident.[10] Interviewed by the BND in 1986, he claimed Honecker was to be overthrown by Naumann and the 'Kremlin was said to have agreed'. In Meissner's version, Egon Krenz was to be installed as First Secretary, but the putsch attempt collapsed during the aforementioned showdown. As to Honecker's reaction at the 'impotent dwarf' jibe, Meissner said the First Secretary shook his head and shrieked: 'There have been people for decades who have tried to oppose me. It did them no good. Get out of here!' In his memoirs, Günter Schabowski noted 'Naumann was a keen drinker but not a hard drinker – he bragged about his plans as general secretary. He already had the list for his Politburo ready.'[11] He had few scruples, according to Schabowski, despite having been close to Honecker since the 1950s. 'Honecker is now firmly determined to stay in office at least until the 1991 party congress,' Meissner told the BND. 'He feels fit aside from high blood pressure because of his age. Moreover, he wants to fulfil one wish. After the 1987 Bundestag elections, he wants to come to the FRG to see the Saarland, his homeland, once again.' (Günter Schabowski became the new East Berlin party chief in place of Naumann)

Evil Partnerships

At 01.44 on 5 April 1986, three people were killed and 153 injured, including sixty Americans, when a powerful bomb exploded in a packed West Berlin nightclub popular with US servicemen. The *La Belle* club in the American sector was torn apart in what was the most shocking and disturbing crime in Berlin for a decade. No one took responsibility for the blast, but intelligence reports filtering through to President Reagan led the United States to blame the attack on Libyans working from East Berlin. As the news broke, phone calls ricocheted back and forth between Honecker and Mielke. It was established that the American evidence stemmed from an intercepted telephone call between Colonel Ghaddafi and diplomats at the Libyan mission in East Berlin, linking Ghaddafi directly to the atrocity. The story became even murkier when it later emerged that Honecker, Krenz and Axen were said to have been briefed in 1985 about a planned attack by Libyan terrorists on a US establishment in West Berlin.[1]

According to *Stern*, the Stasi had warned Honecker repeatedly of a possible bomb attack but by one means or another, he issued repeated instructions not to interfere. In other words, let them get on with it.[2] Even after the incident, he allegedly gave instructions to be kept up to date about operational measures but asked Stasi agents to do nothing which might harm relations with Libya.

Die Welt went further, reporting that a Stasi colonel who, following the attack, wanted to put an end to the activities of the terrorists, was unceremoniously dismissed on the instructions of the SED leadership.[3] In the tumult, Bruce W. Clark, a US Political Advisor on East Germany with the State Department office on Central European Affairs, remembered the US ambassador, Frank Meehan, paying a visit to the Foreign Ministry to ask the GDR to act against the Libyan embassy in East Berlin. 'The officials told him that they had no idea what he was talking about, and if his accusations were true, it was just shocking.'[4] Looking back, Markus Wolf thought the bombing was the 'logical culmination' of the decision to allow extremists to use East Berlin as an occasional base. Mielke never anticipated the gratuitous risks, he explained, but dealings with the terrorists 'simply swung out of his control'.[5] Ten days after the bombing, US President Ronald Reagan ordered retaliatory strikes on Tripoli and Benghazi in Libya. (The action was widely seen as an attempt to kill Ghaddafi.)

Barely three weeks after the *La Belle* atrocity, the fallout was eclipsed by another explosion, this time at the Chernobyl nuclear reactor in Ukraine. As the world confronted the news that radioactive clouds were spreading across Europe, GDR TV kept shtum. Yet again, Western media became an important source of information for East Germans who found themselves helpless in watching the direction changes of the winds carrying radiation-rich clouds from the fallout area. In Ukraine, Russian responders were making up solutions as they went along as the machinery of government stagnated. After five days of torrid headlines in the West, GDR domestic radio launched a blistering attack on 'doom-mongers':

> The accident in the Chernobyl nuclear power station and its tragic consequences for the people employed there is a fact. The readings of radiation measurements are another fact. According to the FRG Nuclear Research Centre in Karlsruhe, the radioactivity level poses no danger to health. Yet media in the FRG, of all countries, are having a field day. Their motives are obvious. *Bild* newspaper is once again serving up horror stories as ordered. Banner headlines are the order of the day: Atom Dust – Fresh Danger; Children's Playgrounds Contaminated; or Mothers, Shower Your Kids.
>
> It conjures up apocalyptic visions against its better knowledge yet well knows what impact its enlightenment will have. Its main purpose is to project the Russians as the power of evil, a sinister menace looming on the horizon. Crop Losses in Prospect; Fear of Poison Rain; Vegetables May be Contaminated; and other horrific reports round out the picture. The gutter press like *Bild* quote from each other, hoping perhaps to enhance their credibility. They run all this under the headline of Nuclear Catastrophe and want to send chills up your spine. The very mention of Moscow is meant to frighten *Bild* readers.[6]

In the midst of the disaster, the growing environmentalist movement became markedly more hostile against nuclear energy, especially given East Germany had a nuclear power station at Greismald, 120km from the south coast of Denmark. Activists also decried the flagrant abuse of nature, factories bellowing out gaseous mixtures, increasing militarisation and urban decay – many historic buildings around the country had gone to seed. True to form, as the government downplayed Chernobyl, it also brushed aside concerns about smog, acid rain and damage to forests.

Later that year, protest action by Greenpeace activists took place in front of the GDR Ministry of the Environment against the leaching of salt into the

Werra River from potash mines in Thuringia, where an average daily quantity of 40,000 tons of brine was dumped into the river, leaving it nearly dead biologically. For campaigners, the appalling effects of environmental neglect could be seen in soot-covered Bitterfeld, in the district of Saxony-Anhalt where chemical factories – using coal-based products to manufacture pesticides, dyes and plastics – turned the town and surrounding region into a hazardous landscape. Ash, soot and dust, chlorine and hydrochloric acid were just a few of the highly toxic substances belched out into the atmosphere.

Most alarming, eye ailments, together with lung and skin diseases were common. Physicians noticed the children of Bitterfeld showed differences in size and weight and that girls showed delayed bone development.

The air in Halle or Leipzig was about twice as dirty as in Duesseldorf or Tokyo. The dirt and smog were mainly produced by soft coal which supplied about 6 per cent of GDR energy and put out much more sulphur dioxide, dust and ashes than other raw materials. There were too few dams and reservoirs, meaning industrial enterprises used the same water up to five times. Add to that the fact that 50 per cent of household sewage flowed unpurified into the environment, deteriorating drinking water supplies. East German drinking water in some regions contained up to 260 milligrams of nitrate per litre – a dangerous amount.

Remarkably, the neglect of environmental protection was even criticised in the official organ of the Central Council of the SED youth organisation. 'For economic and political necessities, it is impossible at the moment to solve comprehensively the discrepancy between the required effectiveness of the national economy and the necessary environmental protection.' Instead of investing to eliminate the damage to the environment, *FORUM* lamented, 'some enterprises prefer to pay high fines regularly, which is considerably cheaper'.[7]

Meanwhile, during the upheaval in the Soviet Union, political clouds gathered over Gorbachev as the conservative old guard accused him of pushing reform too far, too fast. Since taking office, he had launched his restructuring, known as 'perestroika', alongside a crusade against alcoholism, crime, indifference, laziness and mismanagement, and raged about the deficiencies of an economy that, as he put it, could make a spacecraft rendezvous with Venus but 'cannot supply its own people with enough food, consumer goods and healthcare'.

While Honecker agreed Soviet society was ripe for transformation, he was stunned at the giddying speed of change. Of particular concern were reforms reducing the Party's ability to meddle in economic decisions, new press freedoms (which allowed journalists to criticise past mistakes and poke scorn at officials who committed new ones), the slashing of billions spent on subsidising food and the introduction of more 'democracy'. Aggravating his distrust was the appointment of a special party commission to investigate the rights and wrongs of Stalin's purges and the rehabilitation of his victims.

At a Warsaw Pact meeting of Central Committee secretaries in the Polish capital in January 1987, the Soviet delegation was forced to listen to a chorus of disquiet. Fists were shaken as the old guard bemoaned the spill over from perestroika was causing 'political discomfitures'. Opening proceedings, Czech leader Gustav Husák said piously that it was unwise to regard the Soviet reform process as irreversible. Bulgarian leader, Todor Hristov Zhivkov, kept in mind how Khrushchev's reforms resulted in the Hungarian revolt. Having lapped-up Husák and Zhivkov's performances, Honecker put on an energetic one-man show by asserting Soviet reforms might trigger a Yugoslav-style break with Marxist-Leninism. For good measure, he branded Mikhail Shatrov's revisionist new play about Lenin a 'betrayal' of the October Revolution and argued against dissident Andrei Sakharov's release from exile in Gorki. Faced with such opposition, the solution, according to Gorbachev, was to turn perestroika into a success and make the naysayers want to imitate it.

Beyond the artificial calm of the Warsaw Pact meeting, Gorbachev privately warned the Soviet Politburo if the outrages continued, he would stop supplies of gas and oil to the GDR or demand payment in hard currency. By this point, Gorbachev's suspicions of the GDR's impressive economic figures had prompted him to privately liken Honecker to Ostap Bender, a fictional conman and the protagonist in the novel *The Twelve Chairs*.[8] He came to detest Honecker's habit of praising himself in the presence of senior Soviet officials, while continually extolling the GDR's stability and economic prosperity.

An impatient man, Gorbachev found it hard to tolerate such smugness and at one point supposedly even considered overthrowing Honecker. As the story goes, he even sounded out Hans Modrow, the moderate SED leader in Dresden, as a possible successor. At the same time, it was also alleged that diplomats from the Russian Embassy in East Berlin had been spreading the word that Modrow was considered by Gorbachev as Honecker's preferred successor. (Rumours abounded but were never proven that Gorbachev and Modrow had known each other at university in Moscow during the 1950s.) Years later, the *Berlin Morgenpost* claimed Valentin Falin, the former Soviet ambassador to Bonn, confirmed the reports.[9] Further insight was provided by the former Russian ambassador to the GDR, Vyacheslav Kochemasov who divulged in a 1992 *Der Spiegel* interview, that Werner Krolikowski, First Deputy Chairman of the GDR Ministerial Council, had confided that conditions in the Politburo were 'unbearable', and policy was driven by dogma. Discussion and debate, he said, 'had been phased out', and an 'utterly implausible' communications strategy was introduced. The feeling, he claimed, was that something must be done: the leader must be replaced.[10]

However, in the upshot, nothing happened. Interestingly, though, the affair sheds light on an attempt to discredit Honecker by Willi Stoph the previous year. After growing impatience with the SED leader's dalliances with Western personalities, Stoph's mind apparently oscillated from day to day between the two poles of uncertainty: Honecker's romance with the West, which could lead to something like a reunification; and Gorbachev's warming relationship with the USA, which could also ease relations with the FRG. Ever suspicious, it is likely the SED leader knew about Stoph's secret note to Gorbachev in early 1986 detailing Honecker's hostility to Soviet reforms and shoddy economic management. No doubt Stoph had hoped and expected to be rewarded, but Gorbachev never wrote back – an indication that (at that point, at least) he had no desire to support dissent. (But it is possible he knew that if Stoph did mount a successful coup, he would not encourage reforms thereafter. As it was, Stoph became hesitant and indecisive, unwilling to act against Honecker without Soviet backing.)

It is worth noting that Politburo members Heinz Hoffmann, Alfred Neumann, Erich Mielke and the SED's chief ideologue, Kurt Hager, were also unclear about what exactly Honecker was trying to achieve with his foreign dalliances. They were equally weary of a Gorbachev–Reagan summit in Geneva where both leaders committed to an even military balance. In fact, during an interview with the West German news magazine *Stern*, Kurt Hager further distanced the GDR from Gorbachev's policies with a rhetorical question: 'Would you feel obliged to put up new wallpaper in your apartment if your neighbour were to wallpaper his?' The statement left few people in any doubt that Gorbachev's reform policy was not a model for the GDR.

In the wider world that year, Helmut Kohl won the federal elections for the second time in January 1987, prompting Gorbachev to declare his willingness to intensify cooperation 'at all levels' in German-Soviet relations, which he considered of 'central importance' for future foreign policy. By July, FRG President Weizsaecker was embarking on a state visit to Moscow and issuing a reciprocal invitation (which was realised in June 1989).

This marked improvement in ties between Moscow and Bonn, and led Gorbachev to finally grant Honecker permission to make his often-postponed visit to West Germany. Vyacheslav Kochemasov, the Russian ambassador in Berlin, remembered the SED leader displaying a feeling of contentment and relief when the trip was confirmed, 'as if the great tension that had prevailed up to that point had been released'. Almost immediately, Volkskammer president Horst Sindermann, was dispatched on a lightning visit to Bonn to firm out details, while exhaustive talks opened over who Honecker would speak with, subjects for discussion, after-dinner speeches; itinerary; and the text of a joint communiqué at the end of the visit.

Soon, unofficial articles of greeting – including one from Helmut Schmidt – appeared in the West German media. Writing in *Die Zeit*, Schmidt noted 'even if Erich Honecker, and we can never be friends, in terms of party or politics in general, let us receive him honourably. Receive him as one of our brothers!'[11] Likewise, Oscar Lafontaine, the prime minister of Saarland and deputy head of the SPD, noted 'the SED general secretary as a man who, like all natives of Saarland, was capable of not taking things too seriously'.[12]

The Bonn Visit

The moment that had already been so elaborately labelled as historic by the West German media, began at 08.00 on 7 September 1987 at Bonn airport. Under a bright sky, Honecker was welcomed to West Germany with pomp and ceremony as the Bundeswehr band played the East German national anthem 'Auferstanden aus Ruinen' and a military honour guard gave the salute.

Although officially described as a 'working visit', the SED leader was afforded all the protocol honours of a state visitor, making Germany's two-state identity clearly visible throughout the world. At a special lunch, Federal President Weizsäcker welcomed his guest as a 'German among Germans' and called for further 'system-opening cooperation'.

That same night at dinner, using road-tested language, Honecker urged the FRG to accept the reality of two German nations, warning against 'sweet dreams' of reunification. In response, Kohl summed up the issue in a nutshell, saying on fundamental points: 'We are as far apart as ever. No one could expect anything else.' Concluding his speech, he added: 'I want to say once again on behalf of the federal government – we are firm about the unity of the German nation.' In closing, Kohl called for an end to the shooting of would-be escapees from East German territory. Honecker, meanwhile, sat silent.

The trip continued with a visit to North Rhine-Westphalia, followed by a journey to Essen to meet with leading representatives of the FRG economy. The following morning, Honecker was in Trier being feted by Minister-President of Rhineland-Palatinate Bernhard Vogel.

On the final leg of the trip, though, policy took a back seat for a jubilant visit to the Saarland and a pilgrimage to his childhood home. He travelled by motorcade to Neunkirchen, where he stopped in Wiebelskirchen district to meet his younger sister, 70-year-old Gertrud, before visiting the graves of his parents, Wilhelm and Karoline. 'The East German leader was welcomed by a cheering crowd of about 1,000 people who lined the streets as his motorcade drove through the town,' AP reported. 'As he stepped out of the car and went into the green family house, some people waved East German flags but about twenty demonstrators carried signs protesting the shoot-to-kill orders and demanding freedom for East German political prisoners.'[1]

There were encounters with old friends and new admirers at a reception by the Lord Mayor in the Neunkirchen community hall, where – much to the surprise of Moscow and Erich Mielke – Honecker gave an emotional speech in which he spoke – in an off-the-cuff remark – of a day when Germans would no longer be divided by borders: 'The day will come when borders no longer separate us, but unite us, just like the border between the German Democratic Republic and Poland.' Though the remark probably revealed more about Honecker's overwrought nerves than of his true convictions, West German tabloid *Bild* hit the newsstands with the quote: 'Sensation! Erich Honecker: Our border can fall.' *Die Welt* was more cautious, noting the SED leaders' statement on the transitory nature of borders should be viewed carefully. 'The border with Poland is not a dividing line between two different systems that Honecker compared to fire and water. Thus, we might suspect he wanted to suggest reunification under socialist premises.'[2] Honecker's 'Neunkirchen remarks' noted the *Frankfurter Rundschau*, 'show that the man at the top of the GDR now is aware that shots at the Wall are the worst blemish of his state.'[3] Speaking to reporters outside Neunkirchen community hall, Honecker said:

> I was deeply impressed by the friendly reception accorded to me. The reunion with old acquaintances, friends and comrades in arms was a moving moment for me. I am grateful primarily to the mayor of Neunkirchen, Peter Neubert, and the people of the town for giving me this opportunity during my official visit to the FRG. I would like to say that my activities on the Saar have no more faded from by memory than has the time of the anti-fascist struggle in the Ruhr area, in Essen, Baden-Wuerttemberg and Berlin, which I waged with many staunch comrades in arms.[4]

Honecker's travels took him to Munich, where he held talks with Franz Josef Strauss in the Bavarian State Chancellery before visiting the Dachau concentration camp to meet with survivors. He was back in East Berlin that same evening. For all its publicity value, there were no breakthroughs on human rights or disarmament in what was primarily a symbolic gesture of goodwill between the two German states.

It was also clear that despite their close contacts, the two leaders had little natural affinity. However, their 'frank exchange of views' secured agreement on intensifying bilateral contacts in fields such as sports, improving rail connections to Berlin, expansion and repair of motorways and measures for environmental protection, including the desulphurisation of the GDR lignite industry. A further relaxation of travel visas to East Berlin (the FRG wanted tourists to be able to spend two days there) were delayed due to Honecker's concerns over drugs and AIDS – two perils he claimed were spread by the daily flood of tourists from the West. He also expressed reluctance to commit himself fully to Bonn's wish to allow visitors from the West to take bicycles into the GDR. However, it was agreed to ease restrictions on the importation of reading matter (technical or professional periodicals), cassette tapes and videos from the FRG. The visit, for Honecker, at least, had been spectacularly successful. 'In the future,' lamented a Christian Democrat politician in West Germany, 'we will have to do with an even more self-confident GDR.'[5]

In a revealing interview with Belgian journalists on 14 October 1987, the General Secretary was asked, 'The reforms being carried out in the Soviet Union seem not to have hit upon a particularly positive echo in the GDR. Do you think that they are little suited to the country you lead?'[6] Although Honecker assured journalists that they had the 'wrong impression', he explained the restructuring introduced in the Soviet Union was being followed in the GDR with 'much sympathy and great interest':

> As you know, for decades' friendship and constantly deepening cooperation with the Soviet Union have been a basic pillar of our policies. The exchange of information and experiences on the building of socialism is a firm constituent of this close cooperation. In this, we learn from one another, as is usual between friends. Life again and again confirms that socialism is not a rigid and unchanging structure, as it is portrayed in the West. Newly developing issues and problems of social development require new ways and solutions. It is only important that each country recognises this in time and finds solutions that are relevant to the existing concrete conditions.
>
> Of course, we, too, in the GDR, as in other socialist countries, have undertaken necessary structural changes. I would remind you that for years we have been orientated toward the comprehensive intensification of production, as well as toward the speeding up of production and the application of key technologies, microelectronics in particular. This has put us in the position of continuing our tried and trusted course of the unity of economic and social policy, in spite of complicated international conditions. A very important step on our side was the creation at the end of the 1970s and the beginning of the 1980s of the combines, which today form the backbone of our economy. Measures for raising the autonomy of combines and factories were resolved and are having positive effects. Therefore, we are not 'anti-reform', but are constantly checking where changes are necessary and how

they are to be affected. To this end, many broad consultations and discussions are held about this, in which millions of citizens participate. The basic principle is: We will make changes when it is necessary and do that which serves the further strengthening of socialism and the well-being of our people.[7]

During 1988, Honecker's health slipped as he endured several bouts of influenza, muscle weakness and lack of vitality. Even his daily shot of lemon juice failed to ward off illness. Physically, his back was slightly bent, his vocal cords strained, and he had lost considerable weight.

On the work front, while cheered by Moscow's pledge to start a pull-out from Afghanistan and withdraw nuclear missiles from the GDR, he was irked by a stream of homilies on perestroika and glasnost appearing in the socialist press. Among these, the former Czech leader, Alexander Dubček giving his first interview in nearly twenty years, declared the 1968 Soviet-led invasion that ousted him would have been 'unthinkable' had Gorbachev been in power then.

For two decades, Honecker blotted out the memory of the man connected with the 'Prague Spring', but now – splashed on the front page of the Italian communist daily *L'Unita* – Dubček complained of being pushed to the margins of society, working as a forestry official and monitored under police surveillance until Gorbachev visited Prague in 1987. 'After that, I didn't see the police anymore,' Dubček gushed, referring to his newly found freedom.

Equally perplexing was the call of a Moscow weekly for the restoration of citizenship to dissident Alexander Solzhenitsyn. In an unblushingly frank leader, the paper lauded a 'remarkable son of Russia', who should not have been expelled in 1974. An outspoken critic of communism, Solzhenitsyn had helped to raise international awareness of political repression and the dehumanising Gulag system. Honecker, himself, proved unforgiving to his own party comrades seeking rehabilitation. He ignored Konrad Naumann's (the drunken coupist) appeals for a second chance. 'I feel that at 58 years of age, I am able and ready to meet other party duties,' Naumann pleaded in vain – he was never destined to recover office.[8]

Throughout that winter, Honecker continued to gaze West. He succeeded in boosting the GDR's international legitimacy with a three-day visit to France where he was feted by President Francois Mitterrand. In Paris, the two agreed that the superpowers should halve their nuclear arsenals but differed on calls for a freeze on short-range missiles. Honecker also referred to a GDR proposal for a chemical-weapon-free zone in Central Europe but said a global ban 'would of course be even better'.[9] In a front-page commentary, *Le Monde* said the visit was a result of 'normalisation of relations between East Germany and Western

Europe'. Toasting Honecker at the Elysee Palace, Mitterrand pronounced that Europe 'must not be the mute witness or the passive prize of East-West relations', and the occasion showed the desire for reconciliation between 'the French and the Germans, all the Germans, wherever they find themselves'. The only low point came when the Prime Minister, Jacques Chirac, said he hoped the Berlin Wall would fall one day, 'just like the useless and ridiculous walls of fortified cities of earlier times have fallen'.[10] Honecker, who had last seen Paris in 1935, toured the royal palace at Versailles, dined in the Eiffel Tower and attended a performance by famed mime artist Marcel Marceau.

However, on his return to Berlin, he could not settle. That winter, he held other enthusiastic encounters with Western politicians, including FDP federal chairman Otto Graf Lambsdorff and the governing mayor of West Berlin, Eberhard Diepgen, who managed to secure overnight stays for West Berliners visiting the East on day trips. Soon after, the red carpet was rolled out for Rhineland-Palatinate Minister-President Bernhard Vogel in East Berlin.

For these visiting dignitaries, it was quite clear the GDR was still not jumping on Gorbachev's revolutionary train which was beginning to derail regimes across the Soviet bloc. On 19 February, news arrived that more than 100,000 demonstrators in Lithuania rolled out loudspeakers to demand political change and independence. A week later, on 24 February, 3,000 people in the Soviet Republic of Estonia defied a ban to rally in support of independence. Officials were greeted with shouts of 'Freedom now!' By 25 March, demonstrations had spread to Czechoslovakia where Roman Catholic groups marked the first mass protest against the socialist government since the sixties. Even more concerning, news arrived from Hungary; where Honecker's long-time friend Janos Kadar was cast into political oblivion after attempting to censure reformists.

As problems in the socialist world intensified, ARD, ZDF and West German satellite channels devoted more airtime to the unrest. The 'negative occurrences' taking place in Hungary, Czechoslovakia and elsewhere 'immediately enter the German Democratic Republic via Western TV,' Honecker fumed. When speaking with Vadim Medvedev, a Gorbachev aide and ideologist, he asserted the West was 'not happy with the calm in the GDR. We must tackle the problem ideologically.'[11] Meanwhile, new hostile voices began beaming in from the West. Radio Glasnost, a series on the West Berlin station Radio 100, started reporting on taboo subjects and opposition activities using material smuggled into West Berlin. At the same time, Roland Jahn, an earthy, blunt journalist and former opposition activist who had been expelled from the GDR in 1983, smuggled video cameras into the GDR, enabling unique reporting for his show on SFB. As usual, the SED leadership was driven to despair by the RIAS station in the American sector.

For a short period during May, events in Honecker's family overtook work priorities. When his granddaughter Mariana died of a viral infection, amplified by air pollution, he was left devastated. Reinhardt Andert:

> She had, on a regular basis, larynx inflammations, maybe every six weeks. There was a female pediatrist on the other side of the street. She could have given medication and the problem would have been settled. But for Honecker's family, they had to use the government hospital. So, they had to call and everything … it took about half an hour, but the child had already suffocated.[12]

Shortly after Mariana's funeral, Honecker set about keeping the church on a tighter leash. Having already warned Werner Leich, the chairman of the conference of ecclesiastical leaders, to prevent the Protestant church from becoming a place for 'anti-subversive activities,' he ordered censorship measures against religious periodicals.[13] At the same time, to insulate the population from the popular changes, he tightened official state media censorship. Events, including Janos Kadar's dismissal, received only the briefest press notice, while pettifogging was employed when covering speeches and developments in the Soviet Union.

Orations by Soviet foreign-policy expert Vyacheslav Dashichev were banned after he described the Berlin Wall as a remnant 'left over from the Cold War' that had to 'disappear over time'. Ever sensitive, Central Committee secretary Hermann Axen, fired-off a terse rebuke complaining the comments were directed at the 'sovereignty and security interests of the GDR, at the security interests of the Warsaw Pact states, at our joint political defence alliance'.[14] Another crisis burst open when *Sputnik*, a Soviet news agency magazine providing a digest of the Russian press, was removed from distribution in the GDR.[15] The journal had published a damning article on the Molotov-Ribbentrop Pact of 1939 and Stalin's 'mistakes, failures and crimes' before and during the Second World War. The article asserted Stalin 'had been a mere puppet of Hitler', and Germany's communists were culpable in the rise of Hitler by not 'joining together with Social Democrats to stop him'. The decisive factor for the outburst of anger from the SED leadership, however, was *Sputnik*'s question: 'Would there have been Hitler without Stalin?' This was answered with a plausible hypothesis: if the communists had allied themselves with the Social Democrats in Germany before 1933 in the fight against the Nazis, Hitler would not have won the Reichstag elections and history would most likely have turned out differently.[16]

As a veteran of the fight against Nazism, Honecker seethed with rage, calling the article not only stupid but despicable. In a short-fused response, *Neues*

Deutschland declared Soviet history and the history of the German Communist Party had been distorted by *Sputnik*. 'The magazine – and we say this openly – defames German communists ... distorted visions of Soviet history are incompatible with our friendship with the Soviet Union.'[17] Although unsigned, Honecker personally wrote the *Neues Deutschland* text (distributed by the ADN news agency to the media).[18] The open-ended *Sputnik* ban marked the first time a Soviet magazine had been prohibited in the GDR; simultaneously, five Soviet feature films – all with anti-Stalinist themes – were removed from the national cinema circuit. The *Sputnik* decision proved hugely important, not only as a mechanism for open dispute between East Berlin and Moscow but also for dissent within the GDR.[19]

In the ensuing uproar, the SED Central Committee, the FDJ, the Society for German-Soviet Friendship and newspaper offices, received the drumbeat of criticism as thousands of petitions and complaints arrived from companies, universities, schools and individuals demanding *Sputnik*'s return.[20]

Coupled with disenchantment with the economic decline and ecological problems, the *Sputnik* action also led to an unprecedented wave of resignations from the SED. An investigation noted dissatisfaction at the party base where grumblers and complainers made their voices heard. Ceasing to pay dues was the preferred form of passive resignation.[21]

In loyally championing the repute of the KPD in the *Sputnik* debacle, Honecker did his own reputation untold harm with the public, SED members and Gorbachev. Honecker explained in 1991:

> The *Sputnik* decision was very emotional and not carried out because of our overall policy with regard to the Soviet Union. It was outrageous, and I still find that today, that communists were blamed. Those who did everything in illegality to bring into existence a movement for the overthrow of Hitler and who suffered great sacrifices were to be blamed for the outbreak of the Second World War![22]

In the summer of 1988, Honecker's mood was further aggravated during a visit to the Soviet Union where he witnessed discontent and flux. After a visit to Magnitogorsk, he privately scoffed:

> The immediate feeling of the people there gave the definite impression that with perestroika, the economic position had not become better but worse, productivity had risen but there was no salt nor sugar, nor flour nor meat, all the things that people needed to live ... living standards had not improved but had worsened.[23]

In a conversation with Gorbachev, he recalled with heavy sarcasm the success of the five-year plans when he was last in Magnitogorsk in the 1930s.[24] By this point, the Soviet leader was lumping Honecker in with Bulgaria's Todor Zhivkov, Czechoslovakia's Gustáv Husák and Romania's Nicolae Ceauşescu as the so-called 'Gang of Four': a group of crusty, out-of-touch, inflexible un-regenerated Stalinists unwilling to make reforms.[25]

Remarkably, faced with a flurry of persistent rumours, American officials downplayed intelligence of the Gorbachev-Honecker spat. 'But we were proven wrong,' admits Bruce W. Clark, a US Political Advisor on East Germany.[26] 'The reports were accurate. I think we just couldn't believe that the Soviet Union would do anything to destabilise the hard-line communist government of East Germany given its strategic importance and location.'[27]

Meanwhile, on the home front, Honecker endured an increasingly fractious relationship with Gerhard Schürer, chairman of the State Planning Commission who expressed horror at the continued high Western debt when presenting an almost endless catalogue of economic failings. While he warned of imminent insolvency and proposed a drastic change of course in economic policy, Honecker allowed GDR flag carrier 'Interflug' to become the first airline in the socialist block to order two A-310s Airbus planes for its own fleet using a Western banking consortium to handle the sale and put up part of the total amount of US$130million. The cost climbed when the medium-range machines were equipped with an extra tank to serve long-haul routes to Cuba and the Far East.[28] (Vast sums of money had also been squandered on giving the capital a facelift for the fortieth-anniversary celebrations which bled provincial cities dry, causing a resentment.)

On the verge of tears, Schürer also protested the huge sums spent on GDR's lacklustre microelectronics industry and advised freezing funds to the armed forces and changing subsidy policies. However, after an angry discussion, Schürer's proposals were rejected – a decision endorsed by Günter Mittag, the Central Committee economics secretary.[29] As Egon Krenz laments, all fundamental economic decisions were left to a 'small circle' of 'comrades of the Politburo responsible for the economy' led by Mittag.[30] Margot Honecker later acknowledged that Mittag was 'not loved by the majority of ministers because he did not have the skill to come to agreement with his people'.[31]

Meanwhile, as the economy teetered, Honecker celebrated the completion of the 'three millionth apartment', which he handed over in a blaze of propaganda. In a speech carried on television, he gave the wholly unrealistic assessment that the programme was successfully completed – despite the numbers not tallying with the facts. Not only were modernised apartments included in the figures, but places in old people's homes and workers' hostels were also erroneously listed as newly built apartments.

The apartment issue was one of the few domestic topics that interested Honecker. As the year progressed, he paid remarkably little attention to local matters, including the startling revelation that forty-four people in the GDR were infected with the AIDS virus, and three had died from the disease. Concerns were also raised about the slack discipline and increased drunkenness among the Soviet forces stationed in the GDR, a problem which forced Soviet Defence Minister Dmitry Yazov to issue a reprimand.

Meanwhile, on 1 July, the Soviet Union voted to end the Communist Party's monopoly on economic and other non-political power and to further economic changes toward a less rigidly Marxist-Leninist economy. As events moved at a frightening speed, Honecker sought comfort from like-minded allies including Romanian leader Nicolae Ceausescu, who flew into the GDR during November to receive the Karl Marx Medal for his 'achievements'. Commenting on the trip, the London *Times* opined that because Gorbachev had not articulated a coherent policy toward Eastern Europe, Ceausescu was able to join Honecker in 'claiming to be the true keepers of the communist world', and provide opponents of the Gorbachev reforms inside the Soviet Union with a stick to beat him with as the reforms started to go sour. 'So long as old-style leaders remain in power in Eastern Europe, there is a fifth column ready and waiting to assist a retreat in Moscow.'[32] During their talks, Honecker told Ceausescu:

> If people hold the opinion that the history of the communist world movement, particularly in the socialist countries, is a history of crimes they are not only on the false path but are even working into the hands of those who disfigure the face of socialism ... who want to cast a shadow on socialism.[33]

Even as Ceausescu and Honecker enjoyed their tête-à-tête, the wind of change howled across Eastern Europe. During November, the Supreme Soviet of the Estonian SSR adopted the 'Estonian Sovereignty Declaration', in which local laws were declared supreme over those of the Soviet Union, the first declaration of sovereignty from Moscow of any Soviet or Eastern Bloc entity. In response Moscow declared it unconstitutional, but in a two-fingered salute, reformers pushed on and even replaced Russian as the nation's official language.

At a conference of the SED Central Committee in December, Honecker again spoke out against perestroika, thus confirming his place as the leader of a small band of extreme Stalinist leaders. In private, he poured out attack after attack on those who would seek to weaken the GDR. His main target was Gorbachev.

The Winds of Change

Events in the Eastern bloc and GDR moved quickly that winter, leaving the SED staggering from one crisis to the other. Buoyed when independent parties began operating in Hungary, a silent march in Leipzig, ostensibly marking the 70th anniversary of the murder of Karl Liebknecht and Rosa Luxembourg on 15 January, morphed into an appeal 'for the democratisation of our socialist state'. Watching events unfold, Stasi operatives described the march as a 'political provocation' orchestrated by church groups,[1] notably Pastor Christoph Wonneberger's congregation.

Out of touch, tune and temper, Honecker continued to obscure pro-democracy voices through a media blackout. In what seemed almost like an affront to public sentiment, he stated that the Berlin Wall would still exist in fifty and even in a hundred years' time if the reasons for its presence had not been removed. 'It is necessary to protect our republic from robbers, not to mention those who would like to disturb the stability and peace of Europe,' he said, sounding every bit the old Stalinist. 'The protection of borders is the sovereign right of every state, and thus also of the GDR.'[2] Meanwhile, the economy blundered further toward bankruptcy. Stupefied by Honecker's inactivity, Gerhard Schürer secretly met Egon Krenz at his Baltic Sea retreat in February to divulge details of the GDR's crippling debts to the West which were increasing at a rate of over 500 million marks per month. He warned if this trend continued, East Germany could face insolvency by 1991. Krenz, though, was pre-occupied with a series of blistering headlines concerning new escape attempts appearing in the international media. When 20-year-old waiter Chris Gueffroy was shot while trying to flee at the Berlin Wall on the evening of 6 February, the Western Allies called the shooting a 'crime against humanity'. Gueffroy had been desperately trying to scale the wall with a friend when spotted by border guards. Though the bullets fired at Gueffroy were the last fatal shots at the Berlin Wall, a month later, 32-year-old Winfried Freudenberg was killed after his homemade gas balloon fell from the sky over West Berlin, breaking nearly every bone in his body.

In the midst of this horror, the end of Moscow's military involvement in Afghanistan coincided with Soviet reformers – including Boris Yeltsin – defeating conservative communists in multi-party parliamentary elections in the USSR. Elsewhere, as independence movements gained momentum in the Baltic States, the Hungarian government opened its frontier with Austria on 2 May by dismantling the electric fence along the 240-kilometre boundary – presenting the first crack in the Iron Curtain. The move would have devastating consequences for the GDR. Although concerned, Moscow took no overt actions against Budapest.

Meanwhile, local elections were held across East Germany on 7 May, presenting not so much a spectacle as a sham. Berlin district mayors already knew the results before the vote, as 38-year-old Günter Polauke, one of the youngest mayors in the GDR recounted: 'We already had the election result in our pockets.' As historian Stefan Wolle noted, GDR elections were known to be a farce, 'but almost everyone took part to save themselves trouble.[3] What was new on 7 May was that civil rights groups also exercised their right to participate in the public counting of votes.'[4] Following the example of the Polish citizens' movement, activists in Berlin, Leipzig, Jena and Erfurt, had spent months preparing the monumental investigative job of vote monitoring – an effort befitting a military operation. Stasi reports, as usual, documented every detail: 'The individuals made notes on the election results announced by the election commissioners, sometimes using previously prepared forms.'[5] In almost all constituencies, irregularities, exaggerated results and cases of manipulation of voter turnout were recorded.

In the end, after the ballots closed, Egon Krenz – wearing his chairman of the election commission hat – declared the results in a televised address – an incredible 99 per cent for the SED and their allied parties. It was an 'impressive vote,' he said, which endorsed the 'successful course' of the government and a testament to the SED. But behind this bold front, there was a whiff of Gotterdammerung as ARD and ZDF were already on-air reporting egregious examples of ballot boxes being opened early, falsified voter lists and invalid votes.[6] Markus Wolf, the former Stasi operative, who had since resigned, noted the 'rising resentment over the sham electoral procedures that allowed the Socialist Unity Party to continue in power unopposed after the May election'.[7] 'For us,' Honecker rather dishonestly explained, 'a result of 65 per cent would have been a great success. Of course, our opponents would have said so-and-so many are against [us].' Moreover, he insisted falsification of polls was 'something I consider as frightful'.[8] No election was perfect, he contended, but insisted the vote 'was nevertheless, by and large, correct and gave expression to the will of the people'.[9]

Interestingly, Günter Schabowski later insisted the election deception was not ordered by Honecker, who, he said, had confidence in the loyalty of the Party. 'Without his knowledge, the mayors were told that the Party wanted certain results. It was not done at the polls but in the mayors' offices, but the examiners of the opposition parties did their work perfectly; they had counted votes at the polls and spotted the great difference.'[10]

Although everyday life went on, the sham elections marked a turning point in public attitudes. Many people were no longer intimidated by threats and state violence. Almost daily, the FRG press, in particular, *Die Zeit* and *Bild*, published story after story about moral legitimacy and fiddled elections. At the same time, protestors in the GDR mobilised on the 7th of every month calling for 'free elections instead of fake numbers'. On one occasion, a protest march on Alexanderplatz in East Berlin was broken up by a massive police detachment, while in Leipzig, demonstrators displayed a remarkable degree of quiet discipline. Typically, despite calls for change, Honecker took a cautious stand, and the discontent was left to fester.

Meanwhile, Egon Krenz's image – already tarnished after the sham election – was further muddied when he congratulated Chinese authorities for their tough treatment of demonstrators in Tiananmen Square, where tanks were deployed against unarmed democracy protestors.[11] His decision to applaud the brutality – intended as a warning to those in the GDR calling for reforms – only intensified resentment among the public, earning him the moniker, 'Krenz Xiaoping', a name scrawled on placards at an anti-China demonstration on 9 June in East Berlin. During the demo, protestors were arrested, interrogated and fined. Shortly after, a march on the fringes of a church congress in Leipzig saw activists show solidarity with Chinese students. Later in the month, the Church of the Redeemer in East Berlin staged a protest with several days of nonstop drumming against the suppression of the Chinese democracy movement. The Stasi had already broken up three other demonstrations outside the Chinese embassy by force (secret reports decided that the nerves of protestors were getting more frayed).

As if all this were not bad enough, US President George Bush called for the razing of the Berlin Wall in June, while appealing to the SED to bring glasnost to East Berlin. His call encouraged waves of refugees leaving the GDR for Austria via Hungary. At the same time, copying earlier tactics, more than 150 would-be GDR emigrants were holed-up in several West German diplomatic missions in the Eastern Bloc, hoping authorities would let them travel to the West.

Amid all this, Honecker's health took a sudden turn for the worse at a Warsaw Pact summit in Bucharest. Writhing in agony, doctors diagnosed a bout of bilious colic. He later recounted:

> There was the possibility of an operation on me there and then, but they refrained from that and in accordance with my wish, I came back to Berlin by air. At the time it was very hot and during

the whole time on the plane as well as in the ambulance from the airport to my house, I had to lie with an ice pack on my stomach to alleviate the pain.[12]

From this point, Honecker dropped from sight.

Crippled by abdominal pangs, he spent from July to September recovering from surgery to remove his inflamed gallbladder and part of his colon. Medical reports show complications occurred during the operation when his blood pressure dropped off dangerously. He was often confused and disorientated and displayed symptoms of atherosclerosis, a thickening of the arteries. Urologist Peter Althaus later revealed that surgeons left a suspected carcinogenic nodule in Honecker's right kidney due to his weak condition and failed to inform the patient of the suspected cancer.[13]

Honecker's incapacitation led to the longest period of official silence in his political career. He appointed Günter Mittag as his temporary replacement during his absence. Normally, that job went to Krenz but Honecker was wary of his deputy's loyalty so Krenz was side-lined and instructed to take a long vacation (a move which left him seething).

In hospital, Honecker was supposedly oblivious to the strengthening of grassroots opposition movements spurred by events across the Eastern bloc. 'He was cut off from the world,' Bernd Bruckner recalled. 'He couldn't watch TV, read newspapers or his mail. So, he was in a space where no information could get to him – he needed to recover.'[14]

To make matters worse, his appointed deputy, Günter Mittag – who was also ill – ummed and aahed when confronted with problems. (Mittag was severely diabetic and in 1984 one of his lower legs was amputated: the other was removed late in 1989.)

When asked about this period in 1991, Honecker snapped: 'I was on an operating table. I couldn't react perfectly.'[15] As he remained bedridden, the pro-democracy lobby continued to grow at a hellish tempo. Compounding matters, thousands of GDR citizens continued to seek political asylum at West German embassies in Czechoslovakia, Poland and Hungary. By September, Hungary, which had begun dismantling border fortifications with Austria in early May – opened its frontier to the West, thus allowing East Germans to enter Austria and journey unhindered to West Germany. 'When the thing became known to me – I was still in the intensive care unit,' Honecker recounted. 'I phoned up and said: "Now listen here, have you actually made contact with the Hungarians so that they would respect their commitments?" I was told that something would be done.'[16] Nothing happened. Paralyzed from the outset by their leader's illness, the entire SED Politburo sat silent, shocked by the swiftness and gravity of events. As Krenz later acknowledged, the 'system' was tailored to Honecker calling the shots and nobody in the Politburo took any initiatives. Finally, Gerhard Schürer harried Krenz to act against Honecker during a secret meeting in early September. Unsurprisingly, support came from the sly old Prime Minister Willi Stoph and Stasi boss Erich Mielke, and the heads of the SED district leadership of Berlin and Karl-Marx-Stadt, Günter Schabowski and Siegfried Lorenz. Schabowski worked to gauge which party members needed convincing to support the plan. 'It wasn't possible to topple Honecker by a military putsch,' he later explained. 'It was only possible in the politburo. We wanted to make it appear that he [Honecker] had resigned.'[17] The hardest of all to suborn was Schalck-Golodkowski, the currency guru, who eventually pledged support.[18] At that moment, Krenz dispatched Harry Tisch, the powerful trade union boss to inform Gorbachev of the conspiracy. 'He [Gorbachev] welcomed the fact,' Tisch recounted. 'Gorbachev realised we had reached the point where we understood that life had caught up with us.'[19]

Throughout this period, the Americans, unsurprisingly, took a perhaps closer than usual interest in events. US Ambassador Richard C. Barkley recalled:

> After the fact, we realised that the system really demanded someone like Honecker around to make the big decisions. So, for the longest period of time, a lot of the key decisions were postponed. So, at a time when there were great shifts throughout Eastern Europe, there was nobody in East Berlin to give guidance.
>
> Whether they were right or wrong, people knew what was expected of them. But even political instruments like *Neues Deutschland* didn't know what to do. The usual policy among the East Germans if there is foreign news that you didn't want to talk about, you didn't print it. For example, during that period of time, there was no reporting about the elections in Poland that brought Walesa to power. There was no talk about Tiananmen Square in Beijing. The discussions that were going on in the paper were about how to handle the outflow of tourists, which was increasing daily. It was the summertime after all. That is when people went on holiday. So, they were not addressing a lot of these problems. So, they were in some respects put into a box, at a particularly perfect time for those who were against the regime, or who wanted to get out.

From here on, Krenz and his plotters sat tight but were manoeuvring behind the scenes. Honecker hobbled back to work in late September. The overwhelming impression from those near him was of a man who was out of touch, who was all too human – who lectured, changed his mind, spoke too much and yet did too little. After months in hospital, Honecker, the bright political schemer, was nowhere to be seen.

His return to duty coincided with the rise of an independent political party called 'New Forum,' which used a simple battle cry to demand dialogue about democratic reforms and reshaping society. Founded by a disparate collection of artists, intellectuals and environmentalists, the SED dubbed the movement illegal and denied it official recognition. Adding to the chorus calling for reforms, the East German Social Democratic Party (created in July, of which seven of fourteen founders were clergymen), was followed by a group called 'Democratic Re-Awakening'. Meanwhile, on the streets of the GDR, young, braver spirits continued Monday evening protests in Leipzig, taunting the police with cries of 'Gorby will get you', and 'We want out of this shithouse.' When Honecker ordered *Neues Deutschland* to label those emigrating as 'counter-revolutionaries', many protesters changed their tune and began chanting: 'We want to stay', underlining their desire for change at home rather than a new life in the West. To cement that point, New Forum's manifesto demanded greater freedoms within the East German state rather than emigration. And Konrad Weiss, the leader of 'Democracy Now' – another new group made up of intellectuals – feared the GDR could be annexed as a 'state' within the FRG.

Amid all this, Soviet Central Committee secretary Vadim Medvedev, in charge of relations with socialist countries and ideology, was conducting a lighting tour of East Berlin. He returned home 'with grave thoughts', concluding: 'the first thing one should have done – was to take a decision on the change of leadership'[20] (referring to Honecker). Furthermore, he wailed that most of Honecker's cadres were also inflexibly resistant to change.[21] Seemingly oblivious to events, GDR television – still habitually self-censoring – continued to push forward a steady stream of fawning stories about the ruling party. On 2 October, the evening news led with a report on Honecker's 'friendly encounter' with British tycoon Robert Maxwell. However, by this point, individual acts of resistance began to emerge. One man recounted that on 3 October at around 5.15 pm:

> I came out of the delicatessen and onto Pirna's market square where, out of frustration and pent-up anger, I shouted: 'Down with Honecker', 'Honecker you rascal, give the little children bananas', and 'We want free elections'. When the Stasi arrived a few minutes later, a small crowd shouted: 'Leave the man alone, he is speaking the truth!'[22]

A week later, on 7 October, the SED went on with its grandiose celebrations of the 40th anniversary of the founding of the GDR, with guest of honour Mikhail

Gorbachev. From the outset, pro-democracy protestors were itching to send a message to the Soviet leader, and at Schoenfeld airport, the screams of 'Gorby! Gorby! Gorby!' could be heard as the Russians arrived. Later that afternoon, at an open-air event, the strain on Honecker was obvious. His gaunt, withered face was pallid like white leather. 'He behaved like he was in a trance,' Gorbachev recounted. 'It was obvious he was not feeling right.'

The recognition that Honecker had to go grew constantly, according to Horst Sindermann, the GDR Parliamentary President. 'The last impetus was given by Gorbachev's visit on the 40th anniversary,' he explained.[23] Recounting that trip, he remembered a 'very pleasant' talk between Gorbachev and the Politburo where the Soviet leader 'talked of his problems and of ours. He said we would have it easier with perestroika because we had a strong economy':

> Then Honecker replied. He trotted out a speech about the 4-megabit microchip again. I have to say this because he constantly forgot the relative importance of things, the disproportions that arose from the one-sided concentration on microelectronics. In crucial situations, he always produced statistics and said we had higher productivity than the Soviet Union. This was his justification for staying on the old course, that we were getting on very well on our own. He also told Gorbachev this. That decided matters.[24]

Although in pain, the SED leader lumbered to his feet that same evening at a gala dinner at the Palace of the Republic to deliver a bulky oration lauding decades of achievements. He described the GDR as a state with modern industry and agriculture, a socialist education system, with flourishing science, culture and world-class athletics. 'So much is certain for us,' he said. 'The slogan coined in the founding period of the GDR still applies: "Forward ever, backward never."' Concerning economic achievements, he promised to continue his social policy, wherein residential housing construction was a top priority: 'At the same time, we will dedicate more attention to the need for consumer goods and services.'[25]

Though listening with an obliging smile, Gorbachev thought the speech was devoid of anything regarding the present situation, nor contained analysis or conclusions. Schabowski described it as a long and painful recitation of East German successes. When Honecker finally wrapped up, Gorbachev sarcastically enquired, 'Was that everything?'[26]

It is hard to explain this failure of judgment, the most critical mistake Honecker ever made. Publicly favouring the status quo over the promise of reforms was a severe lapse, regardless of whether he was committed to delivering changes or not. His logical powers, his early warning system, crashed. Romanian observers noted visible disappointment among the audience with the fact that the First Secretary made no references to possible liberalisation of the socio-political structure.

As this was all going on, several hundred members of the Free German Youth – the organisation Honecker founded four decades earlier – sprang a nasty surprise by chanting, 'Gorby, help us! Gorby, save us!' outside the Palace of the Republic. Although prevented from reaching the entrance, the protests spilled over into other areas of the city, especially around some churches, where police intervened. Honecker, later claimed, he had 'no idea' about the protests but was convinced 'not only the dissidents' were involved: 'I learned about it only the day after. But that was a very bad thing.'[27] The following morning, Honecker was not lacking in self-confidence during a three-hour conversation with Gorbachev when he balked at the idea of reforms and treated the Soviet leader to a recap of his achievements. Containing his dismay, Gorbachev later claimed his 'cautious attempts' to convince the SED leader to make reforms led to no practical results whatever: 'It was as if I had been speaking to a brick wall.' Over in Moscow, Anatoly Chernyaev, a principal foreign-policy advisor to Gorbachev, unloaded details of the growing spat into his diary on 11 October:

> I have read the record of conversation of M.S. [Gorbachev] with Honecker in Berlin. I spoke with him [Gorbachev] about this. [Georgy] Shakhnazarov was present. M.S. [Gorbachev] called Honecker an 'asshole' [mudak]. He, Gorbachev added, could have said to his [East German] lieutenants: I have undergone four operations, I am 78 years old, the stormy time requires too much strength, let me go, I have done my job. Then he might have kept his place in history.
>
> Shakh [nazarov] and I voiced our doubts that even if he had done so he would have kept his place in history. Two or three years ago, it might have been possible. Today he has already been cursed by his people ... The Politburo [of the SED] is in session for the second day in Berlin. [Honecker's future successor Egon] Krenz has promised 'to raise a question' about changes to our Ambassador [Vyacheslav Kochemassov] for transmittal to Gorbachev. Honecker warned him: [If you do it] you will become my enemy.
>
> However, Krenz seems to have taken the step. What is about to happen?[28]

A few days after the 40th anniversary 'celebrations', 70,000 protestors – squeezed shoulder to shoulder – converged in the centre of Leipzig demanding change. According to some in the SED, Honecker had made no secret of his willingness to fire on protestors if called upon to do so – a claim he later rejected, insisting consideration of the 'Chinese way' (using weapons) never crossed his mind:

> In spite of all the assertions to the contrary, the Chinese solution never had any standing. It was like this. Up to the 7th and 8th of October, the question never arose of dispersing peaceful demonstrations with the application of armed military force. We looked much more for the so-called security partnership, and it has been shown that this path was the only right one. That has nothing whatever to do with the attitude of Egon Krenz. The orders given for this came from me in my capacity as Chairman of the National Defence Council. I held from the start that guns ought not to be needed. Copies of these orders with regard to Leipzig were sent to all those in charge of operations in the county so that they knew what our attitude would be in such an eventuality.[29]

Already looking to his place in history, Krenz was keen to stress his role in keeping the peace. 'On 9 October I was not yet general secretary, but I don't know about any order of that kind to shoot, nor do I believe there was such an order to shoot,' neither, he said, had there been any orders about the issuing of live ammunition.[30] Krenz remembered holding a telephone conversation with the then First Secretary of Leipzig who told him the director of music at the main concert hall (Gewandhaus) had, together with other public figures, appealed for calm and moderation. In a barbed comment, Honecker later accused his deputy of trying to take credit for the peaceful response in an interview with *Bild*:

> Krenz, later on, wanted to stick some kind of feather in his cap this coincides very much with his contribution to the Federal Republic newspaper *Bild* story 'Now I'll tell everything'. So far as I could tell from this, obviously in 'Now I'll tell everything', the truth mattered to him less than the DM1.5 million he was to receive for the tittle-tattle he engaged in there.[31]

In the event, the lack of police intervention boosted demonstrators' courage and on Monday 16 October, more than 120,000 pro-democracy activists took to the streets of Leipzig in the largest single protest in the nation's forty-year history. That same day, *Bild* reported that more than 20,000 East Germans, unhappy over the leadership's rejection of reforms, had cancelled their party membership over the previous two weeks.

The Curtain Falls

In Berlin, events now moved with dramatic swiftness. Krenz's plotters – with the blessing of Gorbachev – moved to decisively eject Honecker and chart a new course. In classic SED fashion, the final act played out at a routine Politburo meeting the following morning, 17 October, when Willi Stoph interrupted Honecker's opening statement to propose a motion that 'Comrade Honecker be relieved of his function as General Secretary.'[1] Although dumbfounded by the abruptness, Honecker quickly composed himself but was sickened that none of his colleagues had had the decency to speak with him beforehand. 'I gave the floor to the comrades, one after another.' There were no scathing indictments, but Kurt Hager uneasily explained that trust in intellectual circles had vanished under his leadership, while Inge Lang, Siegfried Lorenz and Margaret Muller spoke especially sharply. 'All the comrades with one or another reason, including Günter Schabowski, said it was a very hard decision I had to grasp.'[2] The most fiery speech of all, came from Erich Mielke. As his mouth tightened, the Stasi boss dangled the prospect of releasing a cache of documents concerning Honecker's indiscretions and moral laxity if he did not resign voluntarily (Mielke had 'trustworthy colleagues' stationed outside the Politburo in case Honecker attempted to have his personal bodyguard arrest the plotters).[3]

Having vented, Mielke handed the floor to Honecker's supposed anointed crown prince, Egon Krenz. His eyes circled and puffy, he declared 'this was a decisive moment', and after 'considering the matter very carefully' agreed to the SED leader's removal. He later said he felt an odd tenderness towards Erich, which made the episode difficult. At the same meeting, Honecker's oldest pals and veterans of many bitter battles, Günter Mittag, and propaganda head, Joachim Herrmann, were also relieved of their posts.

The First Secretary didn't defend himself and there was no further business. 'A certain liberation took place,' Honecker reflected. 'I felt no kind of desire to continue to work in the kind of collective that had pushed for my release from all responsibilities in a conspiratorial manner.'[4] Crestfallen, he shuffled back to his office, packed some personal papers, and bade farewell to his secretarial staff in an adjacent waiting room. The fact that Mielke, 'a colleague in a common task', became a fellow conspirator was particularly galling. 'That was not just going behind somebody's back anymore but was the preparation of an inner-party and state putsch,' he stormed. [5]

Late on the evening of 17 October, he returned to Wandlitz looking tired. That same evening, he held a tortured phone conversation with Krenz to arrange the text of his resignation statement. The charade continued the next morning when he 'asked' the Central Committee to release him from the function of general secretary, just as Ulbricht had been forced to do two decades earlier. The full text of Honecker's resignation statement was tapped-out by ADN at 2pm on 18 October:

> After mature reflection, and as a result of yesterday's consultation in the Politburo, I have come to the following decision: as a result of my illness and the operation I underwent, the state of my health no longer allows me to apply the strength and energy which the fortunes of our party and the people demand now and in the future. Therefore, I ask the Central Committee to release me from the function of General Secretary of the SED Central Committee, from the office of Chairman of the GDR State Council, and from the function of the chairman of the National Defence Council of the GDR. Comrade Egon Krenz, who is able and determined to meet the responsibility and extent of the work in the way required by the situation, the interests of the party and the people, and the preparations for the twelfth Party Congress, which encompasses all areas of society, is to be recommended to the Central Committee and People's Chamber.
>
> Dear Comrades! I have devoted my whole conscious life in unshakable loyalty to the revolutionary cause of the working class and our Marxist-Leninist worldview, to the creation of socialism on German soil. The foundation and successful development of the socialist German Democratic Republic, the balance sheet of which we drew up on the 40th Anniversary, I regard as the culmination of the struggle of our party and my own work as a communist.
>
> I would like to thank the Politburo, the Central Committee, my comrades-in-arms in the difficult times of anti-fascist resistance, the members of the party, and all the citizens of our country for all the decades of shared and fruitful activity for the welfare of the people.
>
> I will continue to remain at the disposal of my party with my experience and advice. I wish our party and its leadership continued strengthening of its unity and cohesion and further success to the Central Committee. [Signed] Erich Honecker.[6]

After eighteen years at the SED's helm, the state-run press poured balm on some of Honecker's wounds by praising his constancy, dedication and dignity. Having completed a round of handshakes and farewells, he returned to Wandlitz rather naïvely expecting a quiet retirement.

Once victory was his, Krenz took over as General Secretary of the SED, Chairman of the State Council and Chairman of the National Defence Council. Posing as a beacon of decency, Krenz promised quick results, 'We are facing work – work, work and more work – but work that should bring pleasure and serve all people.' In usual lickspittle fashion, state television portrayed Krenz as a modern man, a pragmatist. Over in the West, *Bild* mockingly noted: 'So, the new man is called Egon Krenz. He is to lead the Marx botch-up and shortage republic. For most citizens, Krenz is just as bad as Honecker.'[7] In a blunt editorial, *Frankfurt Allgemeine Zeitung*'s commentator Friedrich Karl Fromm, suggested Krenz would have to show results and could no longer rely on a lethargic population, which had been ruled in a totalitarian way for fifty-six years, 'and which basically only asked whether it was possible to make at least some kind of nice living under the prevailing conditions'. The Germans in the GDR wanted more, he argued, saying Honecker's successor didn't have the privilege of being treated with indulgence to which Honecker was entitled: 'He basically wanted good or tolerable conditions, but failed to attain them.'[8]

A Stasi mood report noted people questioned Krenz's health, 'there's talk of alcohol. He also lacks charisma. Like Honecker, he comes from the youth movement and will continue to spoil them.' Another report compiled on 19 October, noted the first reactions regarding Krenz, 'were often characterised by consternation on the part of citizens. He is said to be a representative of the former leadership, which has landed the country in a tricky situation.'[9] Speaking on FRG TV, an East Berliner in his fifties said it was 'like replacing a lame white horse with a lame brown one', while a spokesman for the New Forum remarked, 'he is, after all, responsible for many things in East Germany which makes him very suspect'.[10] Even the US Ambassador Richard C. Barkley said it was clear that Krenz did not represent a particularly sympathetic figure; 'Although he was only in his late 40s [he was 52], he had been so associated with the Honecker regime that he was not looked to as a sign of change.'[11]

> He was somewhat better than his reputation. He was basically a child of the system and he voted for the system; he expected the system to continue, and that he would naturally become the head of things. In his view that was preordained. Anyway, it became clear that there were a lot of things going on underneath him that he did not understand. It also became clear that he couldn't control them.[12]

Out in the Cold

Before Honecker had a chance to settle into a comfortable retirement, an early whiff of recrimination came on 23 October when the SED's chief ideologist Kurt Hager, issued the first public criticism of the former General Secretary, stating that elements of a personality cult had surrounded him, 'there had been a tendency to give Honecker sole credit for the country's achievements in areas such as peace and disarmament'.[1] Ironically, at a Politburo meeting a day earlier, it had been agreed to arrange an 'extensive celebration in honour of Honecker'. But now events were moving fast.[2] In later life, Honecker vehemently denied he was the focus of a personality cult. 'I arranged that no stamps would be printed with my picture,' he asserted, adding:

> I never put any value on popularising photographs of me. Once at the Leipzig fair there were forty-two pictures of me published in *Neues Deutschland*. They were published because on all the stands the ambassadors stood with me, as well as ministers of the most diverse governments. That was shown afterward to be wrong, such things should not have been started at all.[3]

Meanwhile, under pressure from all directions, Krenz offered to ease travel restrictions, mistakenly believing this would calm protestors who remained on the streets across the GDR.[4] Demonstrators did not budge however, even after the much-publicised resignation of Margot Honecker. (In a letter dated 20 October 1989, Margot asked the Council of Ministers to release her from this position for personal reasons. The Council of Ministers complied and thanked her for her 'many years of responsible work as a member of the Council of Ministers and as minister of public education'.) Other departures included Kurt Hager and Erich Mielke, who was left a broken man, devoid of his unscrupulous finesse. Watching events unfold, Wolf Biermann – the musician unceremoniously banned from returning to the GDR in the 1970s – mocked the 'unbelievable speed with which the old bastards' were transforming themselves.[5]

For Krenz the news got steadily worse, as over a million protestors spilled into Alexanderplatz on 4 November. Watching events from the Interflug building, novelist Stefan Heym said it was as if someone had thrown open the windows after years of 'stagnation, after years of dullness and mustiness, of phrase-mongering and bureaucratic despotism'. On the sixth, growing discontent sent half a million exuberant marchers to the streets and squares of Leipzig demanding an end to the SED's monopoly on power, and more significantly, reunification with the West, instead of the hitherto call for reform in the GDR.

The hostility stunned Günter Schabowski, who later reflected, 'We had engineered a palace revolution without offering a real alternative. We had not swiftly and thoroughly enough whittled away from Stalin's methods.'[6] However, while the demonstrations were going on, an SED working committee did privately agree to announce passport holders would be able to emigrate or just simply visit the West from 10 November.

Schabowski – now acting as a government spokesman – made a monumental blunder on 9 November during a fateful press conference by mistakenly announcing at 6.53 pm that 'effective immediately, without delay' – all citizens were free to travel to the West without prerequisites, conditions, or family relationships. What he should have said is that the new rules would be enacted at four o'clock the next day, 10 November, in an 'orderly manner' when passport offices and checkpoints were open.[7]

After a few brief moments of bafflement and confusion, the news hit the Associated Press wire at 7.05 pm and was relayed by GDR TV at 7.30 pm and West German TV at 8 pm, prompting a sudden rush to border crossings. A few hours later, ARD newsreader Hanns Joachim Friedrichs told viewers: 'The GDR has announced that its borders are open to everyone as of now. The gates of the wall are now wide open.' Honecker remembered sitting open-mouthed at home watching events unfold on TV: 'It was something surreal, something inexplicable for everyone whose future, whose hopes were bound up with the GDR, for those who worked and fought for four decades. And it was an act that practically liquidated the GDR.'[8]

All through the night, East Berliners surged into West Berlin, many dancing along the Kurfurstendamm in a raucous outpouring of joy. Bars offered free drinks to their unexpected guests, while the underground ran all night to cope with the extraordinary mass of people moving around in a stunned, jubilant city. 'It was so simple to come over,' a young East Berliner told TV reporters. 'The feeling is just indescribable.' Former Chancellor Willy Brandt – forcing himself to hold back tears – said the GDR would never be the same again: 'The people of divided Germany have come together.'

From here on, the SED reaped the whirlwind. A week later, Krenz took a swipe at his former boss by declaring the difficult position was not the blame of rank-and-file communists, workers, peasants or intellectuals. 'Our party's leadership is to blame for that,' he said. 'Former party leader Erich Honecker also bears personal responsibility for the mistakes. But considering his age and health, he should be given the right to decide himself when to make a public assessment of his actions.'[9]

On 3 December, the Politburo and the Central Committee resigned and Krenz threw in the sponge as party leader but remained head of state and chairman of the Defence Council. That same day, several senior members of the old guard – including Honecker – were unceremoniously expelled from the SED. Meanwhile, the state prosecutor's office launched a search of Alexander Schalck-Golodkowski's office, who, reluctant to commit his valuable person to authorities, had fled abroad. Proceedings were instituted against him for abuse of office, personal gain and favouritism.[10] As the days passed, more reports emerged about the SED's abuse of power and the magnitude of the dire economic situation. Günter Schabowski remembers the Politburo engaged in some 'aggressive, impatient' discussion on the situation:

> Their special shops, sojourns in the non-socialist world, private use of jets for holidays, remuneration in and ownership of hard currency, and, above all, the privileges granted to the children, grandchildren and relatives of members of the Politburo and government are the subjects of repeated and ubiquitous criticism.[11]

With tempers running ragged, Erich Honecker was placed under house arrest on 5 December, along with Günter Mittag and propaganda chief Joachim Herrmann – all three faced charges of abusing their posts for personal gain and were not allowed to leave Wandlitz. Mittag, for instance, was accused of personal enrichment by giving two state-funded luxury villas to his daughters, while trade union boss Harry Tisch – who was also detained – reportedly 'ran a hunting estate like a feudal baron'. Separate investigations were opened against Honecker's close associate Wolfgang Vogel, who was arrested on blackmail charges. (For years, Vogel had been used as a 'go-between' during delicate swaps of intelligence agents and other prisoners, including American U-2 spy-plane pilot Gary Powers). The news spotlight briefly turned to Honecker's first daughter (with Edith Baumann), Erica Wildau-Honecker, then 39 and wife of the GDR ambassador to the Netherlands, Karl Wildau. Ambushed by paparazzi in The Hague, she declined to comment on her father's fate and gave a beaming smile when asked if her days in Holland were numbered.

On the sixth, more revelations of a huge network of corruption inside the SED forced Krenz to stand down as head of state, representing a further abdication of power by the SED to reformers. With the Socialist Unity Party utterly discredited, Manfred Gerlach, leader of the non-communist Liberal

Democratic Party was appointed his successor and Gregor Gysi, a reformer, became the SED's new leader. In his first speech, Gysi acknowledged that the Party had brought the GDR to ruin. He repudiated everything it had done since 1949 and declared the SED needed to adopt a 'new form' of socialism.

On the following morning, 7 December, as a new parliamentary commission began investigating corruption under the old order, Honecker's mood spiralled downward when members of the security forces arrived to search his home. He noted bitterly:

> The whole procedure upset me so much I was near a heart attack. A nurse was called, she diagnosed high blood pressure. We knew nothing of what they were looking for. Nothing was taken, except radios for our grandchildren. It was said after I had controlled myself, somewhat, that the search was carried out on the grounds of a deposition of the state prosecutor concerning abuse of trust.

Despite the fragility of the former General Secretary's health, he was also slapped with an eviction notice to quit Wandlitz by 31 January 1990.

Three days later, on 9 December, police officers returned to Wandlitz to ransack the lavishly appointed home of Stasi chief Erich Mielke, who almost had a stroke when being arrested in his kitchen. However, his tongue had lost none of its edge as he angrily accused his former underlings of being 'traitors'. At that very same moment, a few streets away, Willi Stoph was being placed in handcuffs as police officers carried out crates of fine whisky, French vintages and exotic liquors discovered in his cellar. Ordinary East Germans – aware that their leaders lived charmed lifestyles – were stunned by the deceit and dishonesty as details dribbled out.

After an unhappy Christmas cloistered in Wandlitz, Honecker was freed from house detention on 5 January 1990 and immediately sent to Berlin to undergo surgery to remove a malignant kidney tumour, leaving Margot and Sonja to pack and prepare the move. 'She had given away a great deal because, in the new dwelling, we did not need and could not use everything. The old house in Wandlitz no longer existed and we needed to look for a new one.' Margot turned down an offer of a two-roomed apartment on Bersarinplatz in Friedrichshain – but always maintained they had been made homeless.[12] (Pressed on this, she later admitted she could not accept the Bersarinplatz offer for 'security reasons'.)[13]

After nearly a month in the infirmary, any last vestiges of hope that Erich Honecker would enjoy a peaceful retirement were dashed on 29 January. Minutes after being discharged, he was arrested outside East Berlin's Charitie hospital and marched into 'investigative custody' at Rummelsburg remand centre, a former men's prison. State prosecutor general, Hans-Jurgen Joseph, announced he would be tried for high treason. At Rummelsburg he was questioned, not once but several times. 'This was not only shameful for my person but also for the GDR,' Honecker later lamented. 'I have to say I was very agitated and obviously could not have imagined anything like it.' After thirty-six hours, the arrest warrant was annulled due to medical reports certifying him unfit for detention.

Homeless, and with their mental state worsening, Erich and Margot Honecker found shelter with the help of the Berlin-Brandenburg Evangelical Church. Pastor Uwe Holmer, leader of the Hoffnungstal Institute in Lobetal, Bernau bei Berlin, offered the couple a room in his rural homestead – an extraordinary gesture given his children had been refused university education due to their Christian faith. 'The responsibility for the present situation of this country is everybody's,' the church said in a statement.[14] 'Some of the things being said today about the Honeckers leave the unavoidable impression that people are looking for scapegoats to make excuses for themselves.'[15] 'At Lobetal,' Honecker reflected, 'we spent most of our time out of doors because most of the entire world press was interested in us. The Holmer family made us very welcome for we had at first no means to cook for ourselves or anything else.' Over the coming months, Margot and Erich not only breakfasted with the family, but also shared lunch and dinner. 'From a Christian point of view, the Holmer family did not understand the whole thing either. That is the refusal of a dwelling and they thought it a Christian duty to take us in.'[16] Recollecting the period, Holmer remembered Honecker was very disciplined, 'although he was certainly angry inside. He soon realised, and so did I, that we had a different political outlook. Spiritually, too, we had no real bridge. So, we both avoided personal conversations'.[17]

While acknowledging that many people were infuriated by his act of mercy, Holmer's parish backed the move. 'Critics and demonstrators, of course, had a wide variety of arguments,' he explained. 'Most of the time they were annoyed, surprised, or angry that we were granting Honecker asylum. For us, the two were a helpless, rather desperate couple who found no other help than in a parsonage.' At Lobetal, another heartbreaking scene had played out after Sonya and Leo had been made redundant. That winter, the couple accepted an opportunity offered by UNHCR which was providing Chilean refugees free flights (and free excess baggage) to return home.

The farewell was emotional. Roberto remembered his grandparents were tense but full of composure. Sonja fretted over what was to become of her parents, especially her sick father. Their relocation, it transpired, added to Margot and Erich's anxiety as Sonja found herself in a bewildering and uncharted world. In letters to her parents, she complained about problems finding a job and her desire to return to Europe.

Meanwhile in the outside world, it was clear that progress toward a united Germany would quicken after multi-party elections in the GDR during March. After the polls, West Germany and the new East German government would talk about the path to unity. Chancellor Kohl – without any consultation with his allies – arrived in Russia in February and won agreement that 'the unity of the German nation must be decided by the Germans themselves'. From this point, nothing could halt reunification. On 13 February, the four Allied powers from the Second World War – Britain, France, the United States and the Soviet Union – agreed to talks on security issues and, in a speech to the Bundestag, Kohl heralded unification as imminent.

Meanwhile, in Bernau, protesters succeeded in hounding the Honeckers out of Holmer's vicarage during March. After frantic pleas to the Russians, the couple found shelter at a Soviet military hospital at Beelitz-Heilstätten, an overgrown Wilhelminian-era compound near Potsdam, sealed by a high wall. 'When we were brought here,' Honecker complained, 'we were only allowed to bring whatever we could carry. Our furniture and the bulk of our personal possessions is being looked after by friends in Berlin.'[18]

From here on, their new home consisted of three rooms on the ground floor of a doctor's villa, decorated with grubby camel-coloured 1940s' wallpaper and outmoded furniture. There was an adjoining kitchenette. Erich slept in a tiny adjacent bedroom, Margot on a camp bed in the hall. 'It was so dark that fluorescent tube lights burned day and night,' Honecker's lawyer Friedrich Wolff recalled. 'In the middle of the living room was an oval table with five chairs, a glass cabinet was crammed with Russian books, and in the corner, two huge armchairs faced the TV set.'[19] Food was delivered thrice daily from the hospital kitchen (usually boiled pork, mint tea and enormous quantities of white bread). Living temporarily apart from reality, the couple padded around in slippers, took midday naps and devoured every book and newspaper they could find. They avoided outside contacts and distrusted the media but remained in regular touch with just a handful of friends and four lawyers.

'On average, we get up between seven and seven-thirty, breakfast is around nine,' Erich said at the time. 'Then we go tramping in the forest. Then the medical treatment and the daily examination by the doctor take place. After lunch, we go for another thirty- to forty-minute walk and after supper too.'[20] Communication with doctors was in Russian and primarily through Margot, who had a decent grasp of the language. If necessary, an interpreter was called in. In the evenings, the couple consumed vast amounts of television from where they learned of the death of two old comrades: former building minister Wolfgang Junker, who hanged himself on 9 April, and Horst Sindermann who died a few days later.

Honecker's first interview since his downfall was given to Heinz Junge, an old communist comrade from the anti-Nazi resistance, who lived in the West, but became one of the few regular visitors to Beelitz. It revealed a sad and bitter man, angry at Moscow for what he felt was a betrayal, irritated at the West German government which was then in charge of his fate, and totally unrepentant about his past. He lamented:

> Everything I did, I did in the knowledge I was doing something for the people and for peace. In the present situation they need scapegoats, and I am being made the biggest one.[21]
>
> ...
>
> We are well enough looked after here by our friends, at least my medical treatment is looked after. But my wife and I do not understand why a basic constitutional right in the GDR is denied to us – that is, the right to a proper apartment of our own. We do not ask too much, and we want no privileges. All we want is a perfectly normal flat like all other citizens have.

With the tensions of the past few months having left their mark on Margot Honecker, she suffered a minor heart attack on 19 April 1990. A quick-witted masseuse gave first aid, as Honecker looked on – paralyzed with fright. 'It was a very terrible situation,' he recounted. 'I would not have survived her death.'[22]

As Margot recovered that summer, the relentless march to reunification continued. The Honeckers met East German Interior Minister, Peter Michael Diestel, during July to discuss the conditions of their accommodation and police measures to ensure their safety. They complained of not being able to exchange old East German currency for Deutsche Marks because their IDs had been confiscated. In September, despite East German doctors deeming Honecker unfit for prison or trial on charges of abuse of power, breach of trust, corruption and treason, GDR authorities handed 500 volumes of files on the former General Secretary and other former leaders to the West German federal prosecutor, who would decide if they should stand trial. On the eve of German reunification, Honecker said he considered all the charges to be untenable and rejected responsibility for the figure, cited by the prosecutor's office, of 200 killed on the GDR borders. 'I have no personal guilt for that.'[23] Responding to corruption charges, he said:

> My wife and I are shocked by the calumnies against us. We are accused of corruption and self-enrichment at the expense of the people. But Margot and I have nothing to reproach ourselves with; we did not lead a life of luxury and we do not have a bank account in Switzerland ... I receive DM510 a month, from my trade as a roofer, and I have been informed that I am entitled to

a further DM1,700 as a pension for having been in the anti-Nazi resistance. [The money was paid into Margot's bank account.] My own account is blocked, and I don't know when I will be able to touch it.[24]

(This public accusation of corruption – one newspaper accused him of raiding the country's treasury – struck him profoundly).

Finally, on 1 December, reunified German authorities issued an arrest warrant for Honecker on charges that he gave shoot-to-kill orders at the Berlin Wall. According to Wolfgang Ziegler, one of his lawyers, Honecker was 'very composed' when he received the news. However, he was shaken to learn German police had arrived at Beelitz to arrest him (the Soviets refused to hand him over). From here on in, the saga became a murky matter. On 7 March, another of Honecker's lawyers, Friedrich Wolff, met him at Beelitz where he thought he looked 'worse than ever before: swollen face and oedema in his legs. He has had problems with his intestines for three weeks.'[25]

Then suddenly, as German authorities pushed for his arrest, Erich and Margot were illicitly spirited to Russia on a Soviet military postal plane in a cloak-and-dagger operation. In Moscow, they were met by an ambulance, and transferred to Sokolniki hospital. It all happened so fast that staff in Beelitz only discovered the news about their sudden departure on television.

Officially, the Soviets claimed the former General Secretary was suffering severe cardiac problems requiring treatment at a better-equipped hospital in the USSR. German authorities, it later transpired, were given one-and-a-half hours' notice before the flight on 13 March 1991. Enraged by his sudden escape, German government spokesman Dieter Vogel said the move would 'cast a certain shadow on relations, at least for a while. But of course, we have a fundamental interest in keeping our relations as positive, friendly and reasonable as possible.'[26]

The deep irony of Honecker's flight was in the fact that he permitted Gorbachev, the man who he considered his biggest ideological enemy, to help him.

In an interview with West German newspapers, Friedrich Wolff expressed surprise at the drama, saying many Soviets had considered the matter embarrassing. 'And, of course,' he added, 'there is also something like solidarity with the old fellow-fighter. Soviet wishes were known, and there has probably long been some kind of secret agreement.'[27] However, when Bonn demanded Russia hand back Honecker on 15 March, Moscow's foreign ministry spokesman Vitaly Churkin admitted moving the East German was a 'technical violation' of Germany's sovereignty, but ruled out sending him back.[28] Bonn then accused Moscow of breaking international law and trampling on treaties between the two countries. For a short while thereafter, the situation cooled. Throughout the summer, Erich and Margot convalesced at a dacha in Moscow's suburbs. It was only after an attempted coup against Gorbachev in August,[29] that Germany ramped-up pressure and sent a new extradition request.

This time, though, the call was publicly supported by Boris Yeltsin, the new President of the Russian Soviet Socialist Federal Republic but opposed by Gorbachev (whose influence was in steep decline) who continued to protect him from extradition.

'I intend to go back to Germany but only if this illegal arrest warrant that is in force for unknown reasons be withdrawn,' Honecker told a journalist from ARD who had travelled to Moscow to conduct what the network billed as 'the interview of the century'. 'I have no intention to quench their thirst for revenge. The Federal Republic of Germany has no right to prosecute the former head of state of the German Democratic Republic for actions he took while in office.' When asked if the political changes in Moscow had created pressure from the Russians for him to quit the country, Honecker snapped: 'There is no such pressure. On the contrary, we are being well treated so far, nothing has changed about that.' In fact, it wasn't long afterward that the Russians unsuccessfully tried to convince him to leave voluntarily. After endless to-ing and fro-ing during October and November, Russian Minister of Justice, Nikolai Fyodorov personally paid a visit to Honecker's dacha on 10 December with an extradition order declaring it must be enforced no later than 13 December 1991, otherwise, he would be 'delivered' to the FRG by force.[30] It was a frosty encounter. With merciless candour, Margot revealed:[31]

> We were informed that the internal situation in the Soviet Union had changed since the attempted putsch. The economic and political pressure of the FRG was growing in all fields. The Honecker issue was becoming a burden to relations between the Russian-German governments. A compromise had to be found. On the Soviet side, the best solution was for Erich Honecker to return voluntarily. Moscow said they would work hard to get him a decent deal.[32]

What most concerned Margot, however, was the consent of the Soviet Union to a 'voluntary return' of her husband, which she said was in essence a deportation and an 'immoral action' from an ally and friend. 'We demanded a lawyer,' Margot added, 'since according to international law, in such a case the person involved must be heard in a court proceeding. But such a demand was ignored.'

Just at the moment when it seemed that there were no stumbling blocks to returning Honecker to Berlin, an unexpected incident happened. On

11 December, during a dinner at the Chilean embassy on Yunosti Street, Erich Honecker supposedly suffered a mild stroke. From then on, he was given sanctuary by Ambassador Clodomiro Almeyda, who himself had found refuge in the GDR during the Pinochet years. Though the Chilean government said it had refused a request for political asylum – the Honeckers remained inside the embassy as 'personal guests' of the ambassador, an action which threw up a whole series of new dilemmas. The embassy's Chargé d'Affaires, José Miguel Cruz, had clear memories of the Honeckers being installed in the best room, a kind of suite with a bathroom, where they listened to Deutsche Welle and received copies of the best West German newspapers daily. The decision to award this shelter was preceded by weeks of intense debate within the Chilean administration.[33]

An early offer of sanctuary from North Korea slipped away because of Russian objections (a special plane from Pyongyang, equipped with medical staff and an oxygen machine sat waiting at Moscow's Sheremetyevo airport).

In the wider world, as all this was happening, Mikhail Gorbachev agreed to the dissolution of the Soviet Union on 25 December 1991 and ceded all the powers still vested in it to Boris Yeltsin. Almost immediately, Russian authorities – against the wishes of the now powerless Gorbachev – again demanded that Honecker leave the country or else face deportation.

Over in Chile, while President Aylwin and a dozen senior Cabinet officials favoured giving sanctuary to Honecker, Bonn – which was perhaps its closest ally in the industrialised world – dangled the prospect of economic consequences. 'It affected the relationship between the president and the cabinet, in whose ranks many of its members had been exiled in the GDR,' recalled James Holger, a high-ranking official from the Chilean Foreign Ministry.

Having got wind of Honecker's predicament, Khalid Bakdash, leader of the Syrian Communist Party, offered the former General Secretary sanctuary in Damascus. The proposal was made in mid-January, when a party envoy pretending to apply for a visa, entered the Chilean Embassy to convey the invitation. According to *Nidal Al-Shab* newspaper, Honecker replied that Moscow had refused to allow him to leave the country, a fact later confirmed by Margot.

On 17 February, Honecker announced he did not want to undergo any more operations, despite his condition worsening – his kidneys had been stricken by cancer, but now other organs, such as his liver, had been affected. He did not want to go to a hospital in Moscow either, because, as Friedrich Wolff explained, 'the conditions there would be too problematical for him'. Apart from the possibility of being arrested, Erich was afraid of being harassed by the press. Wolff again called upon Bonn to allow Honecker to join Sonja and Leo in Chile.

Meanwhile, over in Bonn, Wolfgang von Geldern, a CDU lawmaker, called for a block on a US$69.4 million loan chancellor Kohl promised to Chile 'until the Honecker case is cleared up and Chile extradites him'.[34] During May, Erich – along with Mielke, Stoph, Kessler and Albrecht – was accused, in a 783-page indictment, of taking part in the 'collective manslaughter' of sixty-eight people as they attempted to flee East Germany. A bulging folder containing the indictment was delivered by courier to the Chilean embassy on Yunosti Street. Soon after, a notable chill entered the air when Clodomiro Almeyda – the ambassador who had facilitated Honecker's refuge – was replaced with James Holger. More than anything else, Holger remembered the confinement in which Honecker found himself was difficult, 'because it was very humiliating for someone proud of his status as former head of state being cooped up in a golden cage'.[35]

Finally, as Chile's position became untenable, Aylwin assured Chancellor Kohl in June that Honecker would leave the embassy. Behind the scenes, though, the action continued to be erratic, 'like, two steps forward, one step back,' according to Bonn's Foreign Minister Klaus Kinkel. 'We kept pressing.'

An important moment came during that stiflingly hot summer, when Holger made an appearance at the Chancellery in Bonn on 22 June 1992, to announce to Friedrich Bohl, a senior aide to Kohl, that Chile wanted to act. 'He reported in absolute discretion on the recent change in the attitude of the Chilean government,' Bohl stated.

However, the tipping point came two weeks later at a news conference, when Russian Federation President Boris Yeltsin was asked to expand on the question of Honecker and the issue of Russian-German relations.

> Our position on Honecker remains as it was. He is with the Chileans at the moment. Let Mr. Kohl decide this issue, together with the Chilean leadership. We do not intend to keep him in our country. We intend to hand him over to Germany. They can deal with him according to justice and according to the law in whatever way they feel necessary. It is all a matter for them. But we will not permit him to live illegally on our territory.[36]

Yeltsin's comments were enough for Santiago to draft an official revocation of Honecker's guest status. 'It was a police operation,' Holger recounted, giving a vivid snapshot of events. 'The [Russian] Undersecretary of Justice told me: "You put Honecker at the embassy door. Then the KGB will take him and escort him to a military plane."'[37]

The absurdity came to a head after Aylwin gave the go-ahead for the eviction on the evening of 28 July. The following afternoon, Holger, acting without preamble, thrust the typewritten revocation paper into Honecker's hand. The measure of surprise had its effect. After a surly outburst and mini-lecture, the former General Secretary scrawled: 'acknowledged under protest' on the bottom corner of the paper.[38]

From here on, events moved at lightning speed. With four uniformed Russian security officials looking on, the former General Secretary was given ten minutes to pack and present himself at the front door. Holger reflected:

> Some thought he would commit suicide. When it was time to leave, Honecker went up to the second floor to fix all his belongings. The Russian agents wanted to accompany him, arguing that he could take his own life. I told them no. I was convinced that he would not do it, because he was too proud a man and wanted to defend himself.

The sorry saga ended at half-past five in the afternoon, when Holger – holding Honecker's elbow – escorted him from the building. 'When he said goodbye,' Holger remembered, 'he told me: "You always respected my position as former head of state and you respected me as a person. I am deeply grateful to you."'[39] (James Holger told the author in 2000, that 'Erich demanded' he be transported to North Korea 'half a dozen times' during this encounter.)

After seven months holed up inside the embassy, the former General Secretary of the Socialist Unity Party of Germany – dressed in a navy-blue suit – emerged with his arm raised in a clenched-fist communist salute. One reporter noted his hair – always so scant and grey – had fallen out. Looking on anxiously, Margot waved goodbye. She would remain in the embassy another day before flying to Chile to join Sonja, ending what she described as months of 'psycho-terror'. That evening, at Vnukovo airport, Erich Honecker was placed on a Soviet Tu-134 civil airliner destined for Berlin. He would never see Russia again.

Return to Moabit

'The landing at Tegel was good,' Honecker marvelled, after the Tu-134 touched down and taxied to a remote freight area. 'People were standing on the roadside; I saw banners, red flags. I heard calls from friends and foes. The kind words predominated.' The mood quickly changed when he sped toward Moabit prison to jeers of 'Murderer!' from a noisy crowd of onlookers stationed at the prison gates. The media hysteria resembled the 'reporting of a large sporting event ... especially the landing of the plane with Honecker on board and the prisoner's journey through Berlin,' according to Friedrich Wolff.

'After fifty-seven years, I could see Moabit from the inside again,' Honecker recounted, as his eyes roamed over the prison. 'At Christmas 1935, the Gestapo brought me here from their headquarters on Prinz-Albrecht-Straße. I was in custody here for a year and a half. For how long will it be this time?' he mused. After a preliminary lecture – which was orderly and polite – the new inmate was given the prison number 244/92 and informed he would appear in court the following morning and, after a brief check-up, was pronounced fit for jail.

His arrival in Berlin was the subject of furious commentary in the media. *Neue Zeit*– a one-time GDR daily still in circulation – took up the assault. Noting the political climate was now starkly different, it reminded readers that the former General Secretary, like no other, stood for the collapse of the GDR and the 'vain, senile old men' of the SED leadership. 'His name is associated with the unbearable restriction of freedoms. And yet there remains a contradiction: Honecker was one of too few Germans who actively resisted Hitler.'[1] While observing that youngsters were 'more interested in the return of Batman to the screen than the return of Erich,' *Neue Zeit* conceded interest did not give way to indifference. 'On the contrary,' it asserted, 'the less one hears about the hiccups between Bonn-Santiago-Moscow, the more popular anger rises against this old man, incapable of all insight.'[2] Somewhat facetiously, *Neue Zeit* suggested it wouldn't have been difficult for Honecker to obtain a gun or a poison ampoule in Moscow and bid a 'manly farewell'. 'He would have had good press; tears would have flowed, and the German constitutional state would have been booed. Kinkel and Kohl would be considered bounty hunters. That would have been a more exciting political spectacle than the tough, meticulous days of litigation that will now follow.'[3] In closing, it asserted the former General Secretary would be the last of the Mohicans to defend the GDR. 'An acquittal for a lack of evidence would be like a slap in the face for the East Germans. Justice should take its course. Even if the accused will not show a trace of remorse.'[4]

On the morning of 30 July, though he needed rest and recuperation, Honecker shuffled into 'Room 500' at Tiergarten court in prison trousers, a white shirt and a grey jacket and was arraigned on forty-nine counts of manslaughter, he made no statement. The trial was expected to start in November.

As this was happening, Margot was on the move. 'I want nothing but my peace, and a few nice days with my grandson and daughter,' she told reporters in the lobby of Moscow airport before departing for Santiago. Though her marital spirit was unwavering, German media portrayed a woman abandoning her man in his most desperate hour. In an appalling full-page spread, *Bild* even cobbled together a series of vox-pops from the public to add colourful chunks of moral outrage. 'I would never desert my husband, no matter what happened,' indignant businesswoman Hieke Werbelow told the tabloid. 'That she did is typical.' Similarly, pensioner Lisbeth Reinsch declared Margot must not be a good wife, 'she deserted her husband, even though she is as guilty as he is'.[5]

Over at Moabit, doctors discovered Honecker's tumour had metastasised, prompting his lawyers to unsuccessfully appeal for him to be released until his trial. He was, though, moved to a private cell, containing a mirror, a square of carpet, an electric fire and a wooden table. Apart from treating his existing ailments, Honecker did not bother the prison medics unduly, except for the occasional sleeping tablet. 'Yesterday I was lucky enough to see Erich Mielke after such a long time,' he scribbled in a notepad. 'A nurse accompanied him on a tour of the yard. I called him from upstairs. No reaction. I again shouted: "Erich!" This time with "Red Front!" That rang across the whole courtyard ... Again nothing.' (There is anecdotal evidence that Mielke was trying to work his passage out of the dock by feigning senility. However, the record shows serious questions were asked as to whether the former Stasi chief was sufficiently balanced or emotionally stable to stand trial.)

When defence lawyer Nicolas Becker met Honecker a week later, he saw a man with a fighting spirit which:

> stayed on until he had the opportunity to give his long political statement in this trial, although this spirit was increasingly restrained by his failing health. My impression was that communist leaders were best to bear when they were not in power, during their fighting period. Honecker, in the early phase of his stay in Moabit, showed a bit of the fighting spirit of a communist youth leader.[6]

An unexpected source of comfort was provided by a former schoolteacher, Eva Ruppert, who made contact with Erich after seeing a report about his incarceration on TV. Over the coming months, she visited Moabit five or six times and kept up a vigorous flow of correspondence. 'He never complained about his situation, but showed great humanity,' she recalled, though was astonished at how he had visibly aged. Even in a tracksuit, she thought he 'retained poise and dignity'. Erich took some consolation from reading, writing and from music and – at his request – Ruppert sent books and cassette tapes (music by Vivaldi and spoken Rosa Luxemburg works). He was impressed with bestsellers *Bonfire of the Vanities* by Tom Wolfe, *The Firm* by John Grisham,[7] and Heleno Saha's *Fourth Reich*, which he thought, 'excellently written'. Eva also sent a copy of *Memories*, Andrei Gromyko's newly published autobiography. 'Now I am starting to read it from the beginning,' Honecker noted on 19 September. 'You can't take his praise for Gorbachev seriously,' he cattily remarked, referring to the gushing words drooling from Gromyko's pen.[8] Honecker's own attempt at a written chronicle – scrawled into a school notebook – included a painful amount of brooding but little self-analysis. 'The tragedy of the GDR,' he mused, was 'particularly great because it was – besides the USSR – the most developed socialist country, one real alternative to the imperialist system.'[9] The German Democratic Republic, he contended, was an indispensable part of history. 'No amount of anti-socialist agitation can make history disappear.'[10] He lamented that former citizens would miss 'what was particularly dear to them about the GDR', including affordable housing, social security, vacations for everyone, and university opportunities for the working classes.

In general, Becker told the author, Honecker adapted well to prison life. 'He chose to wear the regulation clothing and never complained. He showed a certain dignity and got on well with the other inmates.' He never showed any regret about the loss of his status and of his privileges, in contrast to 'many fallen businessmen doing time in Moabit who showed the whiny side of their personality. On his birthday, he asked for 'Mon Cheri', a popular chocolate praline with cherry and a small amount of liquor. This wish was denied by the presiding judge because alcohol was forbidden in prison'.[11]

A new CT scan in August 1992 confirmed the existence of a malignant tumour in the right lobe of his liver, prompting defence lawyers to fruitlessly request legal proceedings – as far as they were aimed against their client – be abandoned and the arrest warrant withdrawn.

In fact, until the very eve of the trial's opening, concerns about the health of the defendants eclipsed the actual case. For a few days, Honecker's focus shifted to Margot, after an organisation known as 'Help' (an association for the victims of political violence in Europe) brought a second charge against her in connection with compulsory adoptions. The application was filed on behalf of Carola Jacob, who was given an eighteen-month prison term in 1979 because of 'an attempt to cross the GDR border illegally', and 'antisocial behaviour'. During her incarceration, Jacob was informed that her 7-year-old son, Michael, had been adopted by order. The first charge against Margot had been filed at the beginning of August by Gisela Mauritz concerning the compulsory adoption of her son, Alexander. (There was, however, another story about allegations of children being abused and driven to suicide in a prison-like barrack in Torgau known – according to the Western media – as 'Margot's Concentration camp'. She managed to avoid prosecution).[12]

'In Germany, the hunt against you, my little one, will continue,' Honecker wrote in a short, tender note to his wife. 'That hurts ... The judiciary of the FRG has no right to sit in court over you, who has served your state loyally and successfully.'

In The Dock

The trial of Erich Honecker and five co-defendants – Erich Mielke, Willi Stoph, Heinz Kessler, Fritz Streletz and Hans Albrecht – described by the *Berliner Zeitung* as the 'largest legal process in German post-war history' – began at the Berlin regional court on 12 November 1992.

As the media frenzy developed, it was widely pointed out that excluding Hitler's successor, Admiral Dönitz – Honecker was the first German head-of-state to be put on trial in over 800 years.[1]

Before proceedings opened, Honecker's chief defence lawyer, Friedrich Wolff, told reporters:

> The Berlin Wall was not built by the initiative of anyone in Germany, but by order of Soviet leaders in Moscow. It was a symptom of a political confrontation that has now ended. You can condemn these defendants politically or morally, and historians may also judge them harshly. But they acted under the laws of a country that was internationally recognised, and today's Germany has no legal right to put them on trial.[2]

On entering the court at 9.30am, Honecker scanned the public gallery for a friendly face. After a few seconds, his eyes laid on a young man thrusting his fist skyward in a gesture – he then shouted: 'Hello Erich. Red Front. We will win, not them.' Smiling, Honecker responded with a Marxist-Leninist salute. That morning, the galleries were jammed with over a hundred supporters of the prosecution. They watched carefully as Erich Mielke – wearing dark sunglasses – hobbled into the courtroom on a stick, followed by Hans Albrecht, a District Party Secretary, who claimed to be so deaf he couldn't follow proceedings. Former Prime Minister Willi Stoph was excused, having suffered a stroke the night before.

Watching the spectacle, Friedrich Wolff thought the condition of the accused reminded him of the old East German joke about the start of central committee meetings. 'First point of order: carry in the Politburo. Second point of order: plug in the pacemakers.' As the courtroom grew hushed, the forty-nine charges of manslaughter related to escape attempts were reduced to thirteen to speed the trial. Although no document was found in which Honecker (or anyone else) explicitly ordered guards to fire at fleeing citizens, he supposedly endorsed the 'unhampered use' of firearms to prevent escapes during a meeting of the National Defence Council in May 1974.[3]

However, Hans Georg Brautigam, who led the three judges, ended the session almost as soon as it began to allow ailing Willi Stoph to undergo medical tests. When it recommenced, proceedings were halted again after Honecker suffered a bout of faintness. (The incident immediately touched off mischief, as anonymous letters were sent to several newspaper offices in Bonn and Berlin claiming the former GDR leader had died.)

From here on, the case never really gained steam. Affidavits assessing the state of Honecker's health were repeatedly introduced, and on one occasion, a representative of one of the co-plaintiffs argued that Honecker was not suffering from cancer but rather a tapeworm, and even proposed that the man in the dock was not Honecker but a body double. Nicolas Becker recalled that:

> The trial was exhausting for him, and his appearance deteriorated clearly from day to day. He was more and more marked by his illness. He never expressed fear to be found guilty, because he thought the trial to be a political trial and he considered the thesis of the prosecutors – that he had violated his own GDR-law by giving orders to prevent transgressions of the Wall by deadly force, if necessary – an ideological theory. On the other hand, the question of responsibility did not arise with Honecker, because who would be more responsible than him.[4]

On 16 November – arguing vigorously that his life expectancy was estimated to be three to six months, while the legal process was forecast to take at least two years, Honecker's lawyers questioned whether it was humane to try a dying man. The following day, proceedings were edging toward an ignominious collapse when Erich Mielke was withdrawn from the trial as his memory floundered about dates, people and places. The next morning, another hearing was adjourned after Honecker was quoted as saying: 'I cannot take any more.' A doctor said he was suffering from an irregular heartbeat and high blood pressure. Again, Nicolas Becker filed a motion to throw out the whole case. 'A man is in danger of being tried to death by typically German thoroughness and implacability,' he said. 'The point of continuing this trial can only be to torment the defendant.' However, the judge was in no hurry to end proceedings and, finally, on Thursday, 3 December, Honecker prepared to deliver the speech he had spent months drafting in prison.

'I don't feel any pain or weakness,' he noted in his diary before entering room 700 of Moabit criminal court. After being called over to the dock,

Honecker described his trial as a travesty of justice. 'It is political theatre,' he said, speaking in a soft but authoritative voice. Furthermore, looking directly at the judges, he said the Berlin Wall had prevented an international confrontation. 'Not building the Wall would have meant the risk of a third world war.' With an eye to the history books, he stood by the fact that the 'decision of 1961 was correct and remained correct'.

As his seventy-minute statement continued, he navigated into murkier waters by noting, 'the people being tried today were yesterday welcomed as honoured guests of the state. Either the politicians from West Germany voluntarily and eagerly greeted a murderer, or they did not consider him guilty of murder.' For his closing statement, Honecker crafted these words:

> I am not going to lend this accusation and this court procedure the appearance of legality by defending myself against the evidently unfounded accusation of manslaughter. A defence is also superfluous because I will not live to hear your verdict. The punishment which you evidently have in mind will never reach me. Everybody knows that today. So, for this reason alone any trial against me is a farce.[5]

It was a triumphant performance. Becker recalled:

> This statement is considered to be his best political speech. We two Western defence lawyers, Wolfgang Ziegler and me, were not involved in drafting it. The reading of this speech in court cost him a lot of strength. One had the impression that after giving this speech, his fighting reservoir was exhausted.[6]

Indeed, on the following day – 4 December – Honecker was wheeled to the prison clinic for a tomography and sonography. 'It does not look good,' he gloomily noted in his diary.

Meanwhile, his battle-weary lawyers again requested the trial be abandoned, but to no avail. Their application was rejected on 21 December. Honecker was troubled, too, by a second arrest warrant for alleged corruption, a possible sign that Prosecutors were getting jittery. 'My lawyers continue to be optimistic,' he noted that evening. 'They have been since August. But this has shown repeatedly to be unfounded.' However, media influence on public opinion increased, both in Germany and abroad. *Der Spiegel* – the magazine Honecker had despised so much began relentlessly working for his release. As a last throw of the dice, Honecker's lawyers handed a complaint to the newly created Berlin Constitutional Court on 29 December stating that the decision to proceed violated their client's fundamental right to human dignity – an overriding principle in the Constitution of Berlin, above even the state penal system and criminal justice. (It is based on Article 1, Paragraph 3 of the Berlin Constitution, and Article 1 of the Basic Law, according to which human dignity is inviolable. Shortly before Christmas, the Berlin Regional Court said Honecker would probably not survive the finish of his trial.)

By this point, Honecker was spiralling into depression. In a letter to Margot on 7 January 1993, he complained about his 'witch trial', confessing he could find hardly any words about the attitude and the actions to describe 'those who do this to us'. Above all, health matters crowded his horizon – high blood pressure, cancer treatments and exhaustion stultified everything.

But then, things suddenly changed.

Gute Nacht

After 169 days in investigative custody, Honecker's trial – dogged by blunders and a tangle of paperwork – finally ended on 12 January 1993. The last throw of the dice by petitioning Berlin's Constitutional Court worked. Judges ruled his further imprisonment was inconsistent with respect for human dignity leading to the Berlin District Court abandoning the case.[1] All this was 'extremely stressful for Honecker,' says Becker, as prosecutors tried until the last second to prevent his release and departure:

> A famous medical professor who had agreed to examine Honecker as a private doctor informed the Prosecutors on the night before Honecker's departure by breaking his duty of medical confidentiality, saying that he could 'repair' Honecker to make him fit to stand the trial. We sued him later and this break confidentiality cost him 10,000 Euros. But the prosecutors did not succeed because a reversal of the decisions to release Honecker was legally and politically impossible also, considering the media frenzy where journalists booked every airplane to South America and left in the last minute because Honecker took another plane. The whole affair had taken speed, had accelerated towards his release and his travel to Chile, that it just could not be stopped.

Interestingly, the lead prosecutor told Becker that he would have asked for the maximum punishment of fifteen years for Honecker if the trial had continued.

The next morning, German media opined the trial was, from gavel to gavel, a depressing spectacle. *Leipziger Volkszeitung* gave its verdict:

> Death will not catch up with Honecker in the dock, and this is good. This old, stubborn man was secretly wishing for death in front of the judge and the cameras as his ultimate revenge. Perhaps it was just in time that the constitutional judges halted the trial proceedings to prevent the possibility that Honecker would die during it – and thus become a martyr.

226

The *Tageszeitung* contended that any 'normal person' indicted for manslaughter would long ago have been released from custody. However, in Honecker's case, the 'trial was overburdened with non-juridical considerations from the very start.'

Over in Chile, Deputy Foreign Minister Edmundo Vargas confirmed Honecker could enter the country if he fulfilled the requirements of Chilean law. Clutching his new passport issued by the Interior Ministry in Bonn, Honecker left Moabit prison a free man and was escorted to Tegel airport in a carload of detectives. He caught a connecting flight to Frankfurt, from where the journey to Santiago took twenty hours on Varig flight RG-741.

On touchdown, the other passengers were ushered out before Honecker stepped into the bright Chilean sunlight. Unaided, he walked down the gangway into the arms of Margot, making a victory sign before being rushed off to the VIP lounge where leaders of Chilean communist and socialist parties were waiting, some carrying flowers. 'I find it hard to express my real feelings at this moment,' he told the gathering, adding:

> Behind me lie many difficult years in hospitals and more than five months in jail. Right at the beginning of this ordeal I learned about my illness, but I was comforted and helped by the solidarity expressed by the Chilean people, by friends and fellow-men throughout the world. I never thought I would see my dear wife and brave companion again.[2]

After reiterating his thanks, he was taken to Las Condes Hospital to undergo new medical check-ups and treatment for his kidney cancer. The following day he arrived at his last address – 'House G' on Carlos Silva Vildósola – a small two-floor residence in the condominium of La Reina.

The walls were beige, the furniture plain and simple – a blue-white-red striped sofa, glass table, wicker chair and a sideboard. A large fuchsia bougainvillea stood out in a garden, full of untidy bushes and clothes drying in the sun.

Without skipping a beat, Margot took full control of her husband's care, coordinating his medicine, fixing meals, maintaining finances and scheduling visitors. She hired Diego Aguirre as a live-in secretary to act as an interpreter and personal assistant. From then on, 22-year-old Aguirre – a former exile in East Berlin – helped his new master deal with doctors, translate private discussions, and aid with mail.[3] In those first few weeks, Aguirre was bewildered by the constant surveillance from the German media – only inside, behind closed drapes, was the family hidden from the glare of photographers. Erich was happiest when Sonja and the grandchildren came to visit. 'He wanted to spend his last days with his family,' Aguirre recalled. 'That was the most important thing for him. In those moments he was happy and smiled.'[4] Far from being bored, Honecker devoured the German press, which always arrived with a two-day delay, while Aguirre translated articles from local newspapers. More than anything else, however, Honecker committed himself to organising his memoirs, a colossal effort that never gained traction given his preoccupation with listening to the tides and currents of German opinion via shortwave radio, and turning on the rhetoric, full flood, in defence of socialism to anyone that would listen. 'He talked and talked, and I always had to wait until he stopped,' Aguirre laughed. 'He spoke long, nice German sentences and I had to wait until I translated. Sometimes I had to say: stop!'[5]

Margot kept busy too. She was an avid reader and voracious letter writer. While she loved the South American sunshine, she longed for snow and white forests, a point she later wrote repeatedly from Chile to acquaintances when they ask if she missed Germany: 'Not Germany, but the German winter.'

Good news arrived by post on 23 March when Honecker was informed he was to receive a pension backdated from August 1992. From then on, funds were transferred monthly to his bank account in Chile.[6] Deposits were topped up by occasional donations from political friends which helped pay medical bills and the mortgage. 'Every monetary gift was welcomed, and at least as a gesture of solidarity,' Aguirre remembered.[7] There were also visitors and gifts from countries and organisations which the GDR had helped and since the country no longer existed, the Honeckers accepted their gratitude.[8] On one occasion, Yasser Arafat was asked if he 'contributed a significant sum' to Honecker's old-age pension. 'I did not give him anything, although I would like to. I am proud that Erich Honecker is my friend. I, personally, and the Palestinian people owe him much. The GDR helped us politically and militarily and trained numerous Palestinian students. I am a man who never forgets such things.'[9]

A huge 'contribution' to the Honecker pension pot came from Cuban singer Silvio Rodriguez, who donated money collected after a concert in Santiago. A hat was even passed around at a luncheon bash in April marking Margot's 66th birthday at the 'Rincön de los Teatinos' restaurant – an occasion used as an official welcome party for Erich. In all, around a hundred guests – including many Chileans and political comrades arrived at what turned out to be Margot and Erich's last hurrah. There were other reasons to celebrate that month after the Berlin Regional Court shut down the trial against Honecker for good, saying his 'serious illness' was justification for the trial's closure.[10]

Unshackled from the threat of further action, Honecker used an interview with a West German magazine to let off steam without worrying about the public reaction. Talking to *SUPERillu*, he criticised Mikhail Gorbachev and Egon Krenz, saying they 'betrayed the socialist camp'. As far as he was concerned, 'Gorbachev was finished'. He freely admitted to making mistakes during his time in government but insisted 'one should not put all the blame' on him. 'Many problems were caused by other people; Mr. Kohl knows that.' In unvarnished language, he rattled on about a new united Germany, predicting a 'black, black, black' future, expressing relief he did not have to solve the problems of that country. He had no complaints whatever against life in Chile, but sometimes felt homesick but 'not for the Berlin of today'. He forced a sour smile when revealing he was unsure about returning to Germany – or even if he could live there in freedom. He did disclose, however, that he was composing his memoirs 'for the German youth ... so they could learn the full truth'.

While continuing this revealing dialogue, he snapped at accusations that he was responsible for the deaths of innocent people: 'The West German press is lying through its teeth,' he asserted, closing the subject which remained off-limits. Health wise, he felt 'sometimes well, sometimes less well', he moved more slowly and had gotten used to the pains. 'I still feel strong,' he chivalrously remarked.[11] However, not long after unburdening himself to *SUPERillu*, his health took a dramatic turn for the worse. Indeed, medical records show he received several blood transfusions but was weakened by an ineffable weariness. According to Juan Carlos Arriagada, a Chilean neighbour, Honecker still managed to 'closely follow the fate of his comrades in Germany' and was horrified when Defence Minister Heinz Kessler, and his deputy Fritz Streletz, were found guilty on charges of incitement to commit manslaughter, while Hans Albrecht was convicted of aiding and abetting manslaughter. 'These sentences came as bitter blows to both Margot and Erich,' said Ed Stuhler. 'It certainly didn't help his health.' Over the coming month, Honecker barely left the neighbourhood, his daily exercise was a slow stroll out in the yard and around the house, always alone, always in silence. Then as the cold weather of the southern hemisphere winter set in, he remained virtually bedridden in a small room on the ground floor where the thermostat had been pre-set to 22°C.

On 7 December 1993, he was rushed to the private 'Clinica Las Condes' in Santiago after fainting – doctors installed a pacemaker. For the next six months, he was worn out, apathetic towards his surroundings and sleeping for long periods. As the cancer progressed, the situation looked grave. Furthermore, Honecker did not bother the hospital with his presence again as he prepared himself for his demise. On 25 May, his doctor, Renato Palma, confirmed he turned down a last-minute operation as 'hopeless'.

Finally, the end for Erich Paul Honecker came at 7 am on 29 May 1994 at 'House G' on Carlos Silva Vildósola in the presence of his wife and daughter. Ever stoic, Margot held his hand. She later telephoned the news to her lawyers in Berlin to get the word out. Telegrams of condolence came from staunch friends, including North Korea's Kim Il-sung, who recalled Honecker actively supported the Korean people in the cause of socialist construction and national reunification: 'The exploits he performed in his lifetime would remain forever.'[12]

Over in Bonn, Helmut Kohl's spokesman, Dieter Vogel, stepped forward to declare Honecker had failed in his political goals. 'His policies caused pain to countless people in Germany. Respect in the face of death requires that we say very little at this time about his role in post-war German history.'

Respect was the last thing German TV commentator Juergen Engert showed when describing Honecker as 'a small figure who will turn out to be nothing more than a footnote in history. But what he did and didn't do will keep us busy for a very long time to come.' *Neue Zeit* opined that he represented a state in which very few people had confidence. 'He was not the GDR, and the GDR was not Honecker.' In a blistering editorial, the *Irish Independent* asserted the verdict of historians throughout the world would be a harsh one. 'Erich Honecker imprisoned his own nation. As an epitaph, it is one few people would care to leave behind them.'

Finally, after funeral arrangements were decided, 3,000 people gathered in the summer heat at Honecker's cremation at Santiago's General Cemetery on Monday, 30 May. Around the open casket, wreaths from friends, neighbours and the German Communist Party were carefully spread out. Margot sat without a glance to either side. 'He did not want a funeral in his home country,' Diego Aguirre explained, 'he knew he would die in Chile. They understood that the country they loved no longer existed.'[13]

At the same time, over in Berlin, half a dozen members of the tiny Communist Party of Germany held a small memorial service at the socialist cemetery in Friedrichsfelde, a few metres away from the well-manicured graves of Walter Ulbricht and Edith Baumann.[14]

Looking back, Roberto Yanez said his grandfather was sacrificed to the communist system, which he had helped to create. 'His own secret service kept files on him and his wife. He was the victim of his unwavering belief in his big brother, the Soviet Union.'[15]

The urn containing his ashes remained with Margot, who continued to live a peaceful life in Chile. She seldom gave statements to the press and only spoke a couple of times to sympathetic journalists. She defended the GDR, the Berlin Wall, and said that German unification was a mistake. On the 10th anniversary of the fall of the Wall in 1999, she slammed her front door in the face of reporters asking how she would spend the day. In her only notable TV interview in 2012, she called the fall of the communist regime a 'counter-revolution', and lamented the demise of the GDR: 'It is a tragedy that this country no longer exists.' She also took the opportunity to complain about her monthly pension of almost €2000, a comfortable income in Chile. But by this point, Margot was already battling breast cancer, which returned aggressively in January 2016 and spread up her spine. She rented the La Reina apartment to pay for round-the-clock care from Chilean nurses who administered morphine to relieve the pain: 'I get injected with opium every four hours,' she told one friend. Her death in May 2016, was announced by the Communist Party of Chile:

> Hundreds of exiled Chilean communists remember and deeply appreciate the solidarity and friendship in which Margot Honecker took an active part – solidarity that reached the Chilean people in the difficult moments of the dictatorship that struck our country from September 1973.
>
> Since her youth, she gave her life to the cause of socialism and fought for the sovereignty and development of the German Democratic Republic. After the fall of socialism in Europe, she received political asylum in Chile, where she maintained friendly ties with our party and especially with those of our members who were able to rebuild their lives in the GDR, receiving the welcome and fraternity of the German people … solidarity that is not forgotten.[16]

Characteristically, *Bild* greeted her demise with the headline: 'No tears for the purple witch.' Several newspapers did acknowledge that she, like her husband, remained utterly sincere in her beliefs.

As for Egon Krenz, he was sentenced to six-and-a-half years in prison in 1997 on four counts of manslaughter, connected with East Germans trying to cross the Berlin Wall or the border between West and East Germany. Krenz complained his trial was little more than 'victor's justice'. 'I know that I am being sentenced in the name of the whole of the former East Germany. The verdict is an expression of the political will of reunited Germany. It has been delivered by exclusively West German judges.' He began serving his sentence in 2000 and spent almost four years in prison. 'It was an unjust trial since I acted as the head of the GDR, a sovereign state,' said Krenz, echoing Honecker's earlier sentiments. Now, the former 'crown prince' leads a quiet life in the Baltic Sea resort of Dierhagen in Mecklenburg – West Pomerania. Günter Schabowski was convicted along with Krenz but because he accepted moral guilt and denounced the GDR, he was sent to prison for only three years. He died in West Berlin in 2015. Günter Mittag was accused of using government funds to build a private home but never faced trial. He died in 1994. As for Erich Mielke, the much-feared Stasi boss, he died in May 2000, aged 92, in a nursing home in Berlin. Within hours of his funeral, flowers and wreaths left at his graveside were torn to shreds by persons unknown.

Acknowledgements

There are a number of people and institutions I wish to thank for their help with this book. I am grateful to the staff at the German Federal Archives or Bundesarchiv, DDR Museum, the European School of Management and Technology (ESMT Berlin), Staatsbibliothek zu Berlin, Wandlitz community council, British Library, and the Forschungs und Gedenkstätte Normannenstraße. I am also indebted to Ed Stuhler, Adam Kellet-Long, Jurgen Litfin, Nicolas Becker and Bernard Morley. At Pen and Sword, I would like to thank my commissioning editor Jonathan Wright, and Charlotte Mitchell, who ensured the project was brought together successfully.

Notes

The Miner's Boy

1. *Honecker Cross Examined*. Pleckbond Ltd (London), 1992. p.55
2. The Allied occupation of the Rhineland took place following the armistice that brought the fighting of World War I to a close on 11 November 1918. The occupying armies consisted of American, Belgian, British and French forces.
3. Honecker, Erich. 'Skizze seines politischen Lebens'. Dietz (Berlin), 1977. p.9.
4. Erich Honecker – Kandidat Der Jugend. Cited from Heinz Lippmann's *Honecker and the New Politics of Europe*. Macmillan. 1972. p.14
5. *Saarbrücker Zeitung* 23 August 1977
6. *Neues Deutschland*. 9 February 1989
7. *Honecker Cross Examined*. p.64
8. Ibid. pp.64–65.
9. Dieter Borkowski 'Erich Honecker: Statthalter Moskaus oder deutscher Patriot?' Bertelsmann, 1987. pp.25–26

Mother Russia

1. Established in the mid-1920s by the Comintern – the Soviet-controlled organisation that governed Communist parties around the globe.
2. Typed transcript of 1983 Ogonjok interview, Honecker papers. German State Archives.
3. Honecker, Erich. *From My Life*. Pergamon, 1981. p.45
4. Ibid.
5. Norbert *Pötzl* 'Honecker: Eine deutsche Biographie' Deutsche Verlags-Anstalt GmbH, 2002. p.28
6. Saarbrucker Zeitung. 5 May 1971
7. Born in 1886, 'Teddy' Thalmann a longshoreman and transport worker, joined the KPD in 1920 and became its party chairman in Hamburg in 1921.
8. *From My Life*. p.61

9. Ibid p.70
10. Ibid p.91
11. Ibid
12. Ibid
13. Heinz Lippmann's *Honecker and the New Politics of Europe*. Macmillan, 1972. p.245

The Prison Years

1. *Honecker Cross Examined.* p.88
2. *From My Life.* p.100
3. *Honecker Cross Examined.* p.84
4. Skizze seines politischen Lebens. p.36
5. Ibid
6. *From My Life.* p.101
7. Willi died on 21 April 1944 in Hungary.
8. SS letter to the Chief Reich Prosecutor at the People's Court. November 13, 1942.
9. *Honecker Cross Examined.* p.86
10. Ibid
11. Völkischer Beobachter. Norddeutsche Ausgabe (Berlin), 16 September 1944.
12. *From My Life.* p.110
13. Borkowski. p.128
14. *From My Life.* p.113
15. Ibid p.116
16. Ich schlug meiner Mutter die brennenden Funken ab: Berliner Schulaufsätze aus dem Jahr 1946 – Annett Gröschner/ Rowohlt Taschenbuch Verlag. In 1946, in the immediate aftermath of the war, Berlin students described their personal wartime experiences in essays. In these authentic documents they talk of fear of death, horror and lucky escapes.
17. Skizze seines politischen Lebens. p.38
18. Ibid. p.119
19. Ibid

Climbing the Ladder

1. And it is here that there appears to be some deliberate blotting out of the historical record. An account in Heinz Lippmann's 1971 biography *Honecker* republished a version of events from a Mrs Vera Kuchenmeister which states on returning to Berlin, Honecker stayed with her family in an apartment near the Alexanderplatz – this clearly never happened.

2. Wolfgang Leonhard 'Child of the Revolution,' as cited from *The Berlin Blockade* by Ann and John Tusa. Coronet, 1988. p.44.

3. *Neues Deutschland*, 17 April 1965

4. Ibid

5. Reinhard Müller, Die Akte Wehner. Rowohlt Tb, 1994. p.69

6. *From My Life*, Erich Honecker.

7. His only rival for the post, Paul Verner –a young, dynamic politician – replaced him as KPD youth secretary. Although Paul Verner was widely seen as the more dynamic candidate, Ulbricht appreciated Honecker's submissive, obedient manner. (According to biographer Dieter Borkowski, some observers considered Verner 'downright devious'.)

8. Interview with Nathan Morley, 2016

9. Birgit Wolf: Sprache in der DDR. Ein Wörterbuch. Berlin, 2000 P 62.

10. *From My Life*, p.128

11. Skizze seines politischen Lebens. p.39

12. Ibid

13. Ibid

14. Ibid pp.42–43

15. Neues Leben. 1 November 1945

16. *Daily News*. 11 June 1946

17. Einheit. March 1946

18. *Neues Deutschland*. 22 March 1947.

19. Skizze seines politischen Lebens. p.67.

20. *Neues Deutschland*. 7 August 1947.

21. Lippmann. p.79

22. Honi konnte nicht mal Russisch! *Bild*. 14 September 2011.

23. *Neues Deutschland*. 9 February 1989

24. The first edition was published in February 1947 and the paper expanded later that year.

25. *Neues Deutschland*. 13 February 1947

26. The United States and Britain rejected Moscow's claims that Berlin sat in Soviet territory as being totally without foundation. (A protocol of 12 September 1944 made clear that 'Berlin was not part of, or located on, the territory to be occupied as a zone by any one of the powers under the Agreement on Zone of Occupation in Germany.) Documents of American Foreign Relations 1961. p.147

27. *Berliner Zeitung*. 29 September 1949

28. *Neues Deutschland*. 9 February 1989

29. *Western Morning News*. 13 October 1949

30. *Sheffield Weekly Telegraph*. 12 August 1950

31. This occurred at the First party conference in East Berlin (January 25–18), when the SED completed the transition to a 'new type of party'.

A Girl Called Margot
1. *Honecker Cross Examined* p.110
2. ZDF 'Honecker's Secrets'. 2017.
3. The small secretariat of the SED Politburo, which at that time was made up of seven people (five from the former KPD: Hermann Axen, Franz Dahlem, Fred Oelssner, Horst Sindermann and Walter Ulbricht, two from the SPD: Edith Baumann and Paul Wessel). After this, Baumann would serve as secretary for agriculture at the SED Berlin office and headed the women's work department in the Central Committee from 1955 to 1960.
4. Borkowski. p.206
5. *From My Life*. p.352
6. This event happened on 28 May 1950
7. *From My Life*. p.188
8. Erich Honecker, 'An alle Mitglieder der FDJ', in Junge Deutschland. p.70
9. *Northern Whig*. 6 August 1951.
10. *Neues Deutschland*. 16 August 1951
11. *Daily Herald*. 21 August 1951
12. Ibid
13. *From My Life*. p.23.

The Model Stalinist
1. 1 April 1952. Record of Conversation of Leaders of the Socialist Unity Party of Germany W. Pieck, W. Ulbricht and O. Grotewohl with J.V.Stalin
2. *Daily Express*. 28 May 1952
3. *Junge Welt*. 7 May 1952
4. Ibid
5. Hermann Matern was the same age as Ulbricht and totally devoted to him.
6. By this point, 9,000 companies had been nationalized, including the industrial concerns Wintershall, I.G. Farben, Mannesmann, Flick, Siemens, AEG and Krupp. The big banks, such as Deutsche Bank, Dresdner Bank, Commerzbank, along with savings banks and other financial and credit institutions also became public property.
7. *Dundee Courier*. 10 December 1952
8. *Daily News* (London). 18 November 1952
9. BUP. 8 December 1952

A Fragile Foundation

1. Cable from the Czechoslovak Mission in Berlin to Foreign Minister Vaclav David, 17 June 1953, received 1.45 pm. CET Source: National Security Archive/CWIHP, 'Russian and Eastern European Documents Database (READD)' Collection. Provided by Andreij Edemsky (Moscow); translated by Caroline Kovtun.
2. Ibid
3. *Pravda* Correspondent P. Naumov to Dimitrii Shepilov, 'Report on the Events in Berlin on 16 and 17 June 1953', 22 June 1953 Source: TsKhSD (Moscow), per. 4546, op. 30, pap. 5, 11. 72–86. Published in German in Gerhard Beier, WirwollenfreieMenschensein (Koln Bund, 1993), PP163-168. Translated by Christiaan Hetzner.
4. Lippmann. p.157
5. *Daily News* (London). 18 June 1953
6. Ibid
7. FBIS-FRB-53-119
8. Prague, Czech Home Service. 20 June 1953
9. 'Memorandum from Karl Schirdewan to First Secretaries of the District Leadership of the SED', 21 June 1953, History and Public Policy Program Digital Archive, SAPMO-BArch, DY 30 IV 2/5/530. Translated by Christiaan Hetzner.http://digitalarchive.wilsoncenter.org/document/112614
10. Albert Norden, speech to the Central Committee of the SED, October 1955. As cited from *Honecker* by Heinz Lippmann. p.167
11. *Pötzl*. p.65
12. Ibid
13. *From My Life*. p.193
14. *Honecker Cross Examined*. p.109
15. By the mid-1960s, the Stasi was employing 50,000 full-time staff and had over 100,000 collaborators.

Return To Moscow

1. From this point, Karl Schirdewan, gained influence within the FDJ given his position as the youth secretary in the Central Committee. Schirdewan had long considered Honecker an ineffective windbag, ill-suited to his job. Also, it is worth noting, that with Honecker in Moscow, Albert Norden detailed criticism culminates in the demand that FDJ work must be 'turned inside out', the 'structure of the apparatus to be changed'. Norden's working group had carried out thorough research in several towns and rural communities in order to obtain an authentic picture of the state of the FDJ.

2. Remarkably, the four-man delegation from East Germany – Walter Ulbricht, Otto Grotewohl, Alfred Neumann and Karl Schirdewan – had not been invited to hear Khrushchev, so after dinner, they retired to bed. It was only when a Soviet comrade woke them up at 3 am that same morning that they learned about Khrushchev's outburst. He spoke of how within a few short hours, the man who had ruled supreme for three decades had been unmasked as a despot. After listening intently, the German delegation returned to their beds, without a single word or comment; only Schirdewan stayed up to write a detailed note of the speech. 'Walter Ulbricht and Karl Schirdewan, who stayed in Moscow, said nothing to me about,' Honecker lashed out acidly.

3. Eventually, the town of Stalinstadt was changed to Eisenhuttenstadt and Stalinallee was rechristened as Karl-Marx-Allee and Frankfurter Allee.

4. The hotly tempered Schirdewan was already acquainted with Khrushchev and the pair enjoyed a cordial relationship, while Ulbricht distrusted him – primarily because he had been locked up in Nazi concentration camps during the war – rather than working in Soviet service, making him 'unreliable'.

Highflyer

1. *Honecker Cross Examined*. p.114
2. Skizze seines politischen Lebens. p.104
3. Ibid. p.106
4. Lippmann. p.179
5. Borkowski. p.249
6. Brandt Heinz autobiography. p.326, cited from Volklein. p.259
7. From 1985 to 1989 Wolfgang Herger was head of the department for security issues of the Central Committee of the SED and the first civilian head of this department.

Endless Flight

1. Berlin, ADN, Radioteletype. 29 April 1959. FBIS-FRB-59-088
2. While this prosperity and the international prestige that went with it were widely reported, observers lamented the greatest unsolved problem in Europe remained German reunification. Commentators mourned that no substantive steps had been taken in that direction or toward a rapprochement between the GDR and FRG.
3. Poland, the GDR and the Soviet Union signed an agreement in Moscow on the construction of the 'Friendship' oil pipeline, which secured the supply of Soviet oil to Poland and the GDR.

4. On 16 July 1958, Honecker was also elected a Secretary of the Central Committee. In this capacity, he was occupied with military and security policy, youth policy, trade union policy, the rights of women and the promotion of sports and physical education.
5. Berlin, ADN. 14 July 1958. FBIS-FRB-58-137
6. This would happen, he said, by abrogating the Potsdam Pact and four-power rule and place control of Allied communications to West Berlin in the hands of the East German government (the Allies would not deal with the Ulbricht regime, even as a Soviet agent).
7. *New York Times*. 11 November 1958.
8. *Neue Zeit*. 31 December 1959
9. *Daily News* (London). 26 August 1960

The Sixties

1. The minutes of the Politburo meeting of 28 August 1956 read: 'Measures for a new housing estate are to be prepared.'
2. After Baumann's death in 1973, Politburo candidate Werner Jarowinsky, who was responsible for trade and supplies in the Central Committee Secretariat, moved in.
3. Schabowski, Günter. Der Absturz. Rowohlt Repertoire , 2019. p.105
4. Bernd Brückner. An Honeckers Seite: Der Leibwächter des Ersten Mannes. Das Neue Berlin, 2014. p.161
5. Schabowski. p.104
6. Lothar Herzog. Honecker Privat. Berolina, 2013. p.100
7. Schabowski. p.103
8. Herzog. p.156
9. FBIS-FRB-60-117. 15 June 1960.

1961: A Momentous Year

1. RIAS. 13 May 1961
2. Borkowski. p.253
3. ADN. 1 August 1961
4. Letter from the Soviet ambassador to East Berlin, Mikhail Pervuchin, to the Soviet Foreign Minister, Andrei Gromyko, 19 May 1961
5. Volklein, Ulrich. Honecker Eine Biographie. AV, 2006. p.276
6. Notes on the Conversation of Khrushchev with W. Ulbricht on 1 August 1961. / Wilson Centre.
7. Volklein. p.277
8. ZAIG 4900. Meeting notes, 11 August 1961. MfS archives.
9. *From My Life*. p.210.

10. Interview with Nathan Morley, 2017
11. *From My Life*. p.211
12. Der Bau der Berliner Mauer, MDR. 12 August 2020
13. BArch DO1/28129
14. *Neues Deutschland*. 14 August 1966.

A New Dawn

1. *From My Life*. p.212
2. *Berliner Zeitung*. 12 August 1991
3. The contact was Horst Sindermann, whom, Kellet-Long says: 'I knew and trusted, had advised me not to leave Berlin when I managed to catch up with him following the Volkskammer meeting authorising the government to take any action it wanted'. (Interview with Nathan Morley).
4. *Neues Deutschland*. 14 August 1961
5. *Junge Welt*. 14 August 1961
6. *Cyprus Mail*. 20 August 1961
7. *Belfast Telegraph*. 1 September 1961
8. ARD Interview in Moscow
9. Erich Honecker, *Aus Meinem Leben* (German edition, 1980). p.202
10. Frankfurt Domestic Radio. 18 August 1961
11. US Foreign Relations Documentation 1961. pp.154–155

Plugging the Gaps

1. The end of construction works came as a small relief to Markus Wolf, a lean and handsome intelligence officer who ran East Germany's foreign espionage division. Often regarded as one of the most well-known spymasters during the Cold War, Wolf was known in the West as 'the man without a face' due to his elusiveness. Remarkably, he wasn't informed about the erection of the wall by Erich Mielke and, after 13 August, found the task of running agents across into West Berlin increasingly problematic. The usual process of collecting intelligence – easily contacting sources in the West and personal meetings – faced terrific difficulties and it took months before intelligence operations could properly resume. Wolf lamented the 'paradoxical situation' in which the controls imposed by the GDR were 'far more draconian and difficult to negotiate than those of the West Germans'.

2. They were something of a novelty at the time and resembled an over-sized armoured truck with a crew of four. Two men sat in the driver's cab and two more were placed inside the truck on which a turret was mounted. The water tank was about 3 metres long and had an approximate capacity of 3,000 litres. Although not invented by the East German communists, the border guards

put them to excellent use. Ironically, the trucks were developed in Italy as a method of dispersing communist demonstrators, the only difference being the Italians often added red dye into the water so that clothing was ruined, and a person could easily be identified by the police the next day.

3. Just ten days after Berlin was split, Ulbricht and Honecker were beaming on Stalinalle reviewing a march-past of factory fighting squads, an event broadcast on domestic radio, which described the scene: 'Detachments of 100 men, one after another, are now forming for the march-past in the direction of the clubhouse of the building workers. Flying above their heads are the red flags of the working class, under whose symbol they have mounted guard. Accompanied by armoured cars and trucks, on which heavy machine guns and anti-aircraft searchlights are mounted, they are now marching through the first socialist street of Berlin.' FBIS-FRB-61-164 East Berlin domestic service 1545 GMT 24 August 1961

4. *Die Fischer Chronik Deutschland*. p.292
5. *Neue Zeit*. 17 September 1961
6. Fischer. p.318
7. *New York Times*. 11 October 1963
8. *Birmingham Daily Post*. 15 January 1963
9. *Honecker Cross Examined*. p.112.
10. *Birmingham Daily Post*. 4 October 1963
11. 'Was der BND über Erich Honecker wusste'. Sachsische Zeitung, 24 November 2012
12. Telegraf 19 August 1963. FBIS-FRB-63-161
13. GDR post office workers were responsible for processing the permit applications. Although they were state employees, they did not represent East German public authorities like police or customs officials. As a result, the Federal Republic viewed the border pass agreement as an administrative agreement that did not signify recognition of the GDR. The SED regime, on the other hand, did everything it could to give the agreement the character of an international treaty. A total of four border pass agreements were negotiated up until 1966.
14. East Berlin Domestic Service. 9 October 1964
15. Schabowski. p.112

A Restless Soul

1. *Pötzl*. p.76
2. *Neues Deutschland*. 8 December 1965. FBIS-FRB-65-236
3. *Honecker Cross Examined*. p.112
4. Ibid

5. Ibid
6. *Neue Zeit.* 4 December 1965
7. *Berliner Zeitung.* 7 December 1965
8. Klaus Tauber blog. Retrieved from: https://klaustaubert-wordpress-com
9. Borkowski. p.263
10. *Der Spiegel.* 1 January 1967
11. Ritter and Lapp, *Die Grenze: Ein deutsches Bauwerk.* Christoph Links Verlag, 2009. p.66.
12. GDR Criminal Code, 12 January 1968
13. FBIS-EEU-67-093-S
14. Ibid
15. Daily Report, Foreign Radio Broadcasts, Issues 216–220
16. 28 February 1968. FBIS-FRB-68-041
17. Ibid

The Problem Neighbour

1. *Neues Deutschland.* 8 June 1968
2. *Belfast Telegraph.* 12 August 1968
3. Wenzke, 'Die Nationale Volksarmee der DDR: Kein Einsatz in Prag', in Karner et al., Beiträge, pp.673–86. Cited from *The Prague Spring and the Warsaw Pact Invasion of Czechoslovakia in 1968.* Lexington Books, 2008.
4. *Neues Deutschland.* 27 October 1968
5. A few weeks later, Brezhnev was singing the same tune. He reminded comrades of his 'respect for sovereignty;' but at the same time, defended marching into a nation where socialism was deemed to be threatened. 'When internal and external supporters hostile to socialism attempt to turn the development of any socialist country in the direction of the restoration of the capitalist system, when a threat arises to the cause of socialism in that country, a threat to the security of the socialist commonwealth as a whole – it already becomes not only a problem for the people of that country but also a general problem, the concern of all socialist countries.'
6. *Neues Deutschland.* 29 April 1969.
7. *Neues Deutschland.* 15 December 1969
8. On 21 May 1973
9. Brezhnev, *Pages From His Life.* 1977. pp.215–216

Et Tu Honecker

1. TASS International Service. 18 March 1970
2. *Neues Deutschland.* 18 March 1970.

3. *Munich Suddeutsche Zeitung.* 18 March 1970
4. Ibid
5. Later in the day, as a type of countermeasure, the local SED arranged a few small demonstrations in front of the hotel, where slogans like 'We hail Willi Stoph' were shouted.
6. Egon Krenz: Ein „Kinderstreich" brachte ihn zur SED. Schuld war die CDU. BK. 23 June 2022.
7. Ibid
8. TASS International Service. 20 March 1970
9. Heinz Hoffmann. p.213
10. TASS International Service. 20 March 1970
11. By this point, the Soviet leader had cemented his influence over foreign policy, taking responsibility for relations with the United States and West Germany centred on the theme of European détente and the perusal of economic relations to supply Russian domestic needs for consumer goods and technology. In this regard, there is little doubt the GDR's foreign policy unquestionably suffered from the Bonn-Moscow Treaty, as the Soviets ignored East Berlin's demands for bloc solidarity, a clear signal that Brezhnev would not let the GDR interfere with his own rapprochement with Bonn. (The USSR and West Germany would sign a long-term trade agreement the following year). Honecker ran his eye over the treaty without enthusiasm. The West German-Soviet treaty saw both states give up territorial claims and consider the borders of all states in Europe as inviolable including the Oder-Neisse Line and the border between the West Germany and the GDR. Both parties further announced their desire to normalize the European situation and to develop peaceful relations among all European states. Détente, it seemed, truly operational.
12. FBIS-FRB-70-118
13. Schabowski. p.111
14. Monika Kaiser, Machtwechsel von Ulbricht zu Honecker. (Berlin, 1997.) p.373
15. *Pötzl.* p.46
16. *Pötzl.* p.47
17. ZDF
18. SAPMO-BArch, DY 30/J IV2/2A/3196
19. Ibid
20. Ibid
21. Ibid
22. Ibid
23. *Pötzl.* p.48
24. *Neues Deutschland*, 14 October 1970.

25. Die Sex-Akte von Margot Honecker, *Bild*. 7 May, 2016. Retrieved from: https://www.bild.de/politik/inland/margot-honecker/die-sexakte-margot-honecker-45705598.bild.html
26. Ibid
27. Schabowski, p.111
28. The document dated January 1971 is confirmed by the fact that a copy of it was confiscated on December 7, 1989 by the East Berlin public prosecutor's office in Willi Stoph's house, where it had been kept in a five-fold sealed envelope. The thirteen signatories were Hermann Axen, Gerhard Grüneberg, Kurt Hager, Erich Honecker, Horst Sindermann, Willi Stoph, Paul Verner, Erich Mückenberger, Herbert Warnke, Werner Jarowinsky, Werner Lamberz, Günther Kleiber and economic reformer Günter Mittag who thought Ulbricht's economic policy 'Was no longer responsible and had become megalomaniac' But Honecker and his colleagues were evidently certain that their request would be taken seriously and supported in Moscow. Honecker had also tried – but in vain – to get a signature from the terminally ill Hermann Materil, who was receiving artificial ventilation in the government hospital. Unlike some of his associates, Politburo member Alfred Neumann, an astute politician, clearly grasped the significance of this moment and refused to sign the letter, instead accusing Honecker of 'letting off steam' and 'creating mood against Walter'. Friedrich Ebert, Georg Ewald, Walter Halbritter, Margarete Müller and Albert Norden also refused to sign.

Cometh the Hour

1. Allgemeiner Deutscher Nachrichtendienst. 3 May 1971
2. ADN. 3 May 1971
3. Brezhnev telegram to Honecker, 3 May 1971
4. ADN. 4 May 1971
5. *Neues Deutschland* 4 May 1971
6. Ibid
7. In later years, she was acutely conscious of the poor treatment of Ulbricht and sought gloss-over unsavory details, these personal regrets also haunted Erich Honecker.
8. Reinhold Andert / Wolfgang Herzberg, The fall. Honecker in cross-examination, Berlin / Weimar

The Modern Man

1. Egon Krenz: Ein „Kinderstreich" brachte ihn zur SED. Schuld war die CDU. BK. 23 June 2022.
2. 'Skizze seines politischen Lebens.' p.149
3. Schabowski. p.110

Notes

4. Profile: Erich Honecker, BBC Radio, 21 Febuary 1989.
5. Honi konnte nicht mal Russisch, *Bild*. 14 September 2011
6. Borkowski. p.279
7. Ibid p.284
8. SED Documentation Berlin State library. p.315
9. Erich Honecker: Der VIII. Parteitag and unsere nachsten Aufgaben. 10 March 1972. p.40.
10. Lippmann. p.235
11. *Der Spiegel*. Die Staatszeitung, der ihr Staat abhandenkam. 3 March, 2021
12. *Daily Express*, 6 September 1976
13. Metelitsa, Stranitsy zhizni, pp.316–17
14. Rome L'UNITA 12 January 1975
15. American Foreign Relations 1971. A Documentary Record. p.163
16. 6 June 1973
17. In the end, the number of people employed in the private sector fell from 1.115 million in 1971 to around 594,000.
18. SAPMO-Barch, ZPA JIV 2/202/47

Jetsetter

1. Markus Woolf. Man Without A Face: The Autobiography Of Communism's Greatest Spymaster. pp.263-4
2. https://www.commentary.org/articles/jeffrey-herf/east-germanys-assault-israel/
3. Honecker – Arafat meeting. East Berlin, 15 December 1988. Wilson Centre, 112924.
4. 29 March 1974. Bundesarchive, DY 30 / 2499
5. Interview with former Colonel Rainer Wiegand. Cited from: Stasi: The Untold Story of the East German Secret Police by John O. Koehler. (Westview Press).
6. ARD Television Network. 23 April 1991
7. *Neues Deutschland*. 26 July 1982
8. UD Department of Defense, Soviet Military Power (Washington, D.C.: US Government Printing Office, 1981), p.34.
9. Qaddafi's Utopia: Big Ideas Covered in Naugahyde, *New York Times*. 11 September 1984
10. Speaking in 1990
11. ARD
12. Die Welt, 12 September 1992. The 69-page report, which was completed in August 1992, was drawn up in connection with the investigations against Erich Mielke, Gerhard Neiber and five other high-ranking Stasi officers.
13. FBIS-WEU-90-178

The Refined Hunter

1. Honecker erholte sich beim Töten im Wald, *Die Welt*. 21 April 2018.
2. Was der BND über Erich Honecker wusste. *Die Welt*. 24 November 2012.
3. Interview with Ambassador Richard C. Barkley. Retrieved from the Association for Diplomatic Studies and Training Foreign Affairs Oral History Project: https://tile.loc.gov/storage-services/service/mss/mfdip/2007/2007bar03/2007bar03.pdf

Auf Wiedersehen Walter

1. *The Times*, 2 August, 1973
2. 1973STATE154520_b
3. Draft letter from Willi Stoph to Syrian President Hafez al-Assad in response to al-Assad's 6 and 10 October 1973 letters to Stoph, October, 1973, History and Public Policy Program Digital Archive, BA-SAPMO IV 2/2A/1721
4. Letter from Honecker to Syrian President Hafez al-Assad, 3 November 1973, History and Public Policy Program Digital Archive, BA-SAPMO J IV 2/2.035/147
5. Ibid
6. East Berlin Voice of the GDR Domestic Service 2 October 1973 5pm broadcast
7. Ein Bücher-Tagebuch: Buchbesprechungen aus der Frankfurter Allgemeinen Zeitung 1981
8. BZ. 27 May 1992
9. Lippmann. p.235
10. Yanez p.72

Friends Afar

1. East Berlin ADN International Service. 20 February 1974
2. *From My Life*. p.433
3. *Neues Deutschland*, 23 February 1974
4. 1974BERLIN00386_b
5. Volker Skierka. *Fidel Castro: A Biography* p.204
6. DY 30/J IV 2/2/1493
7. Hamburg Domestic Television Service. 6 May 1974
8. Gary Bruce. *The Firm: The Inside Story Of The Stasi*. Oxford University Press, 2012. p.65
9. *Der Spiegel* 20 May 1974
10. *Birmingham Daily Post*. 13 May 1974
11. 1975BERLIN05263_b
12. Ibid

Notes

The Statesman

1. *Der Spiegel.* 6 September 1971
2. April 18,1975 10:00 ahttps://www.fordlibrarymuseum.gov/library/document/memcons/1553034.pdf
3. Telex: 1975 July 26, 02:57 (Saturday) / Meeting between President and Honecker / 1975STATE176985_b
4. Speech by GDR First Secretary Erich Honecker to the CSCE, Helsinki 1975 OSCE Archives. 1 August 1975.
5. Memoranda of Conversation: July 31, 1975 – Quadripartite Luncheon in Helsinki (US, UK, France, FRG)https://www.fordlibrarymuseum.gov/library/document/memcons/1553190.pdf
6. Schmidt-Honecker discussions at Helsinki summit 1975. Bonn12721_b
7. Ibid
8. *From My Life.* p.394
9. Wednesday, February 4, 1976 https://www.fordlibrarymuseum.gov/library/document/memcons/1553356.pdf
10. Roberto Yanez. Ich war der letzte Bürger der DDR: Mein Leben als Enkel der Honeckers. p.89
11. Ibid
12. 1976BERLIN05335_b
13. In 1971, the GDR had borrowed about $1 billion; by 1977 it reached $5 billion. In 1981, the dollar debt would top 10 billion. From 1970 to 1974 export earnings had increased by 65 per cent, while the prices of raw material imports shot-up by 170 per cent.
14. Julij Kwizinski. Vor dem Sturm. Erinnerungen eines Diplomaten. Siedler Verlag, 1997. pp.258-59.
15. *Coventry Evening Telegraph.* 4 January 1977.
16. Hamburg DPA. 15 July 1993
17. FBIS-EEU-90-066

Veneer of Stability

1. *From My Life.* p.406
2. Directives for the Five-Year Plan for the GDR's national economic development 1976–1980, Dresden 1976, p.147
3. East Berlin ADN International Service. 6 August 1976
4. FBIS-EEU-80-170
5. Western powers insisted Berlin was one city and that there should be no customs controls between the sectors.
6. 1977STATE260833_c NARCOTICS: HEROIN TRAFFICKING TO BERLIN 1977 November 1.

7. 1977STATE260833_c
8. BZ. 24 April 1976
9. FBIS-EEU-76-080
10. East Berlin Voice of the GDR Domestic. 27 March 1976
11. Tagesspiegel, 99 Zeilen Schwerk, 22 December 2001
12. Read, Anthony. Berlin, Hutchinson, 1994. pp.294–295
13. In a lengthy letter from July 1975, she noted: 'We have declared a State of Emergency. This had to be done to ward off disruption and breakdown of our system. For months some of our Opposition parties have been trying to adopt all means to obstruct the Government with the openly declared objective of seizing power. As you know, we have a multiplicity of political parties ranging from extreme right to extreme left – some are regional with no specific policy. Most of these have come together for the common purpose of paralyzing a constitutionally elected government. Even during our elections in 1971, their slogan was 'Remove Indira Gandhi'. But they found that the people were not with them. Last year, with the economic difficulties due to the successive failures of rain and the world oil crisis, they thought that opportunity had come their way once again. They embarked on a policy of obstructing industrial production by fomenting strikes. They exhorted farmers not to sell produce to Government Agencies, the aim being to bring about the collapse of the distribution system in cities.'
14. BStU, MfS, AOP, Nr. 11806/85, Bd. 52, Bl. 125
15. *Der Spiegel.* 21 November 1976
16. On June 28, 1983
17. FBIS-EEU-77-055
18. Ibid
19. *Neues Deutschland.* 28 June 1980
20. Ibid

The Squeeze Begins

1. Letter from Norden to Honecker. 28 June 1977. Bundesarchive ZPA, IV B2/2028/20
2. FBIS-EEU-77-055
3. From 8 to 12 January
4. *Neues Deutschland* 12 January 1979
5. 1979BERLIN00229_e
6. Indeed, Honecker later admitted that Lamberz and another functionary, Paul Markowski, were both considered possible successors. *Honecker Cross Examined.* p.25

7. According to Markus Wolf, Lamberz was the 'favoured candidate of the intelligentsia and many young Party members to succeed Honecker in the distant future'.
8. *Neues Deutschland.*
9. The GDR Solidarity Committee gave 40 million DDM to African countries in the first half of 1978 and flew many guerrilla fighters wounded in Namibia and Rhodesia for treatment in East German hospitals. Honecker's fingerprints were also detected in Nicaragua where he sent Stasi experts to set up an MfS-style secret service along with a planeload of Kalashnikovs, anti-tank guns and military trucks to fight the 'Contras'. Later, the GDR also financed the 'Karl Marx Hospital' in Managua pumping 4 million DDM into the project annually.
10. FCO. German Democratic Republic: Annual Diplomatic Review. Diplomatic report 94/80.
11. East Berlin. ADN International Service. 25 August 1980
12. Former Honecker butler: 'He completely changed his life'. DW, 23 August 2012.
13. Republished in the GDR press on 7 July 1978.
14. FBIS-EEU-80-170
15. There had been periodic expulsions of FRG journalists (Spiegel and ARD) and warnings were frequently made directly to reporters. In January 1978, the Spiegel office in East Berlin was shuttered and soon after, TV reporter Luetz Lehmann was told he could not interview the prominent East German writer, Stefan Heym. At the same time, the GDR authorities used petty vengeful tactics against prominent critics such as humanist Robert Havemann who was placed under house arrest and virtually isolated from the outside world. Writers Bettina Wegener, Rolf Schneider and the aforementioned Heym were denied exit permits to travel to the West, while writer Guenter Kunert privately let it be known to American contacts that he believed that the exit permit denials were the regime's way of punishing writers who had works/interviews appear in the West without prior official approval.
16. DPA. 18 April 1980
17. DPA. 20 February 1980
18. SED 11th plenum: Honecker on GDR economic trends and problems. 1979BERLIN07378_e

The Eighties

1. *Pravda*. 8 May 1980
2. John O. Koehler. *Stasi: Untold Story of East Germany's Secret Police.* Basic Books; Revised ed. Edition. 2000.

3. Ibid

4. On 5 December, he told a special meeting in Moscow: 'We have a common boundary with the Federal Republic of Germany, and we see how the enemy tries to transpose the counter-revolutionary events in Poland in our country. Never have the broadcasting stations transmitted so much news about the events in Poland as they do now, never have they made so much noise in relation to the goings-on in Polish enterprises. They have been saying for five months that Poland's example should also be followed by the German Democratic Republic. In a speech at the meeting of the party active I declared that counter revolution, wherever it may take place, will not remain unpunished.'

5. Die Welt. 20 August 1980

6. MDR. Die BND-Akte 'Honi'

7. Frankfurter Rundschau. 25 August 1980

8. 'Das hat sehr geschmerzt'. *Der Spiegel*. 17 November 1980

9. VK. 12 November 1980

10. Gute Geschäfte im Kalten Krieg, Profil. 19 June 2016

11. SAPMO-BArch, ZPA, J IV 2/202-550

12. East German leader Erich Honecker writes to Soviet leader Leonid Brezhnev requesting that a meeting of the First Secretaries of the Communist Parties in the Warsaw Pact member states be convened to discuss the crisis in Poland. https://digitalarchive.wilsoncenter.org/document/111992

13. Uprising in East Germany. p.420

14. FBIS-EEU-81-070

15. *Der Spiegel*. 11 March 1990

16. *Der Spiegel*. 13 August 1995

17. Herzog. p.179

18. The letter was all the more awkward given Honecker had publicly listed at the 11th SED plenum in 1979 that anticipated deliveries of raw materials from the USSR over the period 1981–5 would include 19 million tons of crude oil, 6.5 billion cubic meters of natural gas and 4.2 million tons of hard coal per year. In fact, the only time Honecker's speech was interrupted by a wave of 'great applause' was when thanking Brezhnev for 'the understanding he showed for the specific problems of the GDR' – a reference to the promised quota of coal and oil imports, spun in the GDR press as a triumph of SED diplomacy. Compared to 1978, imports from the USSR constituted a 7 per cent increase in oil deliveries and a 7.7 jump in hard coal imports.

19. SAPMO-BA, DY 30 / J IV 2 / 2A / 2422.

20. Eventually lifted by President Reagan in June 1981.

21. Ibid. Letter from SED General Secretary Honecker to Brezhnev not to undermine the cornerstones of the existence of the GDR, 4 September 1981
22. On 15 September 1981.
23. Russian State Archive of Contemporary History. TsKhSD, f. 89, per. 42, no. 48, 'Ob itogakh poezdki t. Rusakova, K. V. v GDR, ChSSR, VNR, i NRB,' 29 October 1981, 2. Cited from The Rise and Fall of the Brezhnev Doctrine in Soviet Foreign Policy, Matthew J. Ouimet. University of North Carolina, 2003.
24. PREM19/471 f218 Record of a discussion between Prime Minister Margaret Thatcher and Chancellor Helmut Schmidt in Bonn, 17 November 1980
25. *Pötzl.* p.7
26. *New York Times.* 13 December 1981
27. In contrast, Hans-Dietrich Genscher privately told Margaret Thatcher, that he thought the GDR the 'most unstable state in Eastern Europe'. PREM19/471 f218 Record of a discussion between Prime Minister Margaret Thatcher and Chancellor Helmut Schmidt in Bonn, 17 November 1980
28. By this point, Honecker had established a 'balance of payments working group' to watch over the use of the scarce foreign currency on a weekly basis.
29. Reagan. 'The President's News Conference,' 16 June 1981.
30. Decades later, Jaruzelski rather bizarrely admitted that the worst part of his job had been to kiss Honecker. 'He had this disgusting way of kissing,' he sniffed. The fraternal kiss became famous after Honecker and Brezhnev were photographed exercising the ritual, the image was subsequently reproduced into a graffiti painting on the Berlin Wall with the slogan: 'My God, Help Me to Survive This Deadly Love.'

Do svidaniya Brezhnev

1. *Honecker Cross Examined.* p.40
2. In 2007, *Der Spiegel* reported Honecker was not upset by the incident and was said to have shot nine deer with a steady hand later that same day.
3. *Neues Deutschland.* 31 December 1982
4. Westfalen Blatt. 21 April 1983
5. *Der Spiegel.* 24 April 1983
6. *Pravda.* 27 April 1983
7. Die Erinnerungen , Strauss memoirs. Pantheon Verlag, 2015. p.25
8. Daily Report. FBIS-WEU-83-158-A

9. ZDF Television Network in German. 13 July 1983
10. Ibid

Uncertain Times

1. Published on 27 July 1984.
2. *Bild*. 7 August.
3. Markus Wolf. *Man Without A Face: The Autobiography Of Communism's Greatest Spymaster*. PublicAffairs; Reprint edition, 1999. p.319
4. Honecker Drops His Plan to Visit West Germany. *New York Times*. 5 September 1984
5. UK Embassy in East Berlin to FCO (1984 Annual Report on GDR) [declassified 2007]
6. Ibid
7. Compounding matters, Margaret Thatcher – a politician unrestrained in condemning the USSR as a tyrannical force for evil in the world – also won another term, securing a landslide victory in June 1983.
8. East Berlin Television Service. 11 March 1985
9. *Newcastle Journal*. 14 February 1985
10. He was caught shoplifting from a department store in West Berlin in the summer of 1986 and revealed that he was working as a spy at the BND. After twelve days, he changed sides again and told German television that FRG police had forced him into making a false confession while under the influence of drugs.
11. Schabowski. p.132

Evil Partnerships

1. In 1990, The West Berlin authorities considered a missing MfS file particularly important because it comprehensively dealt with the issue. This file was said to contain hand-written notes by Honecker which proved he knew about the preparations for the attack and ordered the Stasi not to do anything to prevent it. FBIS-EEU-90-170
2. DPA. 7 August 1990
3. DPA. 11 July 1990
4. Interestingly, the *Berliner Morgenpost* (18 October 1990), cited MfS files alleging Honecker and Mielke had, in fact, attempted to prevent the bombing. The files were said to show 'that the MfS leadership exerted political pressure on the Libyan Embassy in East Berlin to prevent the terrorist attack.' After the bombing, the paper continued, pressure was increased to prevent such attacks, prepared from East Berlin territory, in the future.

5. Wolf. p.276
6. Voice of GDR Domestic Service in German. 5 May 1986
7. As cited in *Der Spiegel*. 6 October 1979
8. Dalos, György: *Gorbachev: Man, and Power; a biography*. Beck, 2011. p.105
9. 'Morgenpost': KGB sollte Honecker 1987 stürzen. Retrieved from: https://www.bild.de/regional/berlin/morgenpost-kgb-sollte-honecker-1987-stuerzen 9355828.bild.html
10. Schmeichelei und Unterwürfigkeit SPIEGEL-Interview mit Moskaus Ex-Botschafter in der DDR, Wjatscheslaw Kotschemassow, über Erich Honecker. *Der Spiegel* (online). 16 November 1992.
11. On 24 July
12. Writing in the 24 August edition of *Der Spiegel*

The Bonn Visit
1. East German Leader Makes Emotion Visit to Hometown, Predicts Normal Border. AP. 11 September 1987
2. *Die Welt*. 12 September 1987
3. *Frankfurter Rundschau*. 12 September 1987
4. ADN. 10 September 1987
5. *Der Spiegel*. 13 September 1987
6. Transcript of discussion with Belgian journalist, as recorded in the US government Daily Report/East Europe (FBIS-EEU-87-199)
7. Ibid
8. Letter from Neumann to Honecker. 11 February 1987. Cited from 'Die SED in der Ära Honecker'. Andreas Malycha. p.160
9. *Neues Deutschland*. 8 January 1988
10. Honecker's Paris Trip Nurtures Western Ties, *LA Times*. 9 January 1988.
11. ZPA IV 2/2039/64. Report of a conversation between Honecker and Medvedev, 24 August 1988.
12. ZDF History, 'Honecker's Secrets'.
13. When the Easter edition of the weekly newspaper 'Die Kirche' appeared – huge white blank spaces denoted the areas cut by censors.
14. Die Welt. 9 June 1988.
15. *Sputnik*, published since 1967, appeared as a monthly magazine in seven languages with a total circulation of around one million copies. The German edition sold around 130,000 of these by subscription and around 60,000 in individual sales. The magazine, based on Reader's Digest, with selected articles from Soviet newspapers and magazines, enjoyed great popularity because of its colourful mix of travel reports, cooking recipes,

crossword puzzles and cultural articles. Since the mid-1980s, *Sputnik* has also provided first-hand information about the two pillars of Gorbachev's reform policy – perestroika and glasnost.

16. When Stalin branded the Social Democrats 'social fascists', the KPD, which was subject to Moscow guidance, was unable to enter an alliance with them.
17. East Germany Launches Censorship Drive Against Soviet Reforms. 8 December 1988
18. This was confirmed by the Central Committee Secretary and Politburo member Joachim Herrmann. *Neues Deutschland*. 27 January 1990
19. 'Hidden Hand'. Geoffrey Gedmin. AEI (1992) p.61
20. Mitteilung der Pressestelle des Ministeriums für Post – und Fernmeldewesen der DDR [Sputnik-Verbot]. 19 November 1988.
21. Parteisäuberungen und Widerstand in der SED. (1996). p.91
22. *Honecker Cross Examined*. p.75
23. Ibid pp.31–32
24. Ibid p.32
25. Another episode which throws light on the strained relations between East Berlin and Moscow came when Honecker introduced the concept of 'Socialism in the colours of the German Democratic Republic' at the seventh session of the Central Committee. Designed to illustrate that developments in the socialist world were more varied than many realized, the phrase was used at frequently at public events and in party literature. However, other than thumbing a nose at perestroika, the 'concept' did little other than emphasise the GDR's past achievements.
26. From 1983 to 1987
27. Bruce W. Clark interview, Association for Diplomatic Studies and Training Foreign Affairs Oral History Project. 2004.
28. Interestingly, in 2021, one of the former Interflug Airbus planes took off on what was its last mission – the rescue of 158 refugees from Afghanistan after the Taliban overran Kabul.
29. Schabowski. p.110
30. *Pötzl*. p.135
31. *Honecker Cross Examined* pp.129–.130
32. *Sunday Independent*. 27 November 1988
33. Chronik Der Mauer. https://www.chronik-der mauer.de/en/chronicle/_year1988/_month11/?moc=1

The Winds of Change

1. MfS, ZAIG, Nr. 25/89
2. Chronik Der Mauer: 1989 https://www.chronik-der mauer.de/en/chronicle/_year1989

3. Ironically, even without the fraud, the SED would certainly have received a solid majority. But, as usual, the charade was played out. At every polling station, the mechanics of voting was designed to expose anyone voting against the SED or political parties allied with the communists 'National Front' list of candidates. If the voters wanted to vote 'yes', it was sufficient to simply fold the voting slip into the ballot box. A 'no' vote, on the other hand, only counted if all candidates on the list were crossed out individually in a special voting booth, where the eyes of the election workers were focused. (A 'no' vote was only recognized if the voter neatly crossed out every single name on the list with a pen provided. Any deviation from this would render the voting slip invalid.)

4. Wahlbetrug 1989 – als die DDR-Regierung ihre Glaubwürdigkeit verlor, https://www.bpb.de/politik/hintergrund-aktuell/290562/1989-wahlbetrug-in-der-ddr

5. 'In isolated cases, they accused the election commissioners of electoral fraud and demanded that they be allowed to count the dissenting votes personally. Such provocations were rejected by the election commissioners, whereupon the individuals left the concerned polling stations without further comment.' While there was a general recognition of the seriousness of the situation, the Stasi had extremely little idea that this activity could be more than a temporary irritation.

6. By late evening, opposition observers knew that the results in the individual polling stations had turned out significantly different in some cases. In Berlin-Weißensee, for example, there were 83 per cent 'yes' votes, but also many 'no' votes and abstentions. Ten, sometimes up to 20 per cent, votes against were also documented in other parts of the GDR. The discrepancy was similar in the Berlin districts of Friedrichshain, Prenzlauer Berg and Pankow, but also in Naumburg, Potsdam, Erfurt and Jena. With such values in individual polling stations, a rejection of only 1.15 per cent in total was theoretically practically impossible. The SED made another serious mistake: on 10 May 1989, the party newspaper *Neues Deutschland* published the alleged results with exact numbers down to the level of city districts.

7. Wolf. p.324

8. *Honecker Cross Examined*. p.41

9. Ibid p.42

10. Schabowski. p.142

11. The GDR Volkskammer called the massacre in Tiananmen Square on June 4 the 'putting-down of a counter-revolution.'

12. *Honecker Cross Examined*. p.42

13. Kunze, Thomas. *Staatschef: Die letzten Jahre des Erich Honecker*. Links, 2011. p.77

14. ZDF History 'Honecker'.
15. ARD interview with Honecker, 1991.
16. *Honecker Cross Examined.* p.46
17. Schmemann 'a wistful glance back'. Cited from Jeffrey Gedmin, *Hidden Hand*. p.105
18. The Schalck Papers, Vienna, 1991. p.410
19. FBIS-WEU-91102. 28 May 1991. Cited from Hidden Hand, Geoffrey Gedmin. p.104.
20. Kuzmin, Khrushcnie. GDR. pp.112–13.
21. Even at this point, as the pillars on which the balance of power existed – strong economy, obedient population and strong security – remained in flux, the SED continued to plod on with countless self-defeating policies. Permission for a public reading by popular author Christa Wolf, who had become vocal in her opposition to Honecker was revoked, while at the same time; party ideologist Kurt Hager attempted to override the approval of critical books by Walter Janka, Stefan Heym and Monika Maron. On a visit to Moscow, Hager privately complained that the GDR was at the mercy of a 'massive campaign by the enemy' of psychological warfare against the GDR, the SED and socialism. 'Cultural and artistic-creators, scientists and other members of the intelligentsia, workers and farmers feel there is an inconsistency between word and deed, their everyday experiences do not correspond to official reporting,' he confided to Vadim Medvedev, a Gorbachev aide and high-ranking Communist Party official. 'Consequently, a justifiable discontent forms.'
22. Klenke, Rationalisierung, Krone. p.116 as cited in Gareth Dale's *The East German Revolution of 1989* p.5.
23. ADN 27 December 1989
24. Ibid
25. *Neues Deutschland.* 6 October 1989
26. Schabowski. p.126
27. 'Das Interview,' ARD, 1991.
28. Wilson Center Archives. https://digitalarchive.wilsoncenter.org/document/117207
29. *Honecker Cross Examined.* p.47.
30. DPA 23 November 1989
31. *Honecker Cross Examined.* p.47.

The Curtain Falls

1. Shortly before the Politburo meeting, union boss Harry Tisch had traveled to Moscow and informed Mikhail Gorbachev of the plan to remove

Honecker. The chairman of the CPSU wished the company every success – sealing the fate of Erich Honecker.

2. *Honecker Cross Examined.* p.11
3. Hans-Hermann Hertle and Gerd-Rüdiger Stephan. Das Ende der SED: Die letzten Tage des Zentralkomitees (Links, 1997). p.52.
4. Ibid. p.12
5. Ibid. p.170
6. Honecker Resignation Statement. SED handout, via ADN. 18 October 1989.
7. *Bild.* 19 October 1989
8. FAZ. 19 October 1989
9. BStU. MfS, Berlin, XV, Number: 49
10. *Reading Evening Post.* 19 October 1989
11. Interview with Ambassador Richard C. Barkley. Library of Congress. Frontline Diplomacy, Manuscript Division
12. Ibid

Out in the Cold

1. *Aberdeen Press and Journal.* 24 October 1989
2. *Die Welt* 28 November 1989
3. *Honecker Cross Examined* p.162
4. As this was happening, *Neues Deutschland* began running endless stories about poor social conditions in West Germany, highlighting poverty, homelessness and the shabby treatment of GDR emigrants. Similarly, the FRG was subject to a stream of vitriol on the airwaves of GDR TV and radio.
5. Wir sind das volk. p.90
6. Schabowski. p.172.
7. BStU 000166
8. *Honecker Cross Examined.* p.6
9. Moscow TASS 17 November 1989
10. Further circumstances were being investigated, including arms trading and the question of the whereabouts of the money thus acquired
11. Gareth Dale. *The East German Revolution of 1989.* p.81
12. Ed Stuhler: *Margot Honecker. A biography.* Ueberreuter, Vienna 2003. p.199
13. Staatschef a.D.: die letzten Jahre des Erich Honecker. p.65.
14. For an Ailing Honecker, Two Strange Bedfellows. *New York Times*, 2 February 1990
15. Ibid.
16. *Honecker Cross Examined.* p.29

17. https://www.domradio.de/themen/kirche-und-politik/2020-01-30/eine-neue-epoche-nicht-mit-hass-beginnen-pastor-uwe-holmer-ueber-honeckers-asyl-seinem-pfarrhaus
18. *The European*. 3 November 1990
19. Staatschef a.D.: die letzten Jahre des Erich Honecker. p.106
20. Ibid
21. *The European*. 3 November 1990
22. Staatschef a.D. p.108
23. The European. 3 November 1990
24. Ibid
25. *Bild*. 17 March 1991
26. *Aberdeen Press and Journal*. 16 March 1991
27. Daily Report. West Europe (FBIS-WEU-91-052). 17 March 1991
28. *Aberdeen Press and Journal*. 16 March 1991
29. Gorbachev was briefly placed under house arrest in Crimea by high-ranking members of his own government. He was saved after Boris Yeltsin, the new President of the Russian Soviet Socialist Federal Republic, dispatched armed men by plane to rescue him. He was released and returned to Moscow, but his administration had been dealt a fatal blow.
30. Ulrich Völklein. Honecker: Eine Biographie. Aufbau Taschenbuch Verlag Gmbh. p.404
31. La otra Alemania, la RDA: Conversaciones con Margot Honecker. pp.100-101
32. Ibid
33. Entre protectores y opositores: labor política frente al caso Honecker. Rev. cienc. polít. (Santiago) vol.36 no.3 Santiago. 2016
34. Ibid
35. Ibid
36. Moscow Russian Television Network. 4 July 1992
37. Entre protectores y opositores: labor política frente al caso Honecker. Rev. cienc. polít. (Santiago) vol.36 no.3 Santiago. 2016
38. Völklein. p.405
39. Entre protectores y opositores: labor política frente al caso Honecker. Rev. cienc. polít. (Santiago) vol.36 no.3 Santiago. 2016

Return to Moabit

1. NZ. 30 July 1992
2. Ibid

3. Ibid
4. Ibid
5. German's rip Honecker's wife for not standing by him, *Baltimore Sun.* August 4 1992.
6. Becker, interview with author, 17 November 2021.
7. https://www.fr.de/rhein-main/post-honecker-11016910.html
8. Eva Ruppert. »Liebe Eva«: Erich Honeckers Gefängnisbriefe. Das Neue Berlin, 2017. p.43
9. Notes from Moabit. p.52
10. Ibid
11. Becker, interview with Nathan Morley. 17 November 2021.
12. *Daily Record.* 31 July 1992

In The Dock
1. The Honecker Trial, A. James McAdams. Kellogg Institute. 1996.
2. *New York Times.* 13 November 1992
3. Peter Richter, Kurzer Proze, Berlin 1993. pp.145–51.
4. Becker, interview with the author. 17 November 2021.
5. A History of Political Trials. p.202
6. Becker, interview with the author. 17 November 2021.

Gute Nacht
1. Events sped after one of the judges, Hans Georg Bräutigam, asked Honecker for an autograph sending the trial entirely off the rails. Bräutigam was forced to recuse himself due to accusations of bias, and a few days later all remaining charges, including embezzlement and manslaughter were dropped.
2. Santiago Radio Chilena Network. 14 January 1993
3. Roberto Yanez. pp.187–188
4. MDR Interview.
5. Ibid
6. FBIS-WEU-93-055
7. Yanez. p.191
8. MDR
9. *Der Spiegel.* 8 February 1993
10. FBIS-WEU-93-069
11. FBIS-WEU-93-076 Berlin ADN. 21 April 1993
12. KCNA 1 June, 1994
13. MDR

14. In later years, Honecker's grandson Roberto Yáñez revealed he had differences with his mother about what to do with the ashes of his grandparents. While Sonja wanted to scatter them in the Pacific, Roberto wanted them to be buried in the Socialists' cemetery in Berlin, alongside their comrades.
15. Yanez. p.195
16. http://www.lalkar.org/article/2458/comrade-margot-honecker-1927-2016